Special Issue

Critique and Cosmos: After Masao Miyoshi

Edited by

Rob Wilson and Paul A. Bové

boundary 2

an international journal

of literature and culture

Volume 46, Number 3

August 2019

Duke University Press

boundary 2
an international journal of literature and culture

Founding Editors   Robert Kroetsch and William V. Spanos

Editor   Paul A. Bové
  Elina Zhang, Assistant to the Editor

Managing Editor   Margaret A. Havran

Photo: Emma Bee Bernstein

Cover image courtesy of Susan Bee

boundary 2 congratulates Charles Bernstein on winning the 2019 Bollingen Prize for Poetry, awarded by Yale University.

boundary 2 has benefited in every possible way from Charles's endless talent and generosity. Our pages fortunately abound with his words, in all possible forms, from poems to interviews and essays. Without his contributions, our effort to internationalize our work would have been much harder. His 1999 special issue, "99 Poets/1999: An International Poetics Symposium," is just one example of his work with us. Charles joined our editorial board in 2000. Without him, we would be much poorer.

We know everyone celebrates his work and this award.

Contents

Introduction: "Aftering"

Rob Wilson

"Critique and Cosmos: After Masao Miyoshi" aims to activate some of the energies, tactics, critical forces, geopolitics, comparative poetics, and visions Masao Miyoshi (1928–2009) carried out in his work from the 1970s into the present millennium: coming to terms with *aftering* this impact in temporal, border-crossing, translational, field-reframing, and revisionary senses. *Aftering* (used as a gerundive verb, like *worlding*) here means prolonging, releasing, and transforming impacts across generic, political, cultural, and disciplinary borders of influence, negation, and control. The ten essays and one review in this special issue do not come to terms with Miyoshi's works in any memorial, critical, or honorific sense, although they can do that, as in the differently framed field-surveying essays in solidarity within and beyond Japan studies by Harry Harootunian, Reginald Jackson, and Mary Layoun, as well as the review essays on Miyoshi's photography and cultural criticism by Keijiro Suga and George Solt, respectively. Instead, these works release, amplify, and renew some of the antagonistic energies and critical visions that Miyoshi embodied and distributed as

boundary 2 46:3 (2019)   DOI 10.1215/01903659-7614099   © 2019 by Duke University Press

life force across various domains, fields, studies, and sites of intervention, from Asian to Asian American studies (as here reframed by Stefan Tanaka and Chih-ming Wang) and beyond. Other essays move into the redefining impact of China across the twentieth century (Arif Dirlik) and its attempted geopolitical production and management of Tibet (Tsering Wangmo Dhompa), and into anthropogenic energies and planetary possibilities of the Anthropocene in differing cultural studies works (Christine L. Marran on "the planetary" as critical ethos, and Rob Wilson on the Korean film *Snowpiercer* as ecocidal embodiment of killer capitalism).

Masao Miyoshi's work in scholarship and photography mandates that cultural criticism envision its work broadly and courageously, as what we call here "critique and cosmos." The aim is not just to write and think as discipline-bound professionals following the protocols of a given field or discipline. Rather, the energies empower scholars and writers to act, intervene, reframe, and provoke knowledge making, and empower the polity and world to reject complacency, injustice, and intellective obviousness. From his free speech days as an assistant professor of English in Wheeler Hall at UC Berkeley, to his all the more globally disruptive impact as Hajime Mori Distinguished Professor of Japanese, English, and Comparative Literature at UC San Diego, Miyoshi's work was never just retrospective or normative as such. His aim was always *projective*, pushing the work, the fields, our tactics of interpretation and linkage forward into situations as a world-making activity. Miyoshi's recurring problematics and subject matter (in literature, art, the university, urban architecture, ecology), as well as his committed ethos to stage large-scale encounters between cultures and modes of doing academic work, areas, literatures, and nations, still call out for *aftering* this impact.[1]

The essays presented here express this transformative power as they intervene in differing fields of environmental, Japanese, Asian Pacific, American, literature, art, film, and history as such. The essays by Miyoshi's longtime comrades Harootunian and Dirlik continue to shake up the field-imaginary of Japan and China studies in the trenchant, disruptive, and redefining ways their work has been identified with over the past four

1. For further research and archival purposes, the Masao Miyoshi Bunko (Collection) is now housed at Doshisha University's Faculty of Culture and Information Science in Kyoto, Japan. It can be accessed online at https://doors.doshisha.ac.jp/duar/repository/ir/158 36/?lang=0&mode=1&opkey=R152922533726880&idx=8. We are grateful to Professor Tetsuya Taguchi and John Solt for their leadership on this project.

decades. The *agonistic* power of Miyoshi as a cultural critic always staged disruptive encounters within and across national terrains of global modernity, and we still need to stimulate such courage, impiety, and scope. "Critique and Cosmos" encourages the dismantling of sublimated discourses and superpower nationalisms, as well as the transnational complacencies of neoliberalism, from the US to Japan and China and the European Union. We need this worldly work if the world and planet are to survive our regimes of globalization, inadequate politics of difference, and drives to recolonization.

Some of the problematics we have in mind in this reworlding formation include the transformation of the humanities to challenge the current regimes of globalization, professionalization, and computerization that often are summoned under the neoliberal banner of the digital humanities and all too commonly serve the forces of corporate privatization. We seek to continue the scholarly and creative transformation of what Miyoshi and Harootunian (2002) called "learning places," those areas, sites, and fields that would prod beyond disciplinary, institutional, and nation-centric frames. Such frames can still dominate in Anglo-American terms and often circulate globally to take academic dominion in sites across Asia and the Pacific. Such a reworking of these learning places would challenge what Miyoshi (2010: 205–41) called the incorporatization of the "Ivory Tower in escrow" in sites from California and London to Asia and the Pacific. At a more planetary level, we seek to embody the transdisciplinary turn toward modes of worlding study that Miyoshi called an ecological "totality" (2010: 243–61), which goes beyond more economistic or anthropocentric frames called the Anthropocene. *Aftering* the will to transdisciplinary intervention of Masao Miyoshi, we thus seek to articulate undertheorized or unidentified critical or theoretical objects in emergence. As Ezra Pound once affirmed in "A Pact" (1957: 27), written across the centuries as linked to his antagonistic mentor and transfigurative model of "commerce," Walt Whitman, working within global-local dreams of critique and cosmos:

It was you that broke the new wood,
Now is a time for carving.
We have one sap and one root between us.
Let there be commerce between us.

References

Miyoshi, Masao. 2010. *Trespasses: Selected Writings*. Edited by Eric Cazdyn. Durham, NC: Duke University Press.

Miyoshi, Masao, and Harry Harootunian, eds. 2002. *Learning Places: The Afterlives of Area Studies*. Durham, NC: Duke University Press.

Pound, Ezra. 1957. *Selected Poems of Ezra Pound*. New York: New Directions.

As We Saw Him: Masao Miyoshi and the Vocation of Critical Struggle

Harry Harootunian

In his academic lifetime, Masao Miyoshi was virtually a walking area studies program. It would be difficult to think of a better a model for the reconfiguration of area studies than the traces of his intellectual trajectory. As a Japanese educated in Japan's elite First Higher School, just before it was dismantled by the postwar US military occupation, and Tokyo University, he was an early exile (calling himself a "Japanese war bride") to the United States, where he completed his education in graduate schools with a PhD in English literature. By that time, he had already successfully embodied a knowledge that covered the literatures of three societies. In time, he would add to this inventory. Leaving Japan permanently in the early postwar years was Miyoshi's entry into the world at large. The force that lay behind the impulse to expand his acquisition of knowledge was probably an unrestrained restlessness that prompted a reaching out to know and understand areas and regions of social life that exceeded his chosen academic specialty of Victorian literature. Years later, he turned to photography to capture the various regions of the world he had come to

boundary 2 46:3 (2019)   DOI 10.1215/01903659-7614111   © 2019 by Duke University Press

visit and know. In a display of this particular archive, exhibited at Duke University in 2013 after his death, it is possible to see that what he composed in photos (Miyoshi 2009) was already reflected in his intellectual and academic shifting that took him away from settled specialization to constantly pursue and discover what was out there and not here.

If Miyoshi left Japan behind as a condition of embracing a wider world, what remained with him was a sense of marginality he had experienced as a Japanese, which undoubtedly explains why he described this lifelong quest as a search for margins and thresholds that have escaped the received conventions of knowledge. For Miyoshi, the journey took him away from the claims of narrow expertise that reaffirmed the centrality of some societies over others to the mystery of what was out there but ignored, as he put it, to reach and encounter the "this that is not here."

This is where he wanted to be and defined for him the field of inquiry he wanted to follow. In another time, he might have been called an exotic, looking for those places beyond the horizon of familiar cultures, knowing he would never grasp the mystery or penetrate it. But to describe Miyoshi in this way would be an unfair misrecognition. Behind this ceaseless search to gain access to what, for him, was not here but there loomed a continuous commitment to finding a critical compass that would immediately lead critique into forms of practice and action, whereby criticism and action would be actualized into a unified strategy of resistance—critical struggle—serving humans rather than only intellectuals and the demands of their culture. In this pursuit, Miyoshi was steered by his admiration of Noam Chomsky, Edward Said, and, later, David Harvey.

Miyoshi's desire for the "this not here" was a declaration of solidarity with the marginal and its claims to visibility and equality. While he wanted to be other, his reasons for this desire differed vastly from those who merely sought to lose their own identity in some form of passing. His was a search for a presence that was not present. For those of us locked in the narrow and parochial world of a region defining area studies, an academic discipline still struggling with the promise of certainty guaranteed by a parochial knowledge but going nowhere, and fortunate to have known him, this is how we saw him and the kind of release his conception of criticism's freedom and boundary transgression offered us by his example. In this regard, the critic Karatani Kōjin described him best when he renamed him the "trespasser," a border crosser.

It is interesting to note that Miyoshi, after several decades of teaching English literature, experienced, like many Japanese scholars and intellectuals before him, the imperative of an obligatory "return to Japan." Physically, he had not returned to Japan for twenty-five years, but what I am referring to is not a metaphorical reembracing of his native land, constituting a reunion with Japan through its literary and aesthetic traditions. Unlike other Japanese who have made this sentimental journey to some imaginary reconstruction of Japan's past in the present, his return to the "native place" was not permanent nor driven by any insurmountable nostalgia for a "lost Japan" but signaled only a momentary excursion to see and learn what had taken place in the years of absence. In the more classic examples of returning to Japan (*Nihon kaiki*), the reunion was an affective and intellectual reuniting with the native place (*kyōdo*) that announced a final rejection of a lifetime's absorption in acquiring Western intelligence and the acknowledgment that such learning would always be superficial, resulting only in surface acquisition that distorted and bent one's true nature. This Japanese distrust of foreign learning probably derived from the historical trauma of having Chinese culture imposed on an earlier and original native configuration of the world and the cosmos. The encounter with what appeared as a superior civilization and the ensuing adoption of its exemplars in language, thought, religion, and art has repetitively led to unscheduled reactions calling for a return to and embracing of truer traditional native sensibilities of the "lost home."

By contrast, Miyoshi returned, after several decades of separation from Japan and things Japanese. His brief reencounter resembled the familiar trajectory of the ethnographer returning to the site of original fieldwork years later to see what had changed and what has remained the same. Miyoshi's return was driven neither by a sentimental impulse compelling the search for the person he was when he left Japan nor by the usual cultural conceit motivating Japanese to reunite with what they believed they had abandoned and lost by turning to the destructive lures of Western learning. While it is difficult to know what persuaded Miyoshi to revisit Japan after so long an absence, both in his scholarly activities and his traveling back, it is conceivable that his solidarity with the margins, renamed as the Third World, was induced by the conviction that when he first left Japan in the early fifties, the country was still part of that peripheral world. Coming back twenty-five years later convinced him that Japan had left this earlier classification and had been moved up the scale to join the privileged rank of advanced capitalist nations—that is, it had become part of the center, at long last acquiring a position of equality, which, he observed, Japan was not always willing to accept. But, as he was to note in his later work, Japan would continue to retain the trace of its earlier marginality in the continual repetition of appealing to haunting reminders of what it had left behind. I shall return to this point later.

Miyoshi's plunge back was already announced by the formation of a critical project concerning how Japan and its literature was being taught and written about in the United States. It was during this period that he wrote *Accomplices of Silence* (1974) and the magisterial *As We Saw Them* (1979). While his earlier book *The Divided Self* (1969) focused on Victorian writers, *Accomplices of Silence* concentrated on novels by prominent modern Japanese authors that already had been translated into English and were thus accessible to non-Japanese readers. With this sample of modern Japanese novelistic production (*shishōsetsu*), Miyoshi wanted particularly to illustrate how the preoccupation with the individualized self obstructed any consideration of the surrounding world that led to a studied silence about it. The problem Miyoshi grasped, which others had failed to see, demonstrated that what Japanese fashioned as a novel was more an attempt to fuse received literary conventions with the more formal models derived from the West.

In this regard, the retreat to the interiorized self constituted a solution to what might have appeared as an irresolvable cleft between a prior tradition of prose writing and the conventions of the modern novel. But the effort to accommodate native literary practice to the form of the modern, Western novel was further complicated by the intervening mediations of Japan's modernizing experience. Fredric Jameson has explained Miyoshi's achievement in the following way: "Masao Miyoshi's classic *Accomplices of Silence* marks the gap between the raw materials of Japanese social experience and these abstract formal patterns of Western novel construction that cannot always be welded together seamlessly" (2016: 286). Moreover, at the time this text appeared, Miyoshi also began recording his observations concerning the difficulty of maintaining dialogue and argument with Japanese that ultimately led him to see its connection to their indifference to and avoidance of criticism. In a sense, the novelistic fixation with a self that appeared unconcerned with the immediacy of the external world and the incidence of critical indifference are two sides of the same coin. *As We Saw Them* focused on the account of the first Japanese embassy to the United States in 1860 and how Japanese looked upon the Americans they encountered and saw themselves in this new relationship with others and their world. There is a recognizable identity between the book's subject, the first Japanese going to America and encountering Americans for the first time, and what had been there and not here, and Miyoshi's own desired trajectory and experience.

When Miyoshi turned to explaining Japan's modern literature and the culture it authorized, his attitude toward the rethinking of Japan was reinforced by the recognition of the larger necessity of transfiguring the postwar discipline of area and regional studies. His engagement of area studies as a supposed discipline was preceded by his interest in ethnic studies, which grew out of his own commitment to the Third World liberation movement in the late 1960s and early 1970s on the University of California, Berkeley, campus and the struggle against the war in Vietnam and the university's administration. The immediate occasion was his criticism of the university's Oriental Languages and Literatures Department (as it was then called) and its treatment of students who claimed Asian ancestry and what he charged as their unfair treatment. These concerns led him to consider the larger question raised by area studies as it was being organized and taught in American universities and colleges, especially the graduate programs devoted to producing specialists in Asian studies. Japan had been in the train of new area studies programs in the United States after World War II, and Miyoshi acknowledged both the importance of broadening the world in which Japan had been resituated and the necessity of redefining its relationship to it. But early on, he noticed the transparent nature of a pseudodiscipline that appealed to representing regions and areas when they were in fact organized on the basis of single nation-states. He was responding to the practice of singularizing the study of Japan (or any so-called territory) as if it constituted a wider region or area, when in fact it was nothing more than a new version of national studies. Even in institutional centers that advertised programs that represented a cultural region like East Asia, the actual practice inevitably broke down into a national division of academic labor between China, Japan, and Korea.

Where area studies sought to differentiate itself from more established programs relating to Europe was to see nation/region as the field where students spent time gathering data for their research projects and using the native language in both their work and daily interactions with the nationals. The "field," as it was increasingly called among the cognoscenti and coreligionists of area studies, was, in fact, driven by an unacknowledged ethnographic unconscious constituted by an unsuitable mix of earlier conceits that had previously and habitually classified such regions as less advanced than Euro-America and the World War II obsession of collecting and gathering information concerning the enemy that led to the establishment of service language schools in Japanese, Chinese, Russian, and other strategic and difficult languages. It should be noted that this sense of learning a difficult language was invariably identified with a less developed region and/or an enemy. At the heart of the purpose of area studies was information gathering, which was seen as a useful resource for the national security state during the Cold War epoch. But its apparent difficulty became a sign of an immense difference from the settled and familiar West. Gathering information became the principal purpose and resulted in undermining the ambition of comparability that area studies had initially pledged to pursue as its primary vocation. Instead of bringing the regions of the world together, it kept them separated and ranked according to putatively developmentalist schemes (Euro-American) determined by considerations vital to American interests in the Cold War. It was in this particular context that Miyoshi grasped the process by which Japan had been scaled upward, singularized and exceptionalized when it was promoted as a model for the unaligned to emulate rather than merely being consigned to the Third World and the recently decolonized, failing new nations. Miyoshi knew that Japan, America's former enemy, had managed to escape this dismal destiny by becoming one of the early charter members of the new American imperium inaugurating the Cold War. Moreover, it is important to keep in mind that area studies itself was the stunted offspring of World War II and nineteenth-century geography that arbitrarily organized societies according to older imperial borders and names that the military subsequently employed. In this regard, area studies simply denied the advice of an old Buddhist adage concerning the illusions of the world and thus a knowledge that there was no East and West, to remain chained to a fixed cartographic directional tyranny that sees the East as East, with all its attending prior associations of backwardness and marginality from the dominant centrality of starting from the West.

Miyoshi thus early grasped the fictitious claims of area studies, its fraudulent claims to disciplinary status, its metonymic substitution of the nation for the region, and the way its continued institutional existence in universities was linked to their capacity to secure funding from whatever source they could tap or hold up, which eventually included foreign governments and corporations, and, in the case of Japan, former fascist millionaires. But he clearly saw this as merely a symptom of the larger tendency of universities and colleges to succumb to the temptation to rededicate their putative "mission" by converting knowledge into intellectual property. This epochal transformation of the university was accompanied by and connected to what Miyoshi early perceived as the simultaneous bankruptcy of the humanistic disciplines, which, instead of resolving the emergent crisis, turned to repetitiously valorizing the fetish of difference and separation. He would live to see the acceleration of this failure in institutions of higher learning and various private foundations, whereby the alleged "crisis of the humanities" itself became a regular commodity hawked for steady consumption as a substitute for encouraging any real effort to devise a conceivable solution. In an insular area studies, tainted by a fantasy representation and contaminated by its complicity with the national security state, Miyoshi saw the tightening of enclosures into insurmountable Chinese Walls. The initial disciplinary impulse that had sought to reconstitute their borders to make crossings easier resulted in further bolstering their "untrespassability" in the name of identity and difference. In his thinking, they—the humanistic disciplines—have accomplished nothing in the attempt to reimagine critical programs capable of accomplishing more than simply contesting the new role played by universities in their corporate function. This historical failure has resulted in confirming students as vital consumers in a menu of subjective identities emphasizing a plurality of differences (Miyoshi and Harootunian 2002: 15).

The clearest testament to this mission to reconfigure area studies into a form of critical intervention was Miyoshi's essay "Japan Is Not Interesting," from the year 2000, which also represents his last essay on Japan (Miyoshi 2010: 189–204). The major portion of my account of Miyoshi's thinking is based on this essay. In this remarkable and prescient essay, Miyoshi reminded us of the consequences of narrow area specialization, deliberately withdrawing from the world of diversity, masking its knowledge of exceptional singularity as a metonymical substitute for the whole, and furthering its cognitive failing to align the gathering of local information with critical practices leading to involvement and intervention. His own attitude exemplified how practice united politics with scholarship, as he demonstrated in his own involvement in the Third World movement, previously mentioned, and his tireless work for the PLO that earned him the enmity of many of his colleagues in English and probably contributed to inducing him to take a chaired professorship at the University of California, San Diego. His practice was not simply a reflection of his eccentric personal style, as many of his contemporaries believed. In this essay, Miyoshi turned his sights on Japanese themselves, and whatever shortcomings he charged against them would rebound to the second order of practitioners of Japan-related studies, the foreign Japan specialists and what might be called their single-minded dedication to the custodial care of an untroubled image of Japanese society. In the 1980s and 1990s, any criticism of Japanese society inevitably brought down an avalanche of denunciations of "Japan bashing" from professional Japan specialists, like Miyoshi's former San Diego colleague Chalmers Johnson (who later changed his own position on Japan) and others who feigned scholarly outrage but who sounded more like carnival hawkers peddling the official line for Japan Inc., as if it was the real account and not the academic equivalent of snake oil. On the Japanese side, the indifference to criticism, he noted, was transmuted into accusation.

This anticritical reflex in Japan studies outside of Japan (as well as in Japan) was especially assured by the principal citadels of Japanese studies, already financially obliged to Japanese corporate donors, if not the Japanese state. Additionally, these academic bastions devoted to Japanese studies gestured toward a form of ancestor worship by naming them after pioneers in the field who may have also brought in money for the center, usually from Japan. Moreover, many of these centers were occupied by self-satisfied specialists who, like the ancestral founders they reproduced, had served the Japanese state and already won recognition from the Japanese imperial institution by being rewarded for performing loyal services to the emperor's invisible empire that elevated them into one rank or another in the Order of the Rising Sun (*Kyokujitsu-shō*). Many of them constituted the front line of opposition in the United States against the appearance of critical opinion on Japan to become the designated gatekeepers of the official image, acting in the capacity of a surrogate chamber of commerce for Japan. It is important to note, in this connection, that even though Japan had been stripped of its extensive colonial empire after the Pacific War, the Japanese monarch (*tennō*) retained the title of emperor. He still presided over the invisible empire of deities and ancestors from which he had descended and derived his authority. In Miyoshi's view, Japan specialists merely mirrored the image of Japan that Japanese wished to project and promote. The problem he identified was the disappearance of critical perspective and, as recorded in *As We Saw Them*, the role enacted by a tradition that encouraged reluctance toward the act of interpretation. If Miyoshi reported dissatisfaction with his former homeland, he was particularly troubled by the way Japanese thinking about themselves had been reflected in scholarship and writing by non-Japanese, namely Americans. Apparently, in this connection, Miyoshi dismissed Karatani Kōjin's lecture titled "Japan Is Interesting because Japan Is Not Interesting" (even though he had not read it) because he concluded that, when considered from the perspective that Japan is not interesting, it could *in fact* be said to be of some interest (Miyoshi and Yoshimoto 2007: 290–91).

As a precedent, if not template, for the kind of argument he wanted to make, Miyoshi returned to Victorian England to draw upon the critical writings of Matthew Arnold to formulate his own assessment of why Japan was no longer interesting. Arnold, in the late 1880s, had struck out against American civilization for its lack of "the interesting." The object of his critique targeted a rejection of America's decentralized democracy and its unerring aptitude for stunting lasting cultural growth, a failure to uphold standards of elegance and refinement that would only invite the reproduction of unrestrained cultural dilution. Recognizing the temporal distance separating Arnold from himself, but not overlooking the class conceits that succeeded to creep into Arnold's critical writings, Miyoshi wondered if Japan, like the United States, lacked the truly "interesting" in national life. He concluded that its absence derived not from the character of its democratic endowment but from the nonappearance of dissent and protest. Here Miyoshi may have overstated Japan's new American-sponsored democratic vocation. While the US military occupation supplied Japanese society with a new political template, complete with a new constitution written by non-Japanese, it remained a political solution to Japan's errant prewar order, imposed by foreigners in record-breaking time on top of the basic components of the earlier sociopolitical configuration that had managed to produce fascism, imperialism, and war in Asia and the Pacific. In this regard, the return of the past was the reappearance of history's contamination of the present.

The occupation provided Japan with an infrastructure of democratic procedures that, because it was imposed from the outside over the principal components of an older prewar configuration, created the figure of a palimpsest that allowed the older elements of the past to enter the present's surface. The occupation's policies were far from achieving a substantive transformation that would have required thorough removal of the retained remnants of the older order that continued to contaminate the democratic imaginary. Even in the new Japanese constitution, often described as more democratic than the US Constitution, the drafters retained the position of the emperor as the symbol of unity of the Japanese people, which referred not to a free citizenry that has demanded constitutional representation but to an emperor who has been reassigned a new role to symbolize a unified "nation's people" (*kokumin*). Because a unified nation's people was an abstraction that had no real historical existence as a sovereign political agent, the alleged symbolic emperor could not refer to anything outside of himself. An appeal to such an abstract conception of popular sovereignty now assigned to the Japanese people had never existed historically, serving as the subjective agent positioned to bring about a constitution. The retention of the emperor as a symbolic figure merely constituted a ghostly reminder of the older Meiji Constitution of 1890, which had been enacted as a gift by the emperor to the nation's people, who became his subjects (*shinmin*). With this image of an overstated Japanese democracy, Miyoshi correctly implied the importance of an existing democratic subjectivity that would substantively anchor or ground the sociopolitical system in the individual's rights of critical dissent and protest. In this respect, his political sensibilities were assailed by the spectacle of Japan's steady slide into a frozen cultural emanation—culturalism—that was supposed to explain how Japanese were different from others and how this cultural difference remained as an unchanging immanence immune to history. In other words, beneath the palimpsest's surface procedural democracy, one inflicted by foreigners, persisted a deeper layer comprised of a vast timeless cultural configuration that had not changed since the Stone Age and could easily make its way to the present to continue determining Japanese conduct and supplying the correct knowledge with which to relate to the world. This unchanging cultural configuration yielded a timeless totalizing knowledge that offered the surety of certainty that would both discourage and foreclose the necessity of all criticism.[1]

In the essay "Japan Is Not Interesting," Miyoshi explained that he talked with several representatives from different social strata of Japanese society and concluded that a vacuum of cultural ideas persevered in contemporary Japan (Miyoshi 2010: 191–95). Japan is uninteresting, he asserted, because it is commonly known that in Japan's culture and society, there are wise men (*kunshi*) who are unable to animate and move anyone (Miyoshi and Yoshimoto 2007: 286). What appears lacking in Japan, answering his question, is "dialogue" generated over a topic of conversation, the absence of any genuine aptitude for argumentation. This criticism of various types of Japanese and the incapacity of Japanese society to generate true dialogic encounters prefigured his own later difficulties with Nobel Laureate

1. See Arai 2016 for a compelling and penetrating account of the role performed by psychology and education in operationalizing this knowledge into a remedial ideology for a neoliberal Japan.

Ōe Kenzaburo, in whom he—Miyoshi—had invested great expectations of activism that he believed the writer had failed to fulfill. He had already given up on Ōe's writings, which, he confessed, he increasingly found unreadable. In his discussions with Yoshimoto, he recalls a later interview of the writer Murakami Haruki in the *New York Times*, where the novelist self-importantly declared that in Japan, it has been said that he—Murakami— is a dissenter. For Miyoshi, this only meant that authoritative and knowledgeable people in the literary world had not yet seriously accepted him. Murakami is said to have laughed off Miyoshi's slight; Miyoshi's response to Murakami was that laughing it off was not an argument. Along the way, he— Miyoshi—replied to his face that he thought Murakami was an entertainer (*yokyōka*) and his work worthless (Miyoshi and Yoshimoto 2007: 287–88).

Miyoshi linked the emptiness of this cultural malaise to an observation that pointed to a disproportionate balance between the behavior of large numbers of Japanese tourists traveling abroad and the few foreigners who visited Japan. Everywhere he looked he saw nothing but the signs of somnolent stagnation and cultural self-satisfaction, and he wondered why Japan, at the time the second-largest economy in the world, was getting no respect from the United States, Great Britain, and France, which meant no expression of interest. If the question was why foreigners had no interest in touring Japan, the answer could be found in what he considered the miasma of a debilitating discourse on national identity, whose presupposition had preceded the program of constructing a modern society. This discourse subsequently underscored the importance of a preoccupation with exceptionality of the nation-form, drawing its strength from a long-standing tradition of island isolation and a growing nativism initially spurred by Japan's intensely accelerated contact with the West and the threat of slipping into the colonial status of its Asian neighbors.

Despite a devastating war in Asia and the Pacific, defeat, and reconstruction, Miyoshi argued, the Japanese national *amour propre* and the obsessive fascination with a singularized collective identity and ideology of a unitary and homogeneous ethnicity never disappeared. In fact, it remained such a powerful force that it could strengthen itself at the expense of entertaining other alternatives demanded by changing historical circumstances. Owing to Japan's own growing colonial empire in Asia before the war, it was widely believed that Japanese, like other Asians, were constituted of heterogeneous ethnicities. The idea of a homogeneous race surfaced only after World War II as a support of what many believed was a damaged sense of national identity. Cultural discourse on what it meant to be Japanese was literally empowered to choke off any threat of other possibilities. The problem, as Miyoshi saw it, was a pervasive form of nationalism, condensed in the phrase "We Japanese" (*Wareware Nihonjin*), which seems to have been invested with amuletic powers whenever uttered, deployed as if it was a magical incantation, a mantra, empowered to immediately summon the whole arsenal of exceptional difference derived from mythic origins that are invoked whenever conversations and writings turn to other peoples, however obliquely and indirectly.

Miyoshi overlooked in this insightful observation the fact that the impulse bringing forth the chant "We Japanese" was driven by an imperative to always compare Japan, a kind of automatic reflex derived from having been compelled to live comparatively as a result of the intimate contact with the West, the earlier Chinese civilization, and, undoubtedly, the dominance of Americanization in the long postwar. It could be seen as a form of "colonization of the mind," even though Japanese haven't seen it that way. In this respect, the insistent repetition of an emblematic identity was a necessary reminder and reinforcement of Japanese difference as a sure preventative from its immanent disappearance before the foreign other. According to Miyoshi, the invocation really means Japan, not, as such, the Japanese people and refers generally to everyday life, not as a fixed dogma but rather as a structure of feeling or common sense, which he considered dangerous because it represses history. Its danger lay in its capacity to bring forth an explosion of "repetitious synonyms and verbosity" without whatsoever signifying any meaning (Miyoshi and Yoshimoto 2007: 335). The importance of this common reflex, which came without saying as it goes without saying, was its capacious power to link businessmen, capitalists, and managers of Japan's consumer society to the benefit of the political classes. The recitation of "We Japanese" did not mean or even call for the activation of mutual cooperation but, to the contrary, was used to suppress the real sense of unconcern toward people without capital and power. It resulted in the figuration of an entire ideology of Japanism (*Nihonshugi*) constituted of older staples such as cherry blossoms and sliced raw fish (*sashimi*). Miyoshi reminded readers that in the United States, the phrase "We Americans" is never used as a repetitious mantra.

At the heart of this empowering ideology of national identity appeared the authority of the imperial institution enabled by the US decision during the occupation to retain the emperor (Hirohito) and absolve him of all war responsibility and guilt. In no time at all, the divine monarch shed his inherited charisma derived from an indeterminate archaic time to slip into the slippers of a petit bourgeois family man, spending his spare time puttering with hydroids. Even though in this essay Miyoshi gestured toward addressing the role played by the emperor in the reconstruction of a cultural discourse in the immediate postwar, he was particularly concerned with the intimate relationship between the imperial institution and the organization of the Japanese sociopolitical order. He also recognized in the increasing closing down of any criticism of the emperor a prefiguration of the larger banishment of a critical attitude. In the case of the emperor, criticism invariably risks the threat of coercion leading to injury, intimidation, job loss, and even ostracism, which undoubtedly enforced the larger move of ridding Japanese society of all criticism, which, in Miyoshi's opinion, meant closing off all possibility of resistance. It should be recalled that the emperor had been considered a "living deity" until Japan's defeat in 1945 and his later disavowal of divinity. But the disavowal hardly dissuaded Japanese from forgetting his claim to divinity overnight as a descendant of the sun goddess. Moreover, the decision to retain him and the imperial household meant that he would continue to preside over all those rites and rituals that would connect contemporary Japan to its archaic origins and their principal purpose of beckoning the national deities and ancestors to maintain the well-being and good fortune of the country and expressing thanks for such blessings. In other words, the regular rituals the emperor performed immediately called attention to his divinity, since it was such divine embodiment in the first place that guaranteed their successful enactment. Hence, retaining the emperor resituated the archaic exemplar of the unification of politics and society in the modern present. It is in this way that the new symbolic emperor, who was supposed to refer to the unity of the "nation's people," referred to himself. These rituals functioned to elicit continuing good fortune and bounty for the nation from the deities, binding emperor and people into a unified collective purpose, reflecting the archaic principle that made no distinction between the performance of religious rituals and governance. The emperor's performance of these archaic rituals and ceremonies also signified conducting political affairs. In spite of the occupation's attempt to separate religion and politics, then, the reinstating of the imperial figure insured both the continuing identity of the two in the body of the emperor and the archaic power of divinity that mandated this combination of sovereign authority as the basis of all legitimation.

By the same measure, rescuing and salvaging the imperial institution was accompanied by the occupation's decision to actively return large numbers of prewar bureaucrats to positions of power, which further guaranteed the continuation of the principal governmental form of the old order. Empowered to perform rituals and ceremonies as forms of governance, an investiture of authority that he—the emperor—alone embodied, trumping all other exercises of legitimation, any act or utterance would thus constitute a representation of the unity or identity of interests of the political and social communities, which, in him, were conflated and remained indistinguishable. In other words, state and civil society were cemented into a singular and undifferentiated identity, and the putative will of the people was "integrated" with the will of the emperor (at least in the Japanese translation of the constitution). The importance of the emperor embodying both politics and the social, for Miyoshi, lay in its authorization of a discourse on identity, reflecting a virtual cultural unconscious, which saw the emperor and the Japanese people stretching back in an unbroken lineage to divine origins and its exceptional claim to a reign of unchanging timelessness.

In fact, this arrangement, according to Miyoshi, was continually enhanced and fostered by the US military occupation precisely because it acknowledged in its midst a reminder of a "visible dominant other," an unfamiliar alterity that had to be made familiar. That is to say, the image of the Japanese had to be dramatically and rapidly transmuted from the unfamiliar and strange, which required altering the dehumanized wartime enemy into a familiar and comfortable friend and inverting the previous slogans admonishing the population to fight to the final end, urging national unity and the demands of total sacrifice, into their postwar opposite, calling for "penitence," the formation of "peace nation, "culture nation," even "atomic bomb nation," whereby Japanese claimed nuclear victim status. Here is the nub of Miyoshi's critique of the absence of criticism in Japan, leveled first against an army of occupation that often callously and thoughtlessly pursued a transformation of Japan that was more window dressing than a program directed at the realization of substantive change. On the other hand, Miyoshi had no reluctance in charging the Japanese with accepting the lures of a devil's promise, which resulted in bringing the country within the precinct of the new American imperium. His complaint was really directed against a long history that had repeatedly demonstrated Japan's willingness to bend to the blandishments of what appeared as a superior culture and surrender its own particularistic difference to the guarantee of incorporation into another putative universalism whose claims were no less the product of a specific cultural formation than its own. He also knew that in these epochal cultural transactions, it was always the political elites that benefited. With the US occupation, Miyoshi noticed that the Japanese willingness to capitulate constituted an ideological frame predisposed to manufacturing "consensus," with which the privileged and empowered of Japanese society (all those prewar bureaucrats and businessmen who escaped jail sentences handed out by the War Crimes Tribunal) were restored to their previous positions. In Miyoshi's view, this return of the principal personnel of the prewar system meant they would occupy positions that enabled them to successfully manipulate the political process, concealing the scandal of difference, unevenness, and inequality.

This image of a smooth and unruffled social order in Japan managed by experts was also exported to the United States, where it was valorized in a number of ways, culminating in Ezra Vogel's best-selling book (in Japan and the United States), absurdly titled (for Japanese consumption, to be sure) *Japan as Number One* (1979). But if Vogel's book provided double service to both the American national security state and Japan, Inc., and undoubtedly made his views particularly welcome in both societies, one lone reviewer in the pages of the *New York Review of Books* called it for what it was, exposing its content as ideological trash serving both American and Japanese political interests.

Miyoshi saw through the haze of this fantasy image, which he believed sought to demonstrate the success of the democratic process exemplified by Japan's rapid and successful reconstruction of the country from the ruins of defeat. But the fantasy worked to reveal the exceptionalist native genius that was now paradoxically offered up as a model worthy of imitation among emerging non-aligned nations in the Cold War struggle. Here, he returned to the role of the emperor and rightly pointed to the one effective instrument of control that managed to keep itself veiled yet passed for an unchanging and unpolitical cultural essence, both communal and permanent. At the core of this unpolitical cultural politics was, of course, the restored emperor, who now, as previously mentioned, symbolized the unity of the Japanese "nation's people." During the early years of the postwar, several writers and thinkers, such as the novelist Mishima Yukio and philosopher Tanabe Hajime, proposed that the emperor authorized the making of culture but remained outside of the actual historical process of production, which meant he was both in and out of time. Hence, the emperor was empowered to simultaneously perform in such ways that his enactment fused religious rituals, the ceremony of governance, and the production of culture. As a result, he stood at the top of a pyramid organized into a lasting hierarchy of social classes, compelling the expectation that all segments cohere in this tight communal configuration founded on archaic tribal familistic principles. All, moreover, looked to this Arnoldian conception of culture that permits no disagreement, dissent, or opposition. In this connection, it is important to mention that Miyoshi's good friend Karatani Kōjin took exception with Miyoshi's blanket dismissal of dissent in Japan by claiming he had overstated it by overlooking instances of protest and mobilized demonstrations.

Yet I think Miyoshi was more right than wrong, inasmuch as his analysis explained the reasons for the absence of genuine dissensus formed by the relationship of criticism to the practical struggle of resistance in Japan that Karatani's defense failed to address. Moreover, Karatani's critique by itself could not persuasively show either moments of effective resistance or lasting forms of opposition against the state, but only reaction responses prompted by the immediacy of events that just as quickly dissipated, as the recent example of Fukushima and the spreading dangers of nuclear toxicity amply show. Miyoshi also perceived in this hermetically sealed social scheme (which also resembled the structure of a political Ponzi scheme) the reasons for Japan's removal from its world and the consequential inability to grasp the nature of its isolation. "Culturally and intellectually," he wrote, "the endless regurgitation of Japan's 'tradition' produces nothing that stirs any new enthusiasm" (Miyoshi 2010: 201). It yields nothing but interminable boredom and the lack of the "interesting."

Miyoshi discovered only a few "interesting" people, who, like himself, I would add, were still capable of serious criticism and dissent. But he knew they remained invisible, as he remained distant, remote, and often inaudible from the scene he addressed. What troubled him most about this Japanese example he set before his readers was recognition of the spectacle of people reluctant to talk about any issue other than their own identities in fear of misrepresentation. He saw no discernible kinship between the Japanese obsession with their self-identity, repeating its distinguishing features like a religious chant, as if even a momentary lapse would result in its disappearance, and signifying an indifference to others because it always leads to misunderstanding. Aware of an earlier area studies paradigm that sought to represent others, even at the price of trying to make them look like us, Japan became America's Dr. Moreau's island, a laboratory whereby unconstrained experimentation was conducted to transform lower forms of animal life into humans. It was this episode that prefigured the formation of the subsequently expanded model announcing America's worldly mission to militarily intervene everywhere in what now has resulted in innumerable catastrophically failed attempts at nation formation. Yet Miyoshi also knew that representation was a hazardous dodge and dangerous exercise, just as he was convinced that self-representation belonged to no privileged and authoritative group, that it was pointless to serve as proxy patriotic custodians of another's culture and history.

If he acknowledged, as we must today, that it is precisely this new nativist move that has increasingly occupied the place vacated by the older model of area studies, which lost its purchase with the end of the Cold War, it is also necessary to recognize that along the way it disclosed an imperial conceit and intellectual bankruptcy long before. This is not to say that Miyoshi approved of its function, which he knew shared the same avoidance of criticism as the Japanese preoccupation with identity and a thoughtless "social scientific" acceptance of the most retrograde authoritarian political forms as a step to realizing liberal government, now misrecognized as "democracy" (Tanaka 2002: 102). Paradoxically, this was an inversion of Marxism, which has argued that liberalism leads to oligarchic and authoritarian rule—that is, fascism. Instead, Miyoshi turned away from such negativity to concentrate on the invisible and neglected minorities that majorities invariably overlook and called for an alliance of all the "exploited," despite the claims of difference. This has become the silhouette of another possible conception of area studies, one that might possess the capacity of upholding opposition of any ethnic and cultural group to privatize and monopolize its identity as a permanent emanation.

Above all else, Miyoshi dedicated himself to acting on this perception, by opposing a scholarship devoted to maintaining this image and as a practical activist pledged to changing its terms. "For," as he put it, "the only alliance that is needed now is the alliance of all the exploited, regardless of the categories of difference" (Miyoshi 2010: 204).[2] The defect of indifference he first observed in Japan he saw reflected and reenacted in the United States. And it was his sensitivity to its appalling consequences for both countries that ultimately guided him through the thicket of American academic hypocrisy, the runaway curricular confusion brought on by its commodification and the swamp of routinized administrative corruption masquerading as "leadership" to reinforce his conviction that thinking critically and finding ways to put it into practice were indistinguishable—that is, they were one and the same thing. This is how some of us came to see and know him, and his example offered a gift in the only worthwhile lesson on

2. See also Miyoshi and Yoshimoto 2007: 342, 345, where the only category of importance for Miyoshi is humanity (*ningen*).

which to found a lasting educational project that he feared was already slipping from the scene. In this regard, he more than fulfilled the requirement of "practical struggle," which Gilles Deleuze proposed when he explained why "revolution never proceeds by way of the negative" (1994: 208). "Practical struggle," he advised, "never proceeds by way of the negative but by way of difference and its power of affirmation, and the war of the righteous is for the conquest of the highest power, that of deciding problems by restoring them to their truth, by evaluating that truth beyond the representations of consciousness and the forms of the negative, and by acceding at last to their imperatives on which they depend" (208). Because he was who he was, as we saw him, Miyoshi left Japan for other fields of experience and other cultures in distress, and ultimately turned his attention toward the coming irresolvable ecological crisis, which would preoccupy his energies to the last.

References

Arai, Andrea. 2016. *The Strange Child: Education and the Psychology of Patriotism in Recessionary Japan*. Stanford, CA: Stanford University Press.

Deleuze, Gilles. 1994. *Repetition and Difference*. Translated by Paul Patton. New York: Columbia University Press.

Jameson, Fredric. 2016. *The Modernist Papers*. London: Verso.

Miyoshi, Masao. 1969. *The Divided Self: A Perspective on the Literature of the Victorians*. New York: New York University Press.

———. 1974. *Accomplices of Silence: The Modern Japanese Novel*. Berkeley: University of California Press.

———. 1979. *As We Saw Them: The First Japanese Embassy to the United States (1860)*. Berkeley: University of California Press.

———. 2009. *This Is Not Here: Selected Photography*. Los Angeles: highmoonoon.

———. 2010. *Trespasses: Selected Essays by Masao Miyoshi*. Edited by Eric Cazdyn. Durham, NC: Duke University Press.

Miyoshi, Masao, and H. D. Harootunian, eds. 2002. *Learning Places: The Afterlives of Area Studies*. Durham, NC: Duke University Press.

Miyoshi, Masao, and Mitsuhiro Yoshimoto. 2007. *Teiko no ba e [Sites of Resistance]*. Kyoto, Japan: Rakuhoku shuppan.

Tanaka, Stefan. 2002. "Objectivism and the Eradication of Critique in Japanese History." In *Learning Places: The Afterlives of Area Studies*, edited by Masao Miyoshi and H. D. Harootunian, 80–102. Durham, NC: Duke University Press.

Vogel, Ezra. 1979. *Japan as Number One: Lessons for America*. New York: Harper and Row.

Asia: A Fallacy of Misplaced Concreteness

Stefan Tanaka

One sees nothing if one simply goes somewhere without problematizing oneself.
—Takeuchi Yoshimi, *What Is Modernity?*

Time is everything, man is nothing; he is at the most the incarnation of time.
—Karl Marx, *The Poverty of Philosophy*

Historians write about others, usually from some past that is treated
as dead or foreign. It is a "safe" endeavor, secure in the comfort of recent
methodologies and the accumulation of knowledge and perspective. Even
though historians have some future in mind, we hide behind our methods and assumptions to distance ourselves from our object of study, often
obscuring the subject. That is what makes this engagement with Miyoshi

I would like to thank Paul Bové and Rob Wilson, both for the opportunity and their
patience. Many of the ideas in this essay were honed in the stimulating workshop at the
University of Witwatersrand. My thanks to Dilip Menon, Wang Hui, and Achille Mbembe
for the intellectual exchange.

boundary 2 46:3 (2019)   DOI 10.1215/01903659-7614123   © 2019 by Duke University Press

so hard to write. It brings out my insecurities—the challenges he issued, and then the realization that more often than not, he was right (which of course further exacerbates those self-doubts). I remember when Masao told me about the draft of his 2000 essay "Japan Is Not Interesting" (2010c). I responded with surprise (pleasantly) and admiration that he would have such a title that directly challenges a field known for its -phils and -phobes. I might even have been the befuddled colleague he reports in the essay.

Yet the title "Japan Is Not Interesting" embeds a series of issues that, typical of his thinking, challenge us to query what we think we know. For my focus on his legacy, it is the importance of pasts and how our engagement with pasts must go beyond the discipline of history. Miyoshi placed into practice what Takeuchi Yoshimi, in the epigraph above, understood as the limitation of Japan's prewar and postwar understanding of China. Takeuchi suggests that soldiers and politicians, as well as China scholars, despite being in China or "knowing" China, "saw nothing" (2005: 163).[1] For scholars today, this should be an important question: To what extent is our knowledge system appropriate to societies today, or even to an earlier era? Takeuchi is correct to point out that we know others through ourselves. What we think we know is often just a portion, or worse, a fantasy of what exists. If we return to "Japan Is Not Interesting," my initial reaction was as a historian whose object of study is usually the past of a "Japan." Yet when one reads Miyoshi's essay, perspective becomes more ambiguous—to whom is Japan uninteresting, and to what extent do we, specialists on Japan, "see" or "know" Japan? After all, the essay started from his conversations with friends and former classmates in Japan who casually commented that Japan is uninteresting.[2] Second, this statement raises a question of nation-state: To what extent does a Japan, especially in an increasingly global world, hinder our understanding of others on the archipelago as well as throughout the world? In an age when information is virtually instantaneous and available at our fingertips, what types of places now have meaning for individuals (the nation-state still certainly has meaning for governments that marshal support for armed conflict and for corporations that exploit national boundaries)?

1. Takeuchi was criticizing what is quite possibly the first Asian studies area studies program in the twentieth century. The Japanese study of the continent certainly predates the US area studies programs, which emerged during the Cold War. See, for example, Cumings 2002.
2. The phrases in Japanese were "nihon wa tsumaranai" (Japan is boring/uninteresting) and "nihon wa dame da" (Japan is no good).

A hint toward how Miyoshi offers a way to deal with these issues is in his 1996 essay, "Outside Architecture" (2010e). Miyoshi had a keen eye for and attraction to architecture (and later photography—see his *This Is Not Here* [2009]), but like most things, that did not keep him from seeing limitations or problems. He writes, "Perhaps, instead of building guilty conscience into aesthetically, theoretically, intellectually admirable but useless shapes and forms, we might stroll in the streets of Kawasaki, Keelung, and Puchon (west of Seoul) and learn how people live. . . . There may be more life there than in architecture's patronage houses" (2010e: 156–57). Here, Miyoshi—like Takeuchi—is challenging us to see beyond our comfort zone within the certainty of modern categories: experts, professing on others, often don't see what they claim to know. I see the phrase "building guilty conscience into . . . admirable but useless shapes and forms" as akin to Takeuchi's claim that Japanese in China (many of whom often desired to help/aid Chinese) "saw nothing."[3] Instead, Miyoshi suggests that we stroll among those we have objectified. To stroll is different than going to or knowing; it is to be with, to be willing to interact, to engage and see something new about oneself. Most area studies specialists would say we do this through the learning of the language and culture, in the rite of passage (dissertation research) and subsequent trips. Yet Miyoshi, like Takeuchi, is willing to suggest that we "see nothing"; we see only the category rather than the activity it purports to encompass.

In my effort to look forward through Miyoshi, I see that he spent much of his career querying and moving around the idea of "Asia." In his case, the stroll can be seen as a method; it operates in the postwar knowledge system we think we know, while not being contained within. His career was a long stroll. He left Japan (figuratively and then physically) for English literature, and after becoming well established in that field, he shifted toward Japanese literature and studies, and then he moved to sites of knowledge maintenance and production—area studies, the global economy, and the university. This career embeds methods that we might take more seriously in our overly specialized disciplines. It restores alterity—the possibility of the self interacting with and even becoming the other—rather

3. This issue has profound implications for the future of the university. See, for example, Miyoshi's 2000 essay "Ivory Tower in Escrow" (2010b). I was involved in the work of the Laboratory for Comparative Human Cognition, where concerns about culture and equity were often investigated through community-based research. Such work has the potential both to add a new dimension to the word *public* in a public university and to alter how we conceive of knowledge of others. For a fine overview of such work, see Lassiter 2005.

than the binary form of otherness common to modern society, self vs. other. Through his career, Miyoshi challenged this fixed notion of the modern self, which Michel de Certeau identifies as being maintained by the "repetition of the gesture of exclusion. The 'same' is a historical *form*, a practice of dichotomy, and not a homogeneous *content*" (1992: 18). Miyoshi's wandering to different sites and topics was an interrogation of his own historicity, a refusal to accept the easy dichotomies that led to quick or facile categorization. Instead, this method produced incisive and often difficult questions about our own assumptions. Eric Cazdyn highlights his approach to teaching, which I see as a core principle of his intellectual sojourn: "To see what constitutes the world and to describe it without allegorization is nearly impossible, but such an impossibility is what all of us are conscribed to inhabit" (Cazdyn 2010: xix). This is a riddle of our twentieth-century knowledge system and a challenge for twenty-first-century scholars.

Asia as Spatialized Time

The difficulty of untangling this riddle is located in the conflation within the word Asia, of a relational idea with notions of absolute space (geography) and absolute time (history). In his 1925 Lowell Lectures, Alfred North Whitehead inquired into the place of science in human understanding and exposed the role of time and space as central elements in the mechanistic nature of thought, an epistemology that existed since the seventeenth century and that, in his words, we could "neither live with nor live without" ([1925] 1967: 50). He called this a "Fallacy of Misplaced Concreteness" (51). Whitehead, here, recognized that our current understanding of time and space has been superseded, and he sought another way to understand our world.

We need to question whether Asia, too, is a "misplaced concreteness" that conscribes us.[4] Asia is foundational to the global knowledge system we inhabit; moreover, this system has been built upon principles and ideas that grounded the rise of the liberal-internationalist world during the late nineteenth and twentieth centuries. Yet at the same time, discoveries of special relativity and thermodynamics relegated many mechanistic notions, such as Newton's absolute time and absolute space, to classical science.

4. Sun Ge writes, "As difficult as it is to sort out the question of Asia, it remains an underlying thread running through the intellectual history in the modern world. Hence, we still have to grapple with the question of Asia as one that constitutes a totality in itself" (2000a: 13).

Nevertheless, we still use formalized structures where allegorical accounts comfortably reiterate preconceived forms. After more than thirty-five years since Edward Said's *Orientalism* (1978) (Miyoshi was Said's close friend), various fields have written much, from the early critiques of deconstruction and post-everything, beginning with poststructuralism, to today, where it seems we are no longer re-ing but now un-ing everything. I do not mean to belittle these efforts; my own work fits within some of them. Yet I have been impressed that we always seem to reiterate what has been stated earlier. The forgetting that is a part of our knowledge industry is rather remarkable.

This is particularly true in the case of Asian studies, where the idea of Asia keeps its subfields (Japanese studies, Chinese studies, South Asian studies, etc.) within the Orient; area studies has become a discipline that disciplines its objects. This is the impossibility. We have recognized this to an extent. Simplistically, the nouns have changed from Orient to Asia, and we celebrate that we are in a post-Orientalist phase. Yet the structure of meaning remains despite statements that we know better. We now use Asia as if we have escaped the Orientalist frame. But have we? Unpacking this is harder than simply changing nouns. Unless we develop an understanding of the conflation of relational place and chronological time in how we understand ourselves and others, Asia will continue to be the Orient.

Asia is an accepted "reality"; it is the name of a continent. Yet scholars also understand that Asia is a Western appellation that now applies to this geographical area. But this connection between idea and geography is frequently contested and indeed is rather recent.[5] We can trace the idea of Asia back to the ancient Greeks (who often lived in the geographical region now identified as Asia); for Herodotus, Asia was the land to the east (today, we would call this Anatolia or the Middle East). It is a realm that emerged in the imagination of the ancient Greeks. This Asia is identical with the Orient, an other of a West. But interestingly, even for Herodotus, Asians did not inhabit this land; Scythians, Persians, and the like did. Moreover, people in this Asia did not identify themselves as Asian. They were of a particular community, region, or empire; today they are from particular nations. The word Asia (*yaxiya*) was introduced to the western Pacific by the Jesuits in the seventeenth century. When we move farther east to Tokugawa society, what we now call China was referred to as *shinkoku* (the characters for Qing and country), and one appellation for the people was *tōjin* (the characters for Tang and person). In one eighteenth-century school of scholars

5. For attempts of Russian and Soviet scholars to reframe the Orient, see Tolz 2011, esp. chap. 2.

(*kokugaku*), the use of *chūka* (middle kingdom) was countered with *iteki* (barbarian). *Chūka* was not a place but a condition that was the opposite of *iteki*.

But today, Asia is not just a relational designation, an over there from the ancient Greece or the West. Beginning in the eighteenth century, Asia was located onto a chronology of becoming; it gained temporality. Montesquieu discusses Asia as a static antithesis to the dynamic Europe; Voltaire recognizes it as the beginning of civilization, but one that had never advanced; and Hegel locates Asia (the "Oriental World") as the first stage in the evolution of universal history (Hegel 1956). This shift fixed Asia as a repetitive "gesture of exclusion" that is constantly invoked to reinforce what Certeau refers to as the "same," in this case, the superiority of the West. I invoke Hegel for two reasons. First, he is central in the making of history, more accurately, the spread of historical thinking. Second, his history is the incorporation, the synchronization, of the world into one history, the naturalization of this gesture of exclusion. Rebecca Karl points out that it was not until the late nineteenth century that Asia gained meaning as an autonomous geographical place (1998: 1098–101). D. Graham Burnett calls this synchronized world a geochronocultural tableau (2003: 18).[6]

In this synchronization, Asia becomes spatialized time, a space frozen in the flow of a new historical way of thinking.[7] The recurrence of Asia as Orient, I believe, is from the naturalization of this homogeneous time. This spatialized time is produced from a conflation between the idea of the Orient, the Newtonian notion of time as absolute and external to humans, and geography. This returns us to the epigraph from Marx, about man being an incarnation of time (Lukács 1971: 89).[8] Asia is both a creation of this time as well as a container for such time. Certeau describes the centrality of time in the objectification of ideas such as the idea of Asia: "For three centuries maybe the objectification of the past has made of time the unreflected category of a discipline that never ceases to use it as an instru-

6. Alternatively, Johannes Fabian writes, "In short, *geopolitics* has its ideological foundations in *chronopolitics*" (1983: 144).
7. Numerous intellectuals have discussed the spatialization of time. See, for example, Bergson (1911) 2002; Gross 1982; Fabian 1983.
8. I have relied on the translation from Georg Lukács (1971). The account in the *Collected Works* translates this phrase as "time's carcase" (Marx 1976: 127). The use of *carcase* is common and goes back at least to H. Quelch's translation (Marx 1900: 25), where he uses "carcase of time." I read *incarnation* (or *embodiment*) to be closer to the German: "Die Zeit ist alles, der Mensch ist nichts mehr, er is höchstens noch die Verkörperung der Zeit" (Marx 1974: 85).

ment of classification" (1986: 216). Even though it has been described as "empty" (Benjamin 1968: 261–64), absolute time plays an active role in our knowledge system. History has classified Asia as the first stage, as forever past. Asia shifted from a relational appellation to a fixed place in the ordering of the world. This unified history—the synchronization of the world—depends on the idea of an absolute time for its veracity and uses geography to conflate idea with places to make it "real."

At this point, a detour is necessary. It is important to mention briefly the history of time and the history of history.[9] For my purpose in this essay, it is important to point out that our current understanding of time and of history arose between the seventeenth and nineteenth centuries. The work of Sir Isaac Newton punctuated the abstraction of chronological time from human society in Europe and was a critical move in the rise of science, technology, and capitalism. The turn to a singular, linear chronology became common from the seventeenth century, when Dionysius Petavius, working from Joseph Scaliger's Julian period, proposed the BC/AD system for reckoning years (Wilcox 1987: 203–8; Grafton 2002).[10] A global or universal time emerged in the nineteenth century; in 1884, the International Meridian Conference organized the globe according to one time (synchronized to the Greenwich meridian), divided into twenty-four zones. Acceptance occurred slowly over the next several decades.

The emergence of modern history and its application to the world should be seen in relation to this transformation of time. On the one hand, this mechanical time offered a way for intellectuals such as Hegel to unify the myriad places of the world into one system. It is important to point out that this ordering is far from neutral; chronological time serves as a naturalized metric to emplot and measure development and progress. On the other hand, it provided a new metric for evaluating and ordering information. Events were now verified by dates; seriality, not situatedness, became the common mode of ordering information, and some collective singular (usually the nation-state) became the subject of history, replacing deeds of exemplary figures. Finally, these changes were occurring simultaneously as the European world was discovering science, mapping (and claiming)

9. The literature on each is vast. I discuss these histories in *History without Chronology* (2019).
10. The Anno Domini system was created by Dionysius Exiguus (born in Scythia) in the sixth century, but it was not used widely. I continue to use the BC/AD system in recognition of its historicity. The use of Common Era elides the connection of this form of chronology to the West and Christianity.

the world, and creating new wealth. In short, our understanding of time and history is the foundation of capitalism, liberalism, and imperialism.

One outcome of this rise of a world history is a conflation of the different meanings of the word Asia. The genius of this formulation is to take a relational idea (the Orient) and fix it along a chronological continuum, fixing it as forever the "not yet" (Chakrabarty 2000: 6–11). Otherness shifts from alterity to a fixed other as some past that reinforces the superiority of a modern West. As Asia becomes an autonomous geographical place, it shifts from a relational (and highly unspecified) area to a spatialized time (still rather amorphous). Asia/Orient remains as Hegel's first stage; he cites conditions closer to some idealized originary moment—morality, closeness to nature, and a near absence of subjective will—to "prove" stasis. By temporally marking the otherness of the Orient, it is always already defined by what it does not have or has not yet accomplished in comparison to the West, the most advanced place. History has become an "instrument of classification."

Recognition of the power relationship embedded in the word Asia existed well before Said's powerful exegesis.[11] Intellectuals in the areas designated within Asia (from the Levant to the western Pacific) have long sought to alter the framework or path so that they were not trapped in the first stage. These intellectuals certainly differ considerably, as do the conditions in which they operated. There is a similarity in that each recognized the partiality of what was presented as universal knowledge, and each turned to history to create a knowledge system that did not predetermine the West as supreme. Interestingly, some of the best work on this problematic have come from ascendant modernizing places: Japan, during the first half of the twentieth century; India, especially during the last quarter of the twentieth century; and "China," with its rise at the beginning of the twenty-first century from the Peoples Republic of China and Taiwan (Chen 2010; Sun 2000a, 2000b; Wang 2011c).

From the late nineteenth century, Japanese intellectuals proposed a range of ideas to alter the hierarchy of history (presented to them as universal), and especially during the first decade of the twentieth century,

11. Much of this history of history was recognized by scholars in the non-West, as they sought to write a history of their own society. My *Japan's Orient* (1993) brings out a particular attempt by historians at Tokyo Imperial University during the early twentieth century. For historians at Kyoto Imperial University, the other important school of Sinology, see Fogel 1984. Sun Ge (2000a, 2000b) has written a fine account of Japanese scholars on Asia throughout the twentieth century.

intellectuals from other regions of Asia looked to Japan for hope (only to be later disappointed by Japan's own imperialism) (Tagore 1917; Aydin 2007). For example, in 1891, Inoue Tetsujirō made what is now a rather familiar appeal in a speech entitled "Tōyōshigaku no kachi" ("The Value of Oriental Studies"). Inoue pointed to European ignorance about Asia and believed that filling the lacuna would correct the deeper structural misconceptions, especially Europeans' misunderstanding of Japanese. Here, he recognized the hierarchy that embedded European disdain for Asians, but he believed that by adding histories of the East to world history, it would show Europeans that Japanese were different from Chinese and did not belong in the same category. The limitation of this method is that more information enters existing categories and thus offers greater detail and nuance. It has not upset hierarchical positions.

A decade later, Shiratori Kurakichi began a different corrective. Shiratori, trained in the positivistic (and nationalistic) history of Leopold von Ranke, created what we might call today an alternate modernity.[12] His tōyō-shi (Oriental history) created a history that reordered Japan's subjectivity to be seemingly autonomous but parallel to that of the West. This history used stages of development like that of Hegel but began in ancient China and ended in Japan. It, too, was a dynamic historical process that used Newtonian time as if universal. This alternative modernity changes the subject of who is on top; Japan is the recent and superior place in Asia, and this system also argues that Japan will rise above the West. Tsuda Sōkichi offered a variation by attempting to eliminate the geographical link between Japan and Asia.[13] In 1938, in a move that begins to see the problem in history itself, he divided the past into rekishi (history, or Geschichte) and shigaku (histories, or histoire); argued that there is no Asia but instead a group of nations—India, China, and Japan; and claimed that Japan is an Occidental, not Oriental or Asian, place. This final claim, of course, returned Tsuda to the linearity of history.

One of the most interesting prewar Japanese intellectual/activists to deal with the problem of Asia was Ōkawa Shūmei. He was a leading intellectual in 1930s Japan: director of the East Asia Economic Research Bureau of the South Manchurian Railway, critic of the government, sup-

12. See, for example, Blackbourn and Eley 1984. Discovering an alternate modernity in China's past is also the goal of Wang 2011c. For two fine extended reviews of his work, see Murthy 2006; Zhang 2010.

13. This recalls Fukuzawa Yukichi's well-known essay from 1885 (1970), "Dissociating from Asia." For a fine analysis of this line of thinking in relation to Asia, see Sun 2000a: 14–22.

porter of Japan's leadership of Asia against Western imperialism, translator of the Quran, as well as a keen critic of modernity. He lived his convictions: between 1932 and 1937, he was imprisoned for plotting to assassinate the prime minister and major industrialists, and at the end of the Pacific War, he was arrested and indicted by the United States as a Class A war criminal (he was not tried, having been declared legally incompetent to stand trial). To decenter both the West and Asia, Ōkawa turned to Islam to reestablish the relationality of these categories. He pointed out that Islam in the West is of the Orient, but from his Japanese perspective, it is part of the West: "Islam is frequently called an Oriental religion (*tōyōteki shūkyō*), and that culture is called an Oriental culture. However, Islam is part of a religious family that includes Zoroastrianism, Judaism, and Christianity" (Ōkawa [1942] 1974: 4–5).[14]

These intellectuals understood the myth of universality as well as the unevenness that it maintains. They addressed some aspect of the way that representation was conflated with place. Inoue argued that it was necessary to fill in the gaps of knowledge; Shiratori dug into the Asian past to present an alternative modernity built on the same absolute time and absolute space and historical thinking as Western histories; Tsuda questioned Asia as a spatialized time and emphasized developmental level to position Japan alongside Europe, not China; and finally Ōkawa used other regions of Asia beyond East Asia (today this might be called transnational or inter-Asia) and then pointed to the incongruities between identification and place. In short, they sought to revise the universal, fill in the huge gaps, and reorder world history to eliminate the hierarchy embedded within the word Asia.

These are all arguments that we hear today as well. Dipesh Chakrabarty's important *Provincializing Europe* (2000) and Naoki Sakai's influential work on the universal and particular, *Translation and Subjectivity* (1997), have raised the awareness of the way Enlightenment epistemology constricts the places of Asia. More recently, a decentering of the West has become an important concern among intellectuals on the western Pacific. For example, Kuan-Hsing Chen, invoking Takeuchi in his book *Asia as Method* (2010), calls for an inter-Asian studies program, an Asian studies in and for Asia. Wang Hui goes further, concluding, "The issue of Asia is not simply an Asian issue, but rather a matter of 'world history.' Recon-

---

14. Ōkawa's argument bears several similarities with Russian criticism of East and West. See, for example, the description of Vasilii V. Bartol'd in Tolz 2011: 50–54.

sidering 'Asian history' at once represents an effort to rethink nineteenth-century European 'world history,' as well as an effort to break free of the twenty-first-century 'new imperial' order and its associated logic" (2011b: 62). These intellectuals are correct to point to the unevenness embedded in world history. Many do have promising suggestions—I will discuss some of these below. But we must also recognize that despite the effort of many very smart intellectuals, there is a remarkably stubborn consistency in the way that "Asia" marks Asia. These accounts often echo the work of earlier Japanese intellectuals. For example, in Wang's last clause, if we change "twenty-first" to "twentieth" and eliminate "new" in "new imperial," the statement could easily have emanated from one of the prewar Japanese intellectuals. It does recall the impossibility that conscribes us.

Return of Time

Just as the renaming of Orient to Asia is superficial at best, the fix is elusive. It involves many interconnected components, and, in particular, we need to go beyond the questioning of the content of history and dig into the layers underlying history itself. Certeau hints at the complexity of untangling this misplaced concreteness: "The operation in question is rather sly: the discourse gives itself credibility in the name of the reality which it is supposed to represent, but this authorized appearance of the 'real' serves precisely to camouflage the practice which in fact determines it. Representation thus disguises the praxis that organizes it" (1986: 203). Asia gains a reality (spatialized time as the first stage connected to geography) through this synchronization of the world around a world history, but this "reality" camouflages a part of the practice—Asia never gains a history.

This recalls Miyoshi's allegory. Asia serves as the incorporation of an area as static, the first stage, while in the slyness of the operation, there is a shift to another "reality"—specific cultures or nations within Asia—China, India, Persia, and Japan. History is operating at two levels. In Hegel, China is both the "oldest and newest" (1956: 116), and this emplotment is picked up by intellectuals in the non-West. Fukuzawa Yukichi ([1875] 1973: 142) laments that Japan's past is twenty-five centuries of "continually doing the same thing," and intellectuals on the subcontinent scour their past to write a history of India (Thapar 2013). Specific cultures (or later nations) within Hegel's "Oriental World" offer empirical data. But these nation-states are being constituted as they offer evidence for a reality that gives reality to Asia. This "real" is one step removed from Asia, allegories that further camouflage the praxis. The pioneering world historian Donald Lach points out that "Europeans' view of Asia was not a static one" (1965: xiv). True, there were many variations. But when he gets to specifics, he writes about China, India, Japan, and countries of Southeast Asia as allegories of Asia, as if they are "Asia." This turn to the specific brings out the second level; the nation-states and their history had to be made. They are necessary conditions for a world history, but in their formulation the universalizing structure is elided.

The possibility of writing one's own history is a dream (more accurately, illusion) of possibility fashioned out of this delimited condition; it is a powerful one.[15] The turn to the specificity of a culture or nation-state as allegory for Asia also opened up the possibility/need for these places either to redefine themselves as separate from Asia or to redefine Asia. This is what Inoue did to correct for what he saw as a lack of knowledge. Shiratori formulated tōyōshi in Japan to create an alternate modernity because of the partiality of the Western universal, and Tsuda denied an Asia (as spatialized time) for nation-states—China, Japan, and Korea—to separate Japan from the continent. More recently, Chen (2010) argues for an inter-Asian studies program to "deimperialize" Asia and create a new Asian subjectivity independent of the West. And Wang Hui (2011c) searches for an indigenous history (Song era) for an alternate modernity of China. These and other examples bring out a seduction in this process—to extract oneself from the position of stasis, one gets to write a history of one's own nation. History both traps and seduces as if there is a solution. Nation-states are homogenized into a single process (the geochronocultural tableau) but are allowed to mine the same past for material to claim their own subjective autonomy.

Michel Serres's metaphor of a race to describe this synchronizing world history and the centrality of the nation is apt; it shows the depth of the sly operation described by Certeau: "That's not time, only a simple line. It's not even a line, but a trajectory of the race for first place—in school, in the Olympic Games, for the Nobel Prize. This isn't time, but a simple competition—once again, war. Why replace temporality, duration, with a quarrel? *The first to arrive, the winner of the battle, obtains as his prize the right to reinvent history to his own advantage*" (Serres and Latour 1995: 49). This

---

15. It is important to recognize that the histories of European nations were written during the nineteenth century: for example, Leopold von Ranke's *Geschichte der romanischen und germanischen Völker von 1494 bis 1514* (*History of the Romanic and Germanic Peoples from 1494 to 1514*) in 1824, Thomas Babington Macaulay's *History of England* in 1848, and Jules Michelet's *Histoire de France* in 1855.

metaphor of a race strikes me as particularly apposite to the temporality of the modern, especially as it has imbricated our understanding of the non-West. If for the moment we stay within that modern history, it is seductive or threatening, for it presents a clear path (participate willingly or be swallowed up) of participation in a system that seems to offer all the same conditions: linear, "empty" time. The seduction is the illusion that the creation of one's national history will free oneself from stasis, its status within Asia.

This was the goal of Meiji Japan, *fukoku kyōhei* (rich country, strong military), the horizon of wealth and power. Sun Zhongshan (Sun Yat-sen) was also caught up in this race. At the outbreak of the Russo-Japanese War, he writes, "The Japanese triumph over Russia was the first triumph of an Asian over a European nation in the past several centuries. . . . All the Asian nations are astonished and overjoyed and have become extremely hopeful. . . . They therefore hope to smash Europe and begin independence movements. . . . A great hope for national independence in Asia has been born" (quoted in Wang 2011b: 30). This is part of Hegel's genius as well as the genius of modernity—to establish a goal that brings units into the same order that then uses unevenness and the past to mark place and, especially, to explain why others do not measure up. The race is seemingly place-neutral, or, in Enlightenment terms, universal. It is also scalable, reinforcing its perceived universality. It can be populated by nation-states, regions within nation-states, or individuals vying to succeed within society (it also structures universities and work within universities). The limitation of Japanese intellectuals was not their lack of reflexivity. Instead, they were caught within the slyness of history that obscures the making of Asia. Japanese intellectuals sought a resolution by modifying or changing the content of history, not history itself. They recognized the particularity of History, what Wang Hui calls world history, but the solution was to formulate a new relation of Japan to the world, using history. A Japan (here one can replace any nation-state) remained the central allegory of their work. It is easy to criticize them now, but this is also the very basis for area studies in the United States today—through the existence of an Asia (Asian studies), academics practice through the allegory of the national culture.

These efforts use the same linear, historical process—history of the world/history of a nation-state—but when placed on a different scale, meaning changes. This is one place where the system camouflages "the practice which in fact determines it." On the one hand, in the synchronization of the world, Asia is frozen time; it is forever at the first stage. On the other hand, the national form restores chronological time through the telling of the national becoming. This is the opportunity to create the identity of one's own nation, both in juxtaposition to the West as well as to others within Asia. The hope is evident today in the inquiries of intellectuals such as Wang Hui, who is in dialogue with many in Asia who are asking similar questions about modernity in Asia. In Sun Ge's two essays, perhaps the best historical analysis of Japanese efforts, she ends with a query that recalls the epigraph from Takeuchi that begins my essay: "Whether Asia should be taken as a perspective of instrumental value, and on which level the question of Asia should be broached, is of concern to our own history" (2000b: 337). Sun Ge is well aware of the role of the nation-state in trying to understand the concreteness of the idea of Asia. Yet the allegory of one's own nation-state is also central to the problem. The search for a history of the nation-state masks the way that history fixes Asia as the originary state. Despite our critiques, we have operated within an idea of history that reiterates the chronological framework. Here the historian is operating like the workers in E. P. Thompson's classic essay on time and work. Workers protested abstract labor through the temporal system that served as the basis of it. They accepted the categories of their employers and learned to resist within the metric that created those categories.[16]

The third fold of this sly operation is that the places of Asia are confronted by their past—both as evidence of their lack of as well as data for a history that shows progress. In the writing of their national history, the very conditions that prove the stasis of Asia serve as data for demonstrating historically the uniqueness of the nation-state. All nation-states claim uniqueness—some essential, timeless quality. In Japan, historians and national literature scholars described themes that run through epochs and characterize the cultural becoming of the nation—Buddhism, Bushido, and a selective smattering of Confucianism; an aesthetic that reveres nature and is tied to Shinto; and affiliation with some communal unit, be it family, village, or domain. These map directly onto Hegel's evidence that the Oriental world is static—morality, closeness to nature, and near absence of subjective will. Japanese studies (and by extension Asian studies) has turned to these topics to give Japan specificity, as if it is old and new.

It strikes me that this is where we still are today despite a call from Miyoshi and Harry Harootunian over twenty-five years ago.[17] In the introduc-

16. Thompson wrote, "They had accepted the categories of their employers and learned to fight back within them. They had learned their lesson, that time is money, only too well" (cited in Tomba 2013: 162fn9).
17. My barometer is the work of Wang Hui, perhaps the most conceptually sophisticated

tion to *Japan in the World*, they argue that "national borders and narratives that have been constructed by colonialism during the past two centuries are no longer viable units. Japan in the world as an isolated national entity is no more meaningful than any other claim to a unique national identity" (1991: 7). If a goal is to alter the fixity of Asia as Orient, then we must also recognize that (1) modern history itself was established to shift the subject from humans and their experience to a knowledge about nations; (2) the writing of history (of a Japan or a China) is part of the very sly mechanism that uses time to objectify Asia as past; and (3) in the making of the nation-state, even though we don't call it colonization (the emergence of the idea of settler colonization is an exception), similar conceptual structures and technologies that homogenized the world operate within the nation.

This is one of the lessons from Miyoshi—the impossibility of describing what constitutes the world without allegorization. This is not a reflexivity of history, where we question a particular past or relations of one national culture to another. Instead, it is a recognition that our very subject position is a product of history, not an accumulated past (it is that as well) but an allegory of history itself. This is one reason for the difficulty of writing this essay: the need to question the ways that I myself have both perpetuated and been trapped by history.

The invocation of the nation or history returns us to the presumption of the absolute space and absolute time of Newton. This form of time is now called classical time in the sciences, and geographers have shown us that the space I am discussing here (place) is social. At the very least, we must recognize that absolute time and absolute space are historical, a way of thinking that emerged around three hundred years ago. Even more, we should consider both myth. Certeau writes, "Thus, historical discourse becomes the one possible myth of a scientific society that rejects myths— the fiction of a social relationship between specified practices and general legends, between techniques that produce and demarcate places in society and legends that propose a symbolical ambiguity as an effect of time" (1986: 220). Certeau's statement is central if we are to unpack issues embedded in an Asia, the Orient, or *tōyō*.

The intellectuals I have discussed have called for a reflexivity, a hope that a different engagement with others will help us understand ourselves.

---

of recent attempts within Asian studies to reconsider Asia. Yet his *Rise of Modern Chinese Thought*, despite this sophistication and like some of Japan intellectuals before, is bound by China and is an effort to reconceive modernity there (to find an alternative modernity).

Yet their return to either history as a way to establish an autonomous sub-jectivity or the nation demonstrates the extent to which Newtonian absolute time and absolute space are embedded in our own knowledge system. I see Takeuchi's call for "Asia as method" as a desire to shed oneself from these limiting frames. Yet Takeuchi himself could not outline that method. He elevates, above all, the values of freedom and equality that emerged in Europe but recognizes that even in Europe, these values were partial and weakened, especially through its imperial endeavors. He writes, "The Orient must reembrace the West, it must change the West itself in order to realize the latter's outstanding cultural values on a greater scale. Such a rollback of culture or values would create universality" (2005: 165). This statement recalls the attempts of many intellectuals described above. Yet he concludes the essay with the following: "When this rollback takes place, we must have our own cultural values. And yet perhaps these values do not already exist, in substantive form. Rather I suspect that they are possible as method, that is to say, as the process of the subject's self-formation. This I have called 'Asia as method,' and yet it is impossible to definitively state what this might mean" (165).

If one has followed my argument, there is a circularity in Takeuchi's appeal for "Asia as method." But perhaps it is the impossibility of which Miyoshi warns. If we "change the West" itself (here world history and the nation-state that is an integral component), then it would be impossible to return to either history or the nation. To do so is to use the conditions created by the West in the making of Asia. Even though Takeuchi does not delineate a clear alternative, we should not take the last clause as not knowing but as a recognition of the difficulty, perhaps impossibility, of the endeavor. Asia as method is a reluctance to fall into established struc-tures, patterns, or knowledge systems. It is an insistence on process and an opening into a different notion of subject. But we must also recognize that that process, without examining the centrality of chronological time, returns us to where we started. My current work explores the possibility of writing history that is not built on chronological time (Tanaka 2019). In the quote above, Certeau reminds us that history—the fiction of social relation-ships—is an "effect of time." History as myth, then, is not untrue as much as an accepted truth that lives on because of practices rather than empirical basis (see, for example, Mali 2003). The epigraph from Marx is of modern society; man as an incarnation of time is our acceptance of modern history as myth. Serres writes that our current understanding of time as an irreversible line "is the equivalent of those ancient diagrams . . . which place the Earth at the center of everything" (Serres and Latour 1995: 48).

Wayfaring

As a conclusion that does not provide an answer, but hopefully goes beyond critique or lament, I find in Miyoshi's stroll rich potential for moving beyond the riddle. The stroll is a way to recover uncertainty, heterogeneity, and perspective. Going through some of the neighborhoods often called seedy, dirty, et cetera, is less to glorify some authentic life located in the everyday or a subaltern than to think of a mode of seeing beyond what our modern forms of knowledge guide us to see. Serres offers hope for a method where a stroll helps us move away from our riddle. He writes, "Allow me to say that what drives history is, precisely, failures. . . . As for history, it advances and retreats at a shuffle, like an invalid. Humanity makes progress most often thanks to small children, women, old people, the sick, the simpleminded, and the poorest" (Serres and Latour 1995: 121–22). I hope that this becomes more than a glorification of difference. Serres recognizes that history has been a form of knowledge that maintains the status quo. A recognition of the margins—those outside of history—opens the possibility of change (as opposed to improvement).

Tim Ingold, in his book *Lines: A Brief History* (2007), juxtaposes our modern world, not as the new against the old, modern versus tradition, or linear versus circular—those are points of a linear connection—but through different kinds of lines that do not necessarily impose such a linearity of absolute time. The wayfarer moves *along*, taking in the surroundings, and inhabits that which he traverses. This is juxtaposed to the traveler who moves *across*, from point to point; an apt metaphor here is transport and production (again, status quo). Ingold argues that practices that started as traces of a gesture have evolved into an assembly of point-to-point connectors. He applies this formulation to narrative, and I would extend it to disciplines and spatialized time: "This fragmentation . . . has taken place in the related fields of *travel*, where wayfaring is replaced by destination-oriented transport, *mapping*, where the drawn sketch is replaced by the route-plan, and *textuality*, where storytelling is replaced by the precomposed plot. It has also transformed our understanding of *place*: once a knot tied from multiple and interlaced strands of movement and growth, it now figures as a node in a static network of connectors" (Ingold 2007: 75).

Wayfaring as an approach is an effort to think of the mobility and ways of knowing prior to the nodes that reduce diversity into generalizable units. The study of movement, the stroll, has purpose, yet it is not to go see what one knows (the point-to-point or an alternate modernity that instantiates the nation-state) but to look for what exists (or existed) in and beyond the known. For Asia, it requires us to keep in mind the warning of Certeau, that time is a hidden classifying instrument of history. Miyoshi teaches us the humility that our perspective is but one of several possibilities. His is a methodology that willingly accepts a heterogeneity in the world (but an impatience for those academics who use conceptual structures that homogenize).[18] It requires that we embrace uncertainty, unless our goal is to remain in the circular process that Certeau identified through his "gesture of exclusion."

A growing number of scholars have employed this emphasis on mobility as a way of studying the past. They work from individual movement, from which we can determine connections, commonalities, and regions, rather than from ideal types. Two such recent works are Kapil Raj, *Relocating Modern Science* (2009) and Enseng Ho, *The Graves of Tarim* (2006). Wang Hui moves in this direction when he finds hope in work such as Hamashita Takeshi's focus on trade networks in his study of tributary systems (2011b: 45–49). The results are a much richer understanding of how activities in the past addressed particular needs and desires, sometimes, but not always, morphing into our modern structures.

The emphasis on mobility suggests the need to incorporate different perspectives and questions the subject of scholarship. Indeed, that is a hope. Miyoshi's *As We Saw Them* (1979) is a terrific example. Miyoshi wrote this book in response to a bias he detected in Japanese studies, in which, despite an affinity toward Japan, there is an undercurrent of assumed Western superiority in the way Japan has been judged by Western standards (Cazdyn 2010: xxiii). This recognition echoes those cited above, yet his approach is different. Miyoshi examined the interchange between Japanese and Americans in 1860 through the knowledge system of the actors themselves. Tokugawa travelers were placed in the knowledge system of their *bakumatsu* period; Americans who contacted (or wrote about) these emissaries were also placed within their particularities of pre–Civil War United States. Moreover, there were many perspectives, not just a "Japa-

---

18. Miyoshi criticized those who simplistically operated within such disciplines or places as if they are self-evident categories. A good example is Miyoshi 2010a.

nese" and an "American" view. They included sailors, translators, ambassadors, and reporters; while he finds generalizable propensities, there is no homogenized "Japanese" or "American" view. These multiple interpretations of the new experience depended on the individual's knowledge system (low-ranking samurai, translator, ambassador, etc.), their surroundings and opportunities, and personal proclivities. Wang Hui finds a respect for the significance of the moment in his *Rise of Modern Chinese Thought*. He invokes a "propensity of the times" (*shishi*), a concept that he attributes to Confucianism from the Song dynasty. It emphasizes the particularity of the contemporary conditions and events rather than seeing them through a world history (Wang 2011a: 69–70). Wang invokes this propensity of the times as a temporality different than the teleology of world history or abstract time and recognizes that a different historical thinking would also be a part of this different temporality.

Today, many profess to move beyond the nation-state, often invoking the transnational. Few actually do so, but here, too, we might take some hints from Miyoshi's career. He started with the nation, English literature, then Japanese literature, but he then moved on to intercultural relations, area studies as a knowledge system, global capitalism, and then the university as a site of knowledge production. It is obvious but important to point out that there is a constant movement toward a questioning of the self.

First, we need not find a historical antecedent in a national past. As I have argued, to do so might solve one issue but traps us within other reductive frames of history. Here, it is worth considering Georg Simmel's opening statement in his essay "The Metropolis and Mental Life": "The deepest problems of modern life flow from the attempt of the individual to maintain the independence and individuality of his existence against the sovereign powers of society, against the weight of the historical heritage and the external culture and technique of life" ([1903] 2002: 11). Simmel suggests that the nation and/or the state—historical heritage, sovereign power, external culture—might also be part of the problem.

Second, we can find similar work that argues for experience, learning, and knowing as culturally situated knowledge. This understanding has been growing over the past few decades. For example, Reinhart Koselleck's "space of experience" is a recognition that not all societies (of the present as well as pasts) are organized through modern linear time (1985: 267–88). In psychology, the introduction of the writings of Lev S. Vygotsky (Cole 1985, 1995) (a contemporary of Mikhail Bakhtin) was key to the understanding of culturally inflected modes of knowing, intersubjectivity, and learning.

One important area of cognitive science, distributed cognition, sees cognition as embedded within the immediate environment (Hutchins 1995). And, in anthropology, "figured worlds" have taken up similar interpretations that knowing and understanding are conditioned by what individuals know and the immediate environment (Holland et al. 2002: 49–65). Miyoshi operated both within and beyond the structures of our modern knowledge system; his legacy to us is to continue pushing to move beyond those structures that we now know have been very reductive and homogenizing.

Those who only saw Miyoshi from afar, or through some of his more trenchant writings, would be surprised to see the word *humility* connected to him. Indeed, disagreeing with him was necessary but often harrowing. Yet there is an intellectual humility in the recognition of the impossibility of our (especially) current knowledge system, and he practiced it through a willingness to move beyond the safe confines of the discipline or region of focus. He recognized, like Serres, that the role of our knowledge system is to promote and maintain the status quo. This, Serres argues (and Miyoshi would agree), is not thinking; it is classification and ordering: "Trying to think, trying to produce, presupposes the taking of risks, the living of one's life, precisely, in the surge outside of the classings of the encyclopedias" (Serres 1995: 98). Miyoshi recognized, indeed defended, the importance of literature and Japanese studies, but these were tools that facilitate efforts to know and understand, not institutions (disciplines) that have value in and of themselves. In his last essay, from 2009, "Literary Elaborations" (2010d: 47), he moved again well beyond the issues Serres discussed here, toward the question of the global environment and human survival. He was pessimistic; cockroaches, he asserts, will survive humans. I hope that he will be wrong; I fear as well that like so many times, he again is more correct than I. At least by that time, I will not have to worry about any more of my insecurities.

References

Aydin, Cemil. 2007. *The Politics of Anti-Westernism in Asia: Visions of World Order in Pan-Islamic and Pan-Asian Thought.* New York: Columbia University Press.
Benjamin, Walter. 1968. "Theses on the Philosophy of History." In *Illuminations: Essays and Reflections*, edited and with an introduction by Hannah Arendt and translated by Harry Zohn, 253–64. New York: Harcourt, Brace and World.
Bergson, Henri. (1911) 2002. "The Perception of Change." In *Henri Bergson: Key*

Writings, edited by Keith Ansell Pearson and John Mullarkey, 248–66. New York: Continuum.

Blackbourn, David, and Geoff Eley. 1984. *The Peculiarities of German History: Bourgeois Society and Politics in Nineteenth-Century Germany.* Oxford: Oxford University Press.

Burnett, D. Graham. 2003. "Mapping Time." *Daedalus* 132, no. 2: 5–19.

Cazdyn, Eric. 2010. "Trespasser: An Introduction to the Life and Work of Masao Miyoshi." In *Trespasses: Selected Writings*, by Masao Miyoshi, edited and with an introduction by Eric Cazdyn, xv–xxxiii. Durham, NC: Duke University Press.

Certeau, Michel de. 1986. "History: Science and Fiction." In *Heterologies: Discourse on the Other*, translated by Brian Massumi, 199–221. Minneapolis: University of Minnesota Press.

———. 1992. *The Mystic Fable: The Sixteenth and Seventeenth Centuries.* Vol. 1. Translated by Michael B. Smith. Chicago: University of Chicago Press.

Chakrabarty, Dipesh. 2000. *Provincializing Europe: Postcolonial Thought and Historical Difference.* Princeton, NJ: Princeton University Press.

Chen, Kuan-Hsing. 2010. *Asia as Method: Toward Deimperialization.* Durham, NC: Duke University Press.

Cole, Michael. 1985. "The Zone of Proximal Development: Where Culture and Cognition Create Each Other." In *Culture, Communication and Cognition: Vygotskian Perspectives*, edited by James V. Wertsch, 146–61. Cambridge: Cambridge University Press.

———. 1995. "Culture and Cognitive Development: From Cross-Cultural Research to Creating Systems of Cultural Mediation." *Culture and Psychology* 1: 25–54.

Cumings, Bruce. 2002. "Boundary Displacement: The State, the Foundations, and Area Studies during and after the Cold War." In *Learning Places: The Afterlives of Area Studies*, edited by Masao Miyoshi and H. D. Harootunian, 261–302. Durham, NC: Duke University Press.

Fabian, Johannes. 1983. *Time and the Other: How Anthropology Makes Its Object.* New York: Columbia University Press.

Fogel, Joshua. 1984. *Politics and Sinology: The Case of Naitō Konan.* Cambridge, MA: Council on East Asian Studies.

Fukuzawa Yukichi. (1875) 1973. *An Outline of a Theory of Civilization.* Translated by David A. Dilworth and G. Cameron Hurst. Tokyo: Sophia University Press.

———. (1885) 1970. "Datsu-A ron." In *Fukuzawa Yukichi zenshū.* Vol. 10: 238–40. Tokyo: Iwanami shōten.

Grafton, Anthony. 2002. "Dating History: The Renaissance and the Reformation of Chronology." *Daedalus* 132, no. 2: 74–85.

Gross, David. 1982. "Time, Space, and Modern Culture." *Telos* 50: 59–78.

Hegel, Georg Wilhelm Friedrich. 1956. *The Philosophy of History.* Translated by J. Sibree. New York: Dover Publications.

Ho, Enseng. 2006. *The Graves of Tarim: Genealogy and Mobility across the Indian Ocean.* Berkeley: University of California Press.

Holland, Dorothy, William S. Lachicotte Jr., Debra Skinner, and Carole Cain. 2002. *Identity and Agency in Cultural Worlds.* Cambridge, MA: Harvard University Press.

Hutchins, Edwin. 1995. *Cognition in the Wild.* Cambridge, MA: MIT Press.

Ingold, Tim. 2007. *Lines: A Brief History.* New York: Routledge.

Karl, Rebecca. 1998. "Creating Asia: China in the World at the Beginning of the Twentieth Century." *American Historical Review* 103, no. 4: 1096–118.

Koselleck, Reinhart. 1985. *Futures Past: On the Semantics of Historical Time.* Translated by Keith Tribe. Cambridge, MA: MIT Press.

Lach, Donald. 1965. *Asia in the Making of Europe.* Vol. 1, pt. 1. Chicago: University of Chicago Press.

Lassiter, Luke Eric. 2005. *The Chicago Guide to Collaborative Ethnography.* Chicago: University of Chicago Press.

Lukács, Georg. 1971. *History and Class Consciousness: Studies in Marxist Dialectics.* Translated by Rodney Livingstone. Cambridge, MA: MIT Press.

Mali, Joseph. 2003. *Mythistory: The Making of a Modern Historiography.* Chicago: University of Chicago Press.

Marx, Karl. 1900. *The Poverty of Philosophy: Being a Translation of the Misère de la Philosophie.* London: Twentieth Century Press.

———. 1974. *Das Elend der Philosophie. Antwort auf Proudhons "Philosophie des Elends."* In *Werke,* Band 4, by Karl Marx and Frederick Engels, 63–124. Berlin: Dietz Verlag.

———. 1976. *The Poverty of Philosophy.* In Vol. 6 of *Collected Works,* by Karl Marx and Frederick Engels, 105–212. Moscow: Progress Publishers.

Miyoshi, Masao. 1979. *As We Saw Them.* Berkeley: University of California Press.

———. 2009. *This Is Not Here.* Hollywood, CA: highmoonoon.

———. 2010a. "'Bunburying' in the Japan Field." In *Trespasses: Selected Writings,* edited and with an introduction by Eric Cazdyn, 159–74. Durham, NC: Duke University Press.

———. 2010b. "Ivory Tower in Escrow." In *Trespasses,* 205–41.

———. 2010c. "Japan Is Not Interesting." In *Trespasses,* 189–204.

———. 2010d. "Literary Elaborations." In *Trespasses,* 1–47.

———. 2010e. "Outside Architecture." In *Trespasses,* 151–57.

Miyoshi, Masao, and H. D. Harootunian. 1991. "Japan in the World." In "Japan in the World." Special issue, *boundary 2* 18, no. 3: 1–7.

Murthy, Viren. 2006. "Modernity against Modernity: Wang Hui's Critical History of Chinese Thought." *Modern Intellectual History* 3, no. 1: 137–65.

Ōkawa Shūmei. (1942) 1974. *Kaikyō gairon.* In *Ōkawa Shūmei zenshū.* Vol. 7. Tokyo: Ōkawa Shūmei Zenshū Kankōkai.

Raj, Kapil. 2009. *Relocating Modern Science: Circulation and the Construction of Knowledge in South Asia and Europe, 1650–1900.* New York: Palgrave McMillan.

Said, Edward. 1978. *Orientalism.* New York: Pantheon Books.

Sakai, Naoki. 1997. *Translation and Subjectivity: On "Japan" and Cultural Nationalism.* Minneapolis: University of Minnesota Press.

Serres, Michel. 1995. "The Birth of Time." In *Genesis*, translated by Genevieve James and James Nielson. Ann Arbor: University of Michigan Press.

Serres, Michel, with Bruno Latour. 1995. *Conversations on Science, Culture, and Time.* Translated by Roxanne Lapidus. Ann Arbor: University of Michigan Press.

Simmel, Georg. (1903) 2002. "The Metropolis and Mental Life." In *The Blackwell City Reader*, edited by Gary Bridge and Sophie Watson, 11–19. Malden, MA: Blackwell Publishing.

Sun Ge. 2000a. "How Does Asia Mean? (Part I)." *Inter-Asia Cultural Studies* 1, no. 1: 13–47.

———. 2000b. "How Does Asia Mean? (Part II)." *Inter-Asia Cultural Studies* 1, no. 2: 319–41.

Tagore, Rabindranath. 1917. *Nationalism.* New York: Macmillan Co.

Takeuchi Yoshimi. 2005. "Asia as Method." In *What Is Modernity? Writings of Takeuchi Yoshimi*, edited and translated by Richard F. Calichman, 149–66. New York: Columbia University Press.

Tanaka, Stefan. 1993. *Japan's Orient: Rendering Pasts into History.* Berkeley: University of California Press.

———. 2019. *History without Chronology.* Amherst, MA: Lever Press.

Thapar, Romila. 2013. *The Past before Us.* Cambridge, MA: Harvard University Press.

Tolz, Vera. 2011. *Russia's Own Orient: The Politics of Identity and Oriental Studies in the Late Imperial and Early Soviet Periods.* Oxford: Oxford University Press.

Tomba, Massimiliano. 2013. *Marx's Temporalities.* Translated by Peter D. Thomas and Sara R. Farris. Chicago: Haymarket Books.

Wang Hui. 2011a. "How to Explain 'China' and Its 'Modernity': Rethinking *The Rise of Modern Chinese Thought*." Translated by Wang Yang. In *The Politics of Imagining Asia*, edited by Theodore Huters, 63–94. Cambridge, MA: Harvard University Press.

———. 2011b. "The Politics of Imagining Asia." Translated by Matthew A. Hale. In *The Politics of Imagining Asia*, edited by Theodore Huters, 10–62. Cambridge, MA: Harvard University Press.

———. 2011c. *The Politics of Imagining Asia.* Edited by Theodore Huters. Cambridge, MA: Harvard University Press.

Whitehead, Alfred North. (1925) 1967. *Science and the Modern World.* New York: Free Press.

Wilcox, Donald J. 1987. *The Measure of Times Past: Pre-Newtonian Chronologies and the Rhetoric of Relative Time.* Chicago: University of Chicago Press.

Zhang Yongle. 2010. "The Future of the Past." *New Left Review*, no. 62: 47–83.

"To Relearn the Sense of the World": A Call to Arms

Mary N. Layoun

Masao Miyoshi concludes his essay "Ivory Tower in Escrow: Ex Uno Plures" with the apt—and poignant—observation, "To right the situation, to null the transaction and be just to all on earth, we may have to relearn the sense of the world, the totality, that includes all peoples in every race, class, and gender" ([2000] 2010: 241).[1] Miyoshi qualifies the proposition—"to relearn the sense of the world"—with a conditional, "we may have to." Yet the entire second half of that essay, in his own characterization, "puzzles over the failure of the humanities at this moment as a supposed agency of criticism and intervention" (2010: 205). In a later essay, "The University, the Universe, the World, and 'Globalization,'" Miyoshi follows up on a near decade of analyses of the university, the humanities, and the roles of both

A shorter version of this paper was presented at "The Future of the Humanities" conference, held in honor of the life and work of Masao Miyoshi at the University of California, San Diego Center for the Humanities, October 28, 2011. I am grateful to the organizer, the participants, and the audience for their invitation, their comments, and their stories.

1. Originally titled "Ivory Tower in Escrow" (2000), in his *Trespasses: Selected Writings* (2010), the same essay is more emphatically subtitled with Miyoshi's concern throughout: "Ex Uno Plures." It is this latter version that is cited here.

boundary 2 46:3 (2019)   DOI 10.1215/01903659-7614135   © 2019 by Duke University Press

in the world to consider the terms of his title. That consideration, he proposes, "hopefully . . . offers suggestions for the future of the now defunct
discipline of the humanities" (2007a: 25). The "may have to" has, perhaps
arguably, become an imperative. So then, in the spirit of his observations
there and throughout much of his work, it is not hyperbolic to characterize
Miyoshi's work as "a call to arms." In an effort to "right the situation," "to
null the transaction," "to be just," Miyoshi's reach is nothing short of global
in "Ivory Tower in Escrow." *All* peoples, *every* race, *every* class, *every* gender. For the future of higher education. For the future of the humanities. For
the future, period.

To characterize Miyoshi's work and legacy as "a call to arms" is, in
the first instance, a reference to those arms that are literally the extremities of our upper bodies, as when we link arms with others—friends, comrades, strangers. And also, the arms of that call are those more metaphorical arms which we might link with the nonhuman and the environment in
concert with the human.[2] For if Miyoshi's life and work is that of a powerful
intellectual and academic maverick, that same work nonetheless points at
an effort that cannot but be collaborative. The arms we might link to try to
"relearn the sense of the world" are necessarily many, many arms.

So then, Miyoshi's gentle imperative in his "Ivory Tower in Escrow"—
"we may have to relearn the sense of the world"—is a collaborative call to
arms, to many, in diverse locations. It is surely not coincidental that the
subtitle of the republished essay—*Ex Uno Plures*/from one, many—locates
itself in distinction to *E Pluribus Unum*/from many, one.[3] And if this latter
is a signpost for a distinct and dominant rhetorical stance in the United
States, where Miyoshi spent much of his academic life, it is equally a signpost for intellectual thought and social practice beyond the United States.
Duly noting the historical origin of the phrase *E Pluribus Unum*, the contemporary rhetorical charge of that phrase is something more like "from the
many" *must* emerge "a one."[4] And the hold of that phrase now extends far
beyond the United States, as Miyoshi outlines in "Turn to the Planet: Literature, Diversity, and Totality" (2001). Following on the implications of this

2. See, for example, Miyoshi's concluding comments on the "one single commonality"
that "involves all those living on the planet: environmental deterioration as a result of the
human consumption of natural resources" (2001: 295).
3. See Habeeb 2013 for a shrill and poorly conceptualized but symptomatic statement of
E Pluribus Unum and "admissions quotas" in US higher education.
4. Danielle Allen astutely addresses this "oneness" and reformulates it as "wholeness" in
the context of the US civil rights movement (2004: 13, 17, 20).

weary but still important opposition between the one and the many in the United States, Miyoshi explicitly and astutely indicts a globalization characterized by "the spread of desocialized individualism, or self-interest and self-indulgence, as the rational choice in everyday life" (2001: 289). In this context, it is the *ir*rational choice of *socialized* collaboration that is a necessary turn of our moment. *Ex Uno Plures*—"from one, many"—the *uno* in this planetary *plures* is one distinctly different from that of *E Pluribus Unum*—"from many, one"—which it challenges.

This planetary turn in Miyoshi's work characteristically takes as its points of departure Japan and the United States, coordinates that form the ground from which his work extends. Yet he carefully and persistently qualifies that ground as *not* one of a simple opposition; Miyoshi's work troubles the waters of both locations and of their confluence. "Once again, my criticism of US hegemony had to be tempered by a stricture on Japan's own insular nationalism," he paradigmatically writes in the same essay (2001: 289). But, from that ground, Miyoshi's reach moves decidedly and tenaciously beyond it. "The University, the Universe, the World, and 'Globalization,'" already cited above, concludes on that tenacious note of "the ultimate cohesive totality":

> Environmental deterioration also demands that the planet be understood and experienced as a commonality that belongs to every single being on earth. Here globalization is a compelling actuality. Knowledge and understanding about it, too, ought to be global, or universal, and inclusive. . . . The humanities discipline that was once sustained by the idea of the nation-state can now seize this moment of despondency and reorganize itself around the planet and the universe, the ultimate cohesive totality as the central imaginary. (2007a: 32–33)

It is noteworthy that it is "as the central imaginary" that "the ultimate cohesive totality" of the environmentally deteriorated planet offers critical work to a "reorganized humanities."[5]

There are other points of departure for a consideration of the legacies of Masao Miyoshi's work for the future of the humanities. But I begin here with his essays on the future of the humanities in higher education, on the future of higher education, on the future of oppositional, "irrational"

---

5. See Chiara Bottici's *Imaginal Politics* (2014) for a compelling conceptualization of the work of the imaginal as related to but distinct from that of the imagination or the imaginary.

thought. For they offer a clear illustration of the location of Miyoshi's work as that of a committed intellectual and academic. And they point at Miyoshi's legacy for the critical study of the humanities in higher education. The call there, as throughout his work, is to *thought*, to *analysis*, to *rethinking*, to engaged conversation, to concerted effort. And yet, engagement beyond the academy at which that intellectual work points is always there, implicitly or explicitly, if often not quite elaborated. But in the conclusion of Miyoshi's essay "Writing across Boundaries and Transgression for Peace: Preface" (2007b), that broader engagement is explicit. Introducing a special issue of *boundary 2* that looks back at a conference in Korea in 2000 from the perspective of another conference five years later (2005), Miyoshi concludes,

> The Daesan forums were not just academic. In my memory, two events outside the conference proper still remain vivid. . . . At the first forum [participants] received an invitation to the official residence of then president Kim Dae Jung. . . . There Wole Soyinka made a proposal to the president that Seoul be declared a haven for the world's political refugees. . . . At the second forum, Tibor Meray composed—jointly with Kim Seong-kon—a peace manifesto, which was signed by seventy-eight out of eighty-one participants in the conference. The three dissenters were from Korea, Japan, and Germany. The manifesto, if general and abstract, still speaks powerfully at this time of egregious assaults and occupations in Iraq, Lebanon, and Palestine. (2007b: 213)

Miyoshi's work is clearly that of literary scholar trained in languages and careful textual analysis. That is one legacy. But his work is also and always that of one keenly aware of the contexts of texts and of the location of their reading, of the location of the intellectual and her work. That too is an important legacy of his work. If the implications of Miyoshi's work extend beyond the US/Japan points of departure from which that work sets out, so too the implications of his work reach decidedly beyond the intellectual and the academic.

In rereading Miyoshi's early work on Victorian literature through to the essays collected in Eric Cazdyn's excellent anthology *Trespasses* (2010), the defining characteristics of Miyoshi's thought and work are consistent and consistently striking. They include his voraciously wide reading; his sometimes startling but always pointed and insightful questioning; his increasingly persistent movement between the more local—institutions of higher education and their workings, for example—and the larger global

forces and powers that frame and push at that local; the diversity of cita-
tions that bears witness to his intellectual range; the sometimes unsettling
observations and conclusions (and what I imagine was a kind of delight in
the unsettlement his work could generate). But there is more: there is a
deep and fierce commitment to the effort to critically analyze and to formulate the conclusions of that analysis. To move conversations and debates
forward, sometimes by sheer intellectual will and an unapologetic and
ferocious questioning. It is these exceptional qualities that characterize
Miyoshi's thought and work as well as his intellectual and academic legacy.

So then, in the context of that compelling legacy, what might it mean
to take up Miyoshi's challenge "to relearn the sense of the world" in the
face of "the failure of the humanities at this moment as a supposed agency
of criticism and intervention" (2010: 205)? As Miyoshi himself points out
in a rather more imperative mode, "Literary and cultural critics must look
out at the world and interconnect all the workings of political economy and
artistic and cultural productions. We must keep reminding ourselves that
the 'global' economy is not global at all, but an exclusionist economy. We
must discover the sense of true totality that includes everyone in the world"
(2001: 295).

How might we begin to do this, in fact—"relearn the sense of
the world" and "discover the sense of true totality"? If the commonality
of the planet is its environmental degradation, how does that planetary
commonality-in-degradation work as our "central imaginary"? A tall order
in the academy at present. A tall order outside of the academy. And yet, that
is precisely one of the unequivocal calls of Miyoshi's work.

In a kind of response to that call, and drawing from Miyoshi's own
intellectual example, I would point to four illustrative directions from which
we might begin to consider relearning the sense of the world as a call
to arms. They are certainly not the only directions to trace from Miyoshi's
work,[6] nor are they the only directions from which to relearn the sense of
the world. Nonetheless, they seem to me to bear out in compelling and suggestive ways a fundamental imperative in Miyoshi's work. And they each
point not only to what we see and hear and know but also to what we *don't*

---

6. What is not accounted for in what follows is Miyoshi's critical legacy for the discipline of
Japanese and East Asian studies. Yet that legacy is enfolded in the larger implications of
his work. Miyoshi's location as a scholar first of Victorian and then of Japanese literatures
and cultures was unquestionably the pivot point from which his broader critical corpus
emerged. It did not, however, define the boundaries of that corpus. Yet, too, the impact of
his work on that academic field is unequivocal and compelling.

or *can't* see and hear and know. If that sounds like a narrowly literary or humanities-inflected observation, the first direction cited is deliberately not from the humanities.

In 2011, based on research they began in 2007, Stefania Vitali, James B. Glattfelder, and Stefano Battiston—complex systems analysts then working at the Swiss Federal Institute of Technology in Zurich—published "The Network of Global Corporate Control." Their research initially drew "from a list of 43060 TNCs [transnational corporations] identified according to the OECD [Organization for Economic Co-operation and Development] definition, taken from a sample of about 30 million economic actors contained in the Orbis 2007 database" (Vitali et al. 2011: 2). Using methods from the study of complex networks, their analysis moved from an initial investigation of those 43,000 TNCs to a much smaller group of the top 1,318 transnational corporations with interlocking ownerships. Seeking to map global ownership and estimate control based on ownership, they identified an even smaller number of 147 entities that, they argue, based on the "complicated web of ownership relations . . . which has almost full control over itself," form a "'super entity' in the global network of corporations" (4). In their computation of "the network control that economic actors (including TNCs) gain over the TNCs' value (operating revenue)," they found that "network control is much more unequally distributed than wealth. In particular, the top ranked actors hold a control ten times bigger than what could be expected based on their wealth" (4). In fact, they continue, the extent of that coagulated control constitutes a "super-entity":

> We find that, despite its small size, the core holds collectively a large fraction of the total network control. In detail, nearly 4/10 of the control over the economic value of TNCs in the world is held, via a complicated web of ownership relations, by a group of 147 TNCs in the core, which has almost full control over itself. The top holders within the core can thus be thought of as an economic "super-entity" in the global network of corporations. (4)

Andy Coghlan and Debora MacKenzie published an article in the October 2011 issue of *New Scientist* in advance of the release of that research, that concisely characterizes Vitali, Glattfelder, and Battiston's process.

> Each of the 1318 [TNCs] had ties to two or more other companies, and on average they were connected to 20. . . . Although they repre-

sented 20 per cent of global operating revenues, the 1318 appeared to collectively own through their shares the majority of the world's large blue chip and manufacturing firms—the "real" economy— representing a further 60 per cent of global revenues.

When the team further untangled the web of ownership, it found much of it tracked back to a "super-entity" of 147 even more tightly knit companies—all of their ownership was held by other members of the super-entity—that controlled 40 per cent of the total wealth in the network. "In effect, less than 1 per cent of the companies were able to control 40 per cent of the entire network," says Glattfelder. Most were financial institutions. The top 20 included Barclays Bank, JPMorgan Chase & Co, and The Goldman Sachs Group. (Coghlan and MacKenzie 2011: 8–9)

Not surprising news for some, perhaps, Vitali, Glattfelder, and Battiston's analysis and conclusions are nonetheless a unique and astute quantitative mapping of what some have argued or have suspected for decades. And, though based on data prior to the financial crisis of 2008,[7] their findings emerged in the midst of remarkable public uprisings across the United States and other parts of the world subsequent to that and other crises.[8] Thus, one might have expected their analysis of the extent of global control in the hands of a very few corporate entities to be of considerable interest not only to organizations and community groups demanding greater autonomy and democratic freedoms but also to the mainstream media and the general public. Yet their findings were not exactly at the forefront of public discussion or of political policy debate following its publication.[9]

7. In a comment on his blog about the use of the pre-crisis 2007 database, James Glattfelder notes, "Yes, it would be very interesting to analyze a more recent network snapshot. However, it is also interesting to see the network shortly before the financial collapse in 2008. Moreover, other national ownership network studies have shown that clusters of powerful agents were very resilient and unaffected by external forces ([3] and [4]). So perhaps the observed power-structure in this 2007 dataset is still surviving the turmoil today" (Glattfelder 2011).

8. These included Occupy Wall Street in New York City and the Occupy movement across the United States, as well as popular uprisings in a number of states in the United States and around the world—in North Africa and the Middle East, for example.

9. Project Censored, the long-standing (1976) if occasionally controversial Sonoma State University news-monitoring group, lists the *PLoS* article sixth on its list of twenty-five under-reported news stories of 2011–12 (http://projectcensored.org/6-small-network-of -corporations-run-the-global-economy/). In spite of the relative absence of mainstream news coverage, Glattfelder notes on his blog that the article went viral on the internet.

Nonetheless, their remarkable work serves as a pointed and very specific reminder and verification of those large global forces that Miyoshi's work repeatedly cites and the effects of which he analyzes.

Of course, mapping the ownership and grossly disproportionate control over the global economy of a small group of mostly financial companies doesn't change that economy or alleviate the social misery and gross inequality that that power has caused. Nor does it alter the position of the humanities in higher education or of higher education itself in many parts of the world. Yet it *does* offer a specific focused point of critical leverage in relearning the sense of the world. And it provides a cautionary note to only seeing the thousand and one fragments around us. It is an example of relearning that contributes to Miyoshi's imperative to "discover the sense of true totality that includes everyone in the world."

A second direction that forcefully suggests the need to relearn the sense of the world is not one that emerges from financial institutions but rather from institutions of higher education, specifically in the United States but with a reach far beyond the United States. Miyoshi's work was fiercely perspicacious in its indictment of the complicitous role of higher education in the exercise of global power—from the colonialism that extracted the ivory of the so-called ivory tower in the first place to more recent extractions of profit for the few in multiple forms. "Ivory Tower in Escrow" is, among other things, a succinct critical history of that complicity and extraction to the turn of the century when it was written. So, Miyoshi would be no more surprised by the second instance than he would be by the first. That is the effort to "save the humanities" by taking out a second and third mortgage— to use Miyoshi's escrow metaphor. Or, in light of more recent banking scandals, we might inflect Miyoshi's metaphor of higher education in escrow as a move to refinance the whole muddle with a subprime loan.

Lest this seem hyperbolic, a not so long ago example, one from a champion of the humanities in higher education.[10] In 2010, in his state of the university address, the distinguished president of a leading US research institution and well-known supporter of the arts and humanities advanced, to considerable acclaim, a vision of the importance of the humanities in and beyond the academy.[11] "When I hear military leaders talking about win-

10. See the characterization of Cornell University President David J. Skorton on the Cornell University webpage as "a national spokesperson for higher education, advocating for the importance of the humanities" (http://president.cornell.edu/david-j-skorton/).
11. Cornell University President Skorton, in his 2010 State of the University address. Skor-

ning the so-called hearts and minds of people in other countries, the way I translate that is all based on humanistic and social science disciplines. That requires that we understand the language, the culture, the religion, and the values of those societies—and that is the humanities" (quoted in Jaschik 2010). While, on the one hand, a kind of statement of fact—the role of some academic anthropologists in the US wars in Iraq and Afghanistan is a sorry illustration—this militarized vision of the importance of the humanities surely says much about our impoverished present and about the humanities in that present. I'd suggest that one of the things it says is that the humanities is bankrupt, literally and metaphorically. Let's underwrite its insolvency by taking out a mortgage—"opening an escrow," in Miyoshi's titular metaphor. If this says as much about the future of the humanities, or if the response to the crisis in the humanities is only to help to win the hearts and minds of others (and, of course, of ourselves) for US military missions, then perhaps the humanities *deserve* foreclosure.

Yet here, too, is a compelling reminder of that totality to which Miyoshi's work points and the signposts of which totality his work seeks to trace. If the environmental degradation of the planet creates a "one," as Miyoshi notes, so, too, does globalization as financial degradation of the planet, as the work of Vitali, Glattfelder, and Battiston makes apparent. And, with mortal force, US—but not only US—military interventions around the world contribute, as well, to a planetary "one." The costs and consequences of environmental and financial and military degradation of the planet, though, are borne with ferocious unevenness by the peoples of our "one" (planet).

This is not, of course, to deny a "crisis in the humanities"—about which many words and much anguish have been expended. Though I insist on the double quotes around the phrase, this is not because it has no material reality. It is a crisis of disturbing proportions for institutions of higher education and for those of us who people them and depend on their work. It has wrought terrible consequences for many of our faculty colleagues, for virtually all of our staff and students, and ultimately for our communities. It has highlighted the very "escrow" in which universities have placed themselves and have been placed. (I insist, too, on that double placement.) There is a "crisis in the humanities." Oh yes.

At the land grant institution where I work, the University of Wisconsin–

---

ton has since departed Cornell to serve as secretary of the Smithsonian Institution. While at Cornell, he helped raise over $5 billion for that institution.

Madison, state support for higher education has steadily declined over at least the last two decades and precipitously over the last eight years.[12] While those two decades involve both Democratic- and Republican-controlled state governments, a decisive shift in state funding for public education in general, including higher education, occurred early in the first tenure (2011–14) of Republican Scott Walker as governor of Wisconsin.[13] In the first months of 2011, Walker introduced—and, with his majority in the legislature, ultimately passed—his devastating Senate Bill 10 (SB10, later Act 10). That bill, among numerous other radically conservative moves against health care, social services, public sector (and later private sector) labor unions, and rights of public assembly, also cut state funding for education across the board, K–12 through higher education.[14] In that same period, Walker's budget proposed an additional 38 percent budget cut for the entire university system of twenty-six campuses, over and above an

12. In 2015, the state of Wisconsin's contribution to public higher education was 15 percent. In 2010–11, the state provided 17.6 percent of the total university budget; in 2000–2001, state support was 26.4 percent; a decade earlier, 1990–91, state support for the university was 33 percent. While this decline in state funding for public higher education is scarcely unique, Scott Walker has distinguished himself in his attacks on state public education in general, including higher education. See the Center for Budget and Policy Priorities comparative analysis, "State Funding for Higher Education Remains Far Below Pre-Recession Levels in Most States," www.cbpp.org/state-funding-for-higher-education -remains-far-below-pre-recession-levels-in-most-states and here, www.cbpp.org/blog/tax -cut-states-put-higher-ed-on-the-chopping-block, where the inflation-adjusted cuts to higher education in Wisconsin between 2008–2014 are cited as over 20 percent. More recently, the follow-through on this kind of work is accomplished as well from on-campus, not only from the governor's office and the state legislature.

13. See Figures 2 and 3 and the final data table in Hillman 2017. The state's General Purpose Revenue (GPR) contribution for each "full time equivalent" (FTE) student in 1973 was $12,908; in 2011, it was $6,888. In early 2017, including Governor Walker's projected "increase" in funding for higher education in his assessment, Hillman could still note, "This budget proposal would bring Wisconsin back to 2010 levels and about $170 million behind pre-recession levels. About 32,000 more FTE students enroll in the UWS [University of Wisconsin System] today compared to 1973, yet GPR funds are about $500 million lower than that year. . . . This means state investment is not keeping pace with enrollment growth, as shown in Figure 3. In the 1970s and 1980s, the state invested between $10,000 and $12,000 per FTE, but this changed around 2000 when per-FTE investment has steadily eroded" (Hillman 2017).

14. See Dave Umhoefer's special report on the aftermath of that bill and the struggle against it in his series "Act 10 at Five," in the *Milwaukee Journal Sentinel*, from October 9, 2016, to December 21, 2016, https://projects.jsonline.com/news/2016/10/9/from -teacher-free-agency-to-merit-pay-the-uproar-over-act-10.html.

earlier $47.5 million cut in the same biennial budget. Was it sheer coincidence that this move occurred at the same time as widespread campus participation in and support for the "Wisconsin uprising" against Senate Bill 10? Whatever the fact of that matter, this sorry move on the part of Wisconsin's governor—and subsequent moves in more state educational systems than only Wisconsin's—reminds us once again of what Miyoshi's work so tenaciously illustrates. The humanities must engage with those forces that include us all, not just with our most immediate circles.

If the Wisconsin uprising ultimately failed to either defeat SB10 or, subsequently, to recall Scott Walker,[15] it did succeed in demonstrating the tremendous force of popular opposition to an attempt to punish those state workers with whom citizens and residents usually productively engage on a daily basis: school teachers, librarians, firemen, sanitation workers, and, surprisingly for some, the police. How to work together to focus, sustain, and organize that popular opposition to longer-term ends is, of course, a crucial question. Uprisings do not necessarily mean structural realignment or redefinition. And what occurs in higher education is part of a larger picture that calls for apprehension, analysis, and comprehension—in concerted struggle with others. The academy is one location from which that effort can take place. There are others. And there are larger forces that frame and try to configure those multiple locations. The struggle—"to right the situation, to null the transaction and be just to all on earth"—to change for the better what, from our various vantage points, we together see and understand is probably unending. The double quotes around "crisis in the humanities," then, are to mark its modulated relation to a network of other crises, other struggles. They mark, as well, its modulated relation to a "true totality that includes everyone in the world." Miyoshi's "sense of true totality," even as the scholars in the humanities "look out at the world and interconnect all the workings of political economy and artistic and cultural productions" (2001: 295), remains just that—a "sense" of totality, rather than a sharp image or understanding of its network of relations. But that sense is enough to propel further work, further analysis, further struggle. And that sense is a crucial component of and propellant for what might come after it.

So if "military leaders talking about winning the so-called hearts and minds of people in other countries" is not quite a preferred resurrection of

15. There was, at the time and subsequently, a rich debate about whether that was the appropriate goal in any event. See, for example, the debate in the *Nation* that began on June 15, 2012 (Lafer et al. 2012).

or future for the humanities, there are other illustrative instances in which we can see both the humanities at work and their networks of connection to other fields of struggle. Miyoshi's citation of a shared degradation of the planet as the ultimate totality, as what links us all, is enacted in a more localized way in Hands Across the Divide (HAD), a women's peace and social justice group on the island of Cyprus. A pan-Cypriot and international nongovernmental organization, Hands Across the Divide was founded in 2001 and registered as a nonprofit organization in England in that same year. Refusing generations of charged ethnic nomenclature, HAD speci-fied membership from three regions: north of the Green Line, south of the Green Line,[16] and internationally. That formal organizations of Cypriots from both sides of the Green Line and, indeed, any contact across that line were severely restricted in Cyprus until 2003 is an intense understatement (Cockburn 2004; Hadjipavlou and Cockburn 2006). Yet Hands Across the Divide organized itself nonetheless.

Why turn here to a small women's organization in an out-of-the-way place? The first two suggestions about directions from which to consider Miyoshi's call to "relearn the sense of the world" reference the global reach of the large and the powerful—the intense concentration of global eco-nomic power, the affiliation of humanities in US higher education with mili-tary missions in other countries as a "solution" to crises in higher educa-tion. What can we relearn about "the sense of the world" from a small group in a small place?

In the first instance, Hands Across the Divide offers a suggestive illustration of ways to respond from the ground up to overwhelming out-side force; ways to organize in the face of multiple boundaries; ways to link arms—persistently, often noisily, but also with humor and clever strategy—with others who are our cohabitants. Small, circumscribed, besieged, and determined, HAD sprang from seemingly impossible terrain—nearly fifty years of ethnic and religious division, nearly fifty years of constitutionally specified "protection" by foreign states, over forty years of a UN peace-keeping presence, over thirty years of being physically cut off from homes and friends and neighbors.[17] Of the amazing efforts by the women of HAD which I've had the privilege to witness firsthand or about which I've been

16. The "Green Line" refers here to the United Nations demarcation of a "buffer zone" in Cyprus, first established in 1964 and extended and closed to passage for residents on either side in the summer of 1974.
17. Cockburn 2004 offers a rich and detailed account of the women of HAD and their work.

told secondhand, two I find particularly and provocatively suggestive in this—and any—context.

In the fall of 2002, the coincidence of the birth of a son to one member of HAD and the death of the elderly refugee father of another member was the context for the women of HAD to seek to cross the Green Line to attend a celebration of birth in the north and a funeral in the south. The women asked the authorities for permission to attend both of these events. Their requests were, unsurprisingly, refused. But they made their request and its refusal public as both an exposé and a teachable moment. Sevgül Uludağ, a HAD member and journalist, wrote a newspaper article that circulated widely, locally and internationally, about the refusal to allow women to cross the Green Line (Uludağ 2002) to celebrate a birth and to bury the dead. The members of HAD in the north gathered soil from the village of the elderly refugee who'd died and couldn't be buried in his village as he'd wished and gave it—in a series of transfers between women across the then still closed Green Line—to the HAD member in the south to scatter on her father's grave.

In late 2002, after months of stalled United Nations peace talks on Cyprus at the Copenhagen Summit of the European Council, in a bold gesture of gendered scorn and protest, northern Cypriot women sent "henna to hawks . . . to show their disappointment and anger for the failed efforts to have an agreement on Cyprus." The women sent henna

> to Turkish Republic of Northern Cyprus president Rauf Denktash and foreign minister Tahsin Ertugruloglu, as well as the "Hawks" against a solution in Cyprus like Denktas advisor Prof. Dr. Mumtaz Soysal from Ankara, former Turkish prime minister Bulent Ecevit, former foreign minister Sukru Sina Gurel and Republican People's Party president Deniz Baykal.
>
> Women also sent henna to the "Deep state." (IPS Communication Foundation 2002)

Symbolic *and* practical politics in each instance, intensely locally informed, far more than locally resonant.

A final example of HAD's work, an illustration of, a signpost for, their struggles and accomplishments, is their visionary statement about the future on the eve of the unsuccessful 2004 vote on the "Annan Plan" (the questionable United Nations proposal to resolve the Cyprus problem). The women of HAD decided "to leap over that moment [of always struggling to articulate 'a solution to the Cyprus problem'] and imagine a future when peace is here at last . . . to ask ourselves: what changes would we, as women, want it to bring?" "Imagining a Post-Solution Cyprus: The Gender Dimension" begins, then, with a statement of what is shared:

> Hands Across the Divide is a group of women who share certain values, including: democracy, equality, inclusion and non-violence. We have come together to form a unitary organization, disregarding, so far as is possible, differences of ethnic or national identity, and even geographical location. That said, however, we know that to co-operate effectively we must take account of the inequalities between us and inevitable differences in the needs we prioritize, deriving from our different past experiences and different realities today. (HAD 2004: 8)

The crucial work of imagining the future, not only of accounting for and responding to the past and present of conflict, continues with preliminary outlines of political and legal structures; of statements on the economy, employment, and training; on security, militarism, and violence; on the family, everyday life, and the community; and on education, media, and culture. And, in conclusion, "Imagining a Post-Solution Cyprus" addresses the work of the humanities, of intellectuals and artists and writers, to call for and envision—to demand—a different future. That demand/vision/call is for "associating and working co-operatively in such a way as to shift the understanding of the others' life experiences . . . at the local level in our communities, at the national level in Cyprus, and internationally—where the people of Cyprus can make the island known as a centre of inclusion and of equality—in short, of peace" (11).

In the context of Miyoshi's call "to relearn the sense of the world" and beyond that context as well, Hands Across the Divide is a unique vision and practice of that relearning. This small group of women not only intellectually explores but puts into practice an ongoing process in which its members are continually called on to "relearn the sense of the world"—and further, to act on what they relearn. And it offers a material example of a process—however difficult and fraught with challenges—by which to begin to engage in that relearning.

The fourth and final direction here from which we might imagine the work of relearning the sense of the world is as deliberate in its citation as in its sequential position. The direction originates in Nazareth in the West Bank, a place marked, even more than Cyprus, by international significance and stunning ignoral simultaneously. It is a tremendous, "small" poetic direction to which we might attend. It is, as well, a lovely response to HAD's call "to shift the understanding of the others' life experiences." The last section of an exquisite eleven-part poem by the late Palestinian poet Taha Muhammad Ali entitled "The Falcon" continues the direct address throughout the poem to an ever-returning falcon of "sadness" or "grief"— *ya hazn*. And in that direct address is a call to arms for recognition not only of the situation of my grief and sadness but also of our collective situation.

> 11
> Most
> probably, sadness,
>> you are not my sadness alone.
>> And as long as you are mine and theirs
>> how can I
> dispense with
> you alone?
> (Ali 2008: 100)

Historically, there has not exactly been a rush to link literal or metaphoric arms with the persistently excruciating situation in Palestine— especially from the United States.[18] Yet from the places in and through which we speak and write and see and engage, we might yet recognize the poetic—and political—gesture that calls out our cohabitation. And recognizing that situation of cohabitation, what might we do, "as long as you are mine and theirs"? The responses to that question are as many as we are, on the one hand. On the other hand, though, Miyoshi's characterization of the pathology of globalization is intensely appropriate. It bears repeating. "The spread of desocialized individualism, or self-interest and self-indulgence, as the rational choice in everyday life" (2001: 289) appears to stymie collective recognition, to come to a dead stop at the wall of "individual response."

In a late interview, Miyoshi reformulates his opposition and response to that pathology. "What is important is the willingness to go outside one's national, cultural, and disciplinary borders. . . . We should be everywhere" (2010: 284). That, in its visionary impossibility and tense contradiction, in its counterintuitive structural implications, is surely also a legacy of Miyoshi's

18. Miyoshi's trip with Edward Said to the West Bank in the late 1970s was a remarkable exception to what was then pretty much a rule for those who had no connection political or by accident of birth to Palestine and Israel. This situation has shifted more recently.

work—a future for which we "may have to"—no, *must*—struggle. For the humanities, for higher educations, for social education, for social justice. It is a struggle and a future we cannot "dispense with alone." It is a grave and urgent demand "to relearn the sense of the world." And yes, it is a call to arms—"mine and theirs."

References

Ali, Taha Muhammad. 2008. *So What: New and Selected Poems, 1971–2005* (Arabic edition). Port Townsend, WA: Copper Canyon Press.

Allen, Danielle. 2004. *Talking to Strangers: Anxieties of Citizenship Since Brown v. Board of Education*. Chicago: University of Chicago Press.

Bottici, Chiara. 2014. *Imaginal Politics: Images beyond Imagination and the Imaginary*. New York: Columbia University Press.

Cockburn, Cynthia. 2004. *The Line: Women, Partition and the Gender Order in Cyprus*. London: Zed Press.

Coghlan, Andy, and Debora MacKenzie. 2011. "Revealed—the Capitalist Network that Runs the World." *New Scientist*, October 19, 2011. www.newscientist.com/article/mg21228354.500-revealed--the-capitalist-network-that-runs-the-world.html.

Glattfelder, James B. 2011. "The Network of Global Corporate Control—Revisited." J-node: a random slice of reality . . . (blog). October 3, 2011 (with comments through August 6, 2013). http://j-node.blogspot.com/2011/10/network-of-global-corporate-control.html.

Habeeb, Lee. 2013. "Ex Uno Plures?" *National Review Online*, January 29, 2013. nationalreview.com/articles/339052/ex-uno-plures-lee-habeeb.

Hadjipavlou, Maria, and Cynthia Cockburn. 2006. "Women in Projects of Co-operation for Peace: Methodologies of External Intervention in Cyprus." *Women's Studies International Forum* 29: 521–33.

Hands Across the Divide (HAD). 2004. "Imagining a Post-Solution Cyprus: The Gender Dimension." *Committee for Conflict Transformation Support Review* 24: 8–11. https://www.c-r.org/downloads/newsletter24.pdf.

Hillman, Nick. 2017. "State Funding Trends for the UW System." Nick Hillman (blog). February 9, 2017. https://web.education.wisc.edu/nwhillman/index.php/2017/02/09/state-funding-trends-for-the-uw-system/.

IPS Communication Foundation. 2002. "Turkish Cypriot Women Send Henna to Hawks." *Bianet English*, December 17, 2002. http://bianet.org/english/politics/15372-turkish-cypriot-women-send-henna-to-hawks.

Jaschik, Scott. 2010. "Call to Defend the Humanities." *Inside Higher Ed*, November 10, 2010. www.insidehighered.com/news/2010/11/01/call-defend-humanities.

Lafer, Gordon, Doug Henwood, Jane McAlevey, Bill Fletcher Jr., Mike Elk, and Adolph

Reed Jr. 2012. "OpinionNation: Labor's Bad Recall?" *Nation*, June 15–July 3, 2012. https://www.thenation.com/article/opinionnation-labors-bad-recall/.

Miyoshi, Masao. 2000. "Ivory Tower in Escrow." *boundary 2* 27, no 1: 7–50.

———. 2001. "Turn to the Planet: Literature, Diversity, and Totality." *Comparative Literature* 53, no. 4: 283–97.

———. 2007a. "The University, the Universe, the World, and 'Globalization.'" *Global South* 1, no. 1: 24–37.

———. 2007b. "Writing across Boundaries and Transgressions for Peace: Preface." *boundary 2* 34, no. 1: 209–13.

———. 2010. *Trespasses: Selected Writings of Masao Miyoshi*. Edited by Eric Cazdyn. Durham, NC: Duke University Press.

Uludağ, Sevgül. 2002. "If We Cannot Bury Our Dead, We Shall Share Our Soil." *Yeniduzen*, October 14, 2002.

Vitali, Stefania, James B. Glattfelder, and Stefano Battiston. 2011. "The Network of Global Corporate Control." *PLoS ONE* 6, no. 10: e25995. doi:10.1371/journal.pone.0025995: 1–25.

Solidarity's Indiscipline: Regarding Miyoshi's Pedagogical Legacy

Reginald Jackson

Although I didn't know him well personally, I have thought about Masao Miyoshi quite a bit since he passed away, particularly in terms of pedagogical legacies, as my own graduate advisor, Hideki Richard Okada, counted him as his most important teacher and as a savior of sorts during the bad old days of Berkeley's Japanese studies regime. Now that Hideki, too, has died, it feels important to attempt to account for his own style of pedagogy in relation to his mentor's lessons. The goal of this project is not to indulge nostalgia. Rather, it is to take up the question of teaching so as

I thank Paul Bové and Rob Wilson for inviting me to participate in this special issue and Michael Bourdaghs for putting us in touch. I also thank the University of Michigan undergrads in ASIAN 381 (Winter 2019) for their patient engagement with these ideas. This piece presents in revised and extended form ideas that were initially presented as part of the "Hideki Richard Okada Memorial Panel on Critical Pedagogies," held at the 2013 annual conference of the Association for Japanese Literary Studies. I thank the panel participants, Christine Marran, Steven Chung, and especially Jim Fujii, for sharing their ideas and reminiscences. I also express heartfelt thanks to Azusa Nishimoto, Okada's partner, for sharing her stories and thoughts about his past with me. For more on Okada as a person and a teacher, see Jackson 2014.

boundary 2 46:3 (2019)   DOI 10.1215/01903659-7614147   © 2019 by Duke University Press

to chart its role in shaping the development of notions of academic territory, valuation, exploitation, and resistance addressed in Miyoshi's scholarship. My hope is that this preliminary consideration of pedagogy might both thicken our understanding of Miyoshi's commitments and foreground resources for future critical work.

The occasion of this volume, dedicated to "legacies of the future" evoked by Miyoshi's thought, presents a ripe opportunity to chart Miyoshi's shifting conception of sites of resistance in relation to the university as he both imagined it and intervened within it. To be sure, essays such as "Ivory Tower in Escrow" (2000) and "Literary Elaborations" (2009) assess in compelling ways the university's priorities, failings, and transformative potential. But as a counterpoint to those essays' more macrolevel assessments of the university system, I want to consider their historical relation to an incident in which Miyoshi responded to a graduate student's request for help in contesting unfair treatment within the academy. I focus on this incident as a crucible that prefigured and amplified movements within Miyoshi's critical consciousness, particularly those related to a pursuit of justice within and beyond the university.

Setting the Scene: Opposition on the Ground

What Miyoshi calls his "battle" with Berkeley's Oriental Languages (OL) Department in the mid-1970s represents a turning point in how Cold War imperatives conditioned notions of excellence within one sector of the American academy. Miyoshi dismantled these notions not only conceptually in his writings but also on the ground during his involvement in that case, which revolved around Hideki Richard Okada's threatened dismissal from the program. I want to read this incident in relation to Bill Readings's notions of excellence, as inflected by a reductive notion of expertise operative at the time. This incident stages a primal scene in which Miyoshi's personal political commitments to teaching and supporting students on the ground collided with institutional and ideological constraints in a way that prefigured more explicit criticisms of area studies and the corporatization of the university later in his career. This essay thus ventures a partial genealogy of the pedagogical praxis that foreshadowed development of the theory.

We begin with Miyoshi's account of the incident. Given its pivotal importance, I quote from Kuan-Hsing Chen's "A Conversation with Masao Miyoshi" (2000) at length:

K: You never had a post in East Asian studies at Berkeley?

M: My god, I completely forgot I spent a whole year fighting with the Oriental Languages Department there. It was an amazing fight. This was in the mid-1970s. I had been teaching in the English Department but the OL Department asked me to teach a course in the Japanese novel, which I did. There were quite a few students. It was an undergraduate course, but there were graduate students in the course as well. One of them, who now teaches at an Ivy League university [Hideki Richard Okada], happened to mention that the OL Department at Berkeley took an awful long time to produce PhDs. I suggested he apply for a grant from the student association to do a comparative study of how long the oriental languages departments at the major campuses in the US took to produce their PhDs. He thought that was a great idea and did it. He found out that Berkeley took the longest, something like twelve years, if I recall. Well, when the chairman of the OL Department [William McCullough] found out about the study, he gave the student, who was taking one of his classes, a C on his term paper. The student was rather shocked, not only because he had never received anything but As before but because of the university rule that any PhD student who received a C or less in a graduate course was out of the program. He came to me and asked me to look at the paper. It wasn't a great paper but when I compared it to the A papers he had written for the same chairman, I couldn't discover any significant difference in their quality to justify the poor grade. So I concluded that the grade was revenge for the comparative study the student had undertaken.

That started my fight with the Oriental Languages Department. I first tried to find out what the departmental requirements for graduate students were but I couldn't find anything in print. So I started writing letters to the chairman about this, and, when he didn't respond, I started writing open letters. But all they could come up with was a list of requirements drafted in pencil. As far as I was concerned requirements written in pencil could hardly be regarded as official requirements since they could always be erased. Finally, I went to the graduate dean, told him about the strange goings-on in the OL Department, and asked him to conduct a departmental review. Since he knew something about the department and me, or at least my work, he agreed to form a review committee.

K: Were you on the committee?

M: Certainly not, since I was the one who had instigated it. But there were quite a few established scholars on the committee, one of whom was a friend of mine who quietly passed on to me the committee reports and other paperwork. It took a hell of a long time— I don't know, maybe a year—but after an incredible number of interviews and so on, the committee recommended receivership, which is where a department loses autonomy over its own affairs, which are turned over to someone appointed by the graduate dean. So I won, in other words. But then, the dean chose not to act on the committee's recommendation and simply threw the whole report into a safety deposit box somewhere. The only upshot was that the OL Department was told that it would come under review two years hence, which, of course, wasn't good enough for me. You cannot believe how long this fight lasted.

K: What happened to the graduate student?

M: He wasn't expelled because he was protected during the review process, but the department refused to write recommendation letters for him or to support his PhD thesis. He wrote his thesis, an excellent one, but his department never recognized his existence. He had to find all of his readers outside the department. Nevertheless, he did manage to find a job at an Ivy League university [Princeton], but I think that was because of the close relationship I had with a faculty member there at the time [Earl Miner]. And his case was but one of several. During the course of this review, the OL Department chair's wife, who was a professor in the department [Helen Craig McCullough], wrote a letter to one of her female graduate students who had attended one of the faculty student meetings which I had organized to talk about what to do about the OL Department. The letter said that since she had attended this meeting, she was obviously one of my followers and therefore she could henceforth consider herself one of my students, not hers. In other words, the student could no longer expect any support from the OL Department. I think I directed five or six PhDs by OL Department students writing on Japanese literature that had to look outside their own department to find readers. At times, we did this through the Comparative Literature Department. It was a hell of a fight, and I don't know if it did anything good. Some of these students want to forget their treatment in the OL Department, because it is such a powerful ongoing bureaucracy upon which they depend for job placement and career advancement. I would like to think that my battle with the department had some positive repercussions among a few Japanologists in this country, but I can't say for certain that it has. (Miyoshi 2010b: 273–76)

One struggles to do justice to the complexity of this narrative, involving as it does a diverse matrix of issues: wartime legacies, Cold War configurations, expertise, authority, jurisdiction, ethnicity, loyalty, retribution, shame, justice, solidarity, and an abiding uncertainty about the intervention's greater good. With this scene set, however, I will attempt to delineate the ways in which these issues intersect, with an eye toward how they conditioned Miyoshi's pedagogical commitments.

"Tenacious Difference," Contaminated Postwar Legacies, and Appeals for Justice

Miyoshi was acutely aware of the ways in which racism, nationalism, xenophobia, and unchecked capitalism could suffocate critical engagement and buttress inequity. Even as he was skeptical of the ways in which diversity as promoted along atomizing identitarian lines could be limiting, however, he also knew how opposing diversity often indexed prejudices far worse than multiculturalism's limitations.[1] What Miyoshi resisted was the impulse to think connection in some prefabricated identitarian way. Based partly on his boyhood memories of interwar Japan, he felt that this kind of logic of connection based on ethnicity was perniciously insular, not to mention collusive with nationalist sentiment. To frame it another way: this logic of shared history or destiny could promote uncritical, *unimaginative* inquiry, insofar as it relied on known identities that were all too familiar and therefore liable to breed complacency. Miyoshi assesses this problem in "Japan Is Not Interesting" (1999), in which he asserts that unchecked capitalism has nurtured "an obsession with the idea of Japan among its people and its cognate development, the absence of critical discourse inside Japan" (Miyoshi 2010d: 196).

Against this myopic propensity, Miyoshi's analyses looked to class as a total category that cut across racial, national, and gender lines. Ultimately, this interest was incorporated into a more expansive analysis of

1. This is evidenced by his statement that "multiculturalism that rejects the discrimination of marginal groups is a democratic improvement over the majoritarian monopoly that had long suppressed all but dominant history and culture" (Miyoshi 2010c: 234).

the planetary in "Literary Elaborations," where ecological consciousness and class consciousness converged in a quest for social justice: "Environmentalism cannot exist without social justice, but social justice cannot be expected to prevail without ecological consciousness" (Miyoshi 2010e: 46). These contiguous concepts ground Miyoshi's charge in "Ivory Tower in Escrow" that "critics and scholars in the humanities must restore the public rigor of the metanarratives" in order "to launch a challenge to this seamless domination of capital" and "combat the corporatization of the university and the mind" (Miyoshi 2010c: 240).

Long before ecological consciousness and social justice converged within Miyoshi's prose, however, he sought justice elsewhere as he developed a transformative metanarrative of pedagogical commitment at the site of the Okada conflict. Jim Fujii frames the conflict in the following fashion:

> Richard, I learned, was involved in what can accurately be called epochal and heroic disagreements with his department advisors who were steadfastly opposed to letting theory inform his reading of Heian literature. . . . At the same time, it is important to note that as late as the early 1980s, race and gender played decisive and determining roles in articulating what was a distinct hierarchy of positions in Japanese studies in the United States. Very few people of color taught so-called content courses—history, religion, political science or literature—while almost exclusively Japanese women were appointed as lecturers to teach language courses (a practice that remains to this day). Richard's struggles in his department at what was then called Oriental Languages cannot be divorced from such longstanding postwar institutionalized realities that shaped Japan studies. (Fujii 2014: 195)

Where Miyoshi's description emphasizes the abuse of power taking place in attempting to expel Okada from the program, Fujii's assessment stresses a different but related element of the scenario. Namely, it points to the ways in which hierarchy within the field affected not just what types of analysis were deemed licit but also which types of people were deemed suitable to teach them. "Suitable" here, though, had at least as much to do with academic qualifications as it did with the desirability of gendered, racialized bodies as determined by their superiors' undisclosed rubrics. Whatever the particular manifestation of these assignments was at Berkeley, it is important to recognize their asymmetrical character as a nationwide motif conditioned in large measure by wartime structures of knowledge production.

These structures were consolidated by the Occupation and promulgated within universities as Cold Warriors formerly employed and trained by the American military received posts in the American academy.

Hence the trend of assigning native, mostly female, informants the task of teaching language (along with the reduced status, pay, and job security that that entailed), while the teaching of content fell to a higher class of knowledge workers, echoing earlier institutional bifurcations. One example involves the US Navy Japanese Language School at the University of Colorado at Boulder: "As for Boulder's students, whereas the US Army recruited mostly Japanese Americans as language students for military intelligence, the Navy enrolled only European American students with top grades, many of whom were also born and raised in Japan" (Mercado 2010: 1; McNaughton 2006: 6). With this bias in mind, we might flesh out Fujii's description further by recalling that Helen McCullough was a white 1944 graduate of the Navy's Boulder school (Krogh 1998: 102), while Miyoshi himself explains in his "Conversation" with Chen (2000), "I came [to the US from Japan] in 1952. During the seven years after the war I had worked as an interpreter for the US Army" (Miyoshi 2010b: 268); Okada was nisei, born at the Heart Mountain War Relocation Center in July of 1945.

Crucially, the academy, and the Cold War American Japanese Studies Department, more specifically, embodied a singular site at which these people could encounter one another. Reading this convergence of lives within the primal scene of the OL fight, we should pause to "recognize and cherish the tenacious difference between the two cultures," as Miyoshi recommends in *As We Saw Them*.[2] Recognition represents the first step toward a clear-eyed acknowledgment of asymmetrical power relations structuring the conflict, before we even broach the academic institutional scenario in which questions of belonging, merit, loyalty, and jurisdiction were debated. To cherish the tenacious cultural difference between these figures would be to keep that asymmetry front and center, refusing to either forget or elide it for harmony's sake.

Such a refusal matters because it sustains historical cognizance of long-standing currents dominant within the formation of Japanese studies. Furthermore, it matters because it inoculates against an unwitting yet none-

2. The full quotation refers to the encounter between Americans and the first Japanese embassy to the United States in 1860. It runs as follows: "Before all cultures are made indistinguishable by the ingratiating blight of technology and consumer culture, one might even now recognize and cherish the tenacious difference between the two cultures" (Miyoshi 1979: 186).

theless malevolent ignorance that can accompany the scholarly privilege to translate Japan—for others and for ourselves. Miyoshi explains things this way:

> The lineage of the Japanologists in America began with the religious and industrial missionaries who went to the Far East to civilize and democratize the barbarians. Then the imperial evangelists of civilization took over the role of teachers and advisors on their return home around the turn of the century. Their godsons, who had been dormant for a while, were mobilized into a cadre of interpreters and administrators during the Second World War and the postwar years. A noticeable advance in Japanology was made by this generation of Occupation-trained specialists, and their impact on scholarship remains both powerful and definitive. Because of the historical circumstances of mission and conquest, this genealogy has no shortage of those uncritical (or even unaware) of their own ethnocentric and hegemonic impulses. (Miyoshi 1991: 67)

These tacit or unconscious impulses can be difficult to track, especially when an early Cold War rhetoric of international friendship or a later one of celebrating diversity sits close at hand, ready to camouflage supremacist inklings. Given the banality of anti-Japanese racism in American culture throughout World War II, it seems plausible to posit its survival in sectors of the postwar academy. However, even without focusing on institutional racism per se, we can detect hegemonic impulses in the ways in which other borders were policed, often as part of a containment strategy designed to marginalize certain voices within the academy under the aegis of scholarly pertinence or merit. As Fujii recounts,

> In a rather draconian step Richard was forbidden by his department advisors to continue studying with Masao (a professor in the English department). They would withhold their signatures and consent for a thesis "contaminated" by critical theory, and he faced many other acts designed to impede his progress at every turn. Adding a few years to completion of his degree, their punitive measures extended beyond graduation. Employment opportunities were far better then compared to now, but he was made to languish at a prep school for many years until he would finally secure tenure track employment at a university. In ways only he would know, Richard paid heavily for his principled stand and perhaps his ethnicity. (Fujii 2014: 195–96)

Poetically enough, in this context, Okada's punishment for straying out of line by writing the untimely seminar paper and embracing critical theory was being made to suffer the same soul-killingly slow disease he'd diagnosed at Miyoshi's encouragement. Like other students who associated with Masao or took his classes during this fraught period, the McCulloughs gave Okada the ultimatum to choose between them and Miyoshi. He made what he felt was the right choice but was ostracized for doing so.

From Critical Supplements to Priceless Support

In describing his encounter with Miyoshi, David Palumbo-Liu provides a sense of the depleted landscape within which Miyoshi's presence mattered both for students and for the demarcation of institutional borders:

> I first met Masao Miyoshi in the late 1970s at Berkeley. It was sobering for me to read his account of those times in this volume. Yes, it was called the Oriental languages department (as Miyoshi indicates, OL for short, or, as we students called it, "Oh, Hell") and housed in the former law-school building, Durant Hall. . . . The gold placard above the [student lounge] entrance read, "The Chaos Room." What Miyoshi writes is perfectly true—in those days, many of us advanced undergraduate and graduate students were hungry not only for theory but for any critical perspective that might in some way present another angle onto literary studies, especially of "the Orient."
>
> At that time, faculty who could provide that were few and far between, so we formed our own reading groups, bought titles from presses such as Éditions du Seuil, and read the Poétique series and the magazines *Tel Quel* and *Glyph*. This was before *Representations* was a twinkle in Stephen Greenblatt's eye. Masao Miyoshi was not only someone who could talk to us about Marxism, historical materialism, and a demystified notion of East Asia; he also had the personal brashness and the politically active, iconoclastic stance to which many of us aspired. He was so close to our interests and sequestered right next to us in Wheeler Hall. Yet disciplinary boundaries, not to mention professional jealousies and turf wars, made it impossible for Miyoshi to be formally appointed in OL, and those who did work closely with him were, as he recounts in these pages, marked pejoratively by his antagonists as *his* students. (Palumbo-Liu 2012: 343–44; emphasis in original)

Palumbo-Liu's account adds a dimension that clarifies Miyoshi's importance and appeal within a broader context of student malaise and institutional strife. An intellectual closeness shared with students regarding critical perspectives eventually engendered more formal bonds as "professional jealousies and turf wars" fueled the formation of cross-generational and cross-disciplinary coalitions. The feudal nature of OL at that time, evidenced most strikingly in the way the McCulloughs forced students to pledge exclusive allegiance or risk peril, inadvertently pushed Miyoshi past the bounds of his field of expertise. It also sent him outside his home department, and even his institution, as he took up a position as visiting professor at the University of Chicago beginning in 1978—making the annual trip east by car. By his own admission, he was no expert on Japanese literature. However, he was nevertheless willing to take on an advisory role to support the orphaned students who sought his help once all hell broke loose in OL.

Miyoshi's support of Okada extended far past a few kind words or a single petition signature. Masao served as Okada's dissertation advisor when the McCulloughs cut him off. As it happens, these experts' abandonment launched Miyoshi into the realm of authority—by default. Miyoshi's willingness to direct the dissertation stands out in part because of his wry recommendation at one point that Okada take old books like *Genji* and burn them, so that the graduate student might migrate to fresher, less embattled sites of inquiry. But this willingness also marks a kept promise to see the project through and to stand by a student who held promise and deserved better treatment. Indeed, this commitment contributed to Miyoshi's decision to stay on at Berkeley as a sentry until Okada safely submitted the dissertation in 1985; Miyoshi decamped promptly for UC San Diego in 1986. Some causes were apparently worth fighting for, despite Miyoshi's increasing preference for more current, more discernibly worldly texts.

Constraints and Expanses We Inherit

Despite Masao's advice to burn those old books, Okada maintained a commitment to Heian texts that fueled rather than forestalled his exploration of new intellectual terrain. The bad Berkeley days Okada lived through emitted negative energy that was refurbished toward more positive ends as he tried to propose better trajectories of critical engagement. To talk a bit about this background is not to apologize or mythologize but rather to historicize a connection to that formative institutional context of OL as a frame for the space Okada worked to build in his best seminars—for which Miyoshi's own courses served as touchstones.

There are any number of questions that seem imprudent or uncomfortable to ask when attempting to excavate oppositional sites of learning. Among these are questions that foreground the dubious desire to discipline students through an insistence on expertise. Indeed, we often forget the extent to which the spaces we inhabit condition the questions we're most inclined to ask—or resist. For Okada, the silo that was OL foreclosed the exigent questions about language, subjectivity, history, and power that captivated him as a graduate student. Worldly concerns that he learned to regard as central in Miyoshi's seminars were judged peripheral or even inimical to the scholarly training he underwent in OL.

Theory thus became a means of escape. At a superficial level, it comprised a range of critical thinking whose nourishing alternatives were preferable to the stale rations habitually doled out in his so-called home department. But at a deeper level, theory supplied tactics for surviving a toxic intellectual atmosphere. To hear Okada or Miyoshi tell it, the diverse thinking beginning to flourish in other departments on campus, not to mention the activist political consciousness burgeoning within other sectors of the broader Berkeley community, was maligned within OL, which disparaged it as marginal to the immediate area of specialization and the educational mission at hand. From this official standpoint, theoretical and worldly concerns were akin to invasive species whose incursion was to be either adamantly ignored or quashed lest it derail business as usual. Remember that this was before interdisciplinary scholarship had landed the cachet it boasts today, back when ethnic, gender, postcolonial, and performance studies' nascent interventions were still struggling to congeal within the US academy. The *post-* had yet to fasten firmly to terms like *structuralism* or *colonialism*, and areas like premodern Japanese literary studies were effectively administered as garrisons assigned to hold the wider world at bay.

In retrospect, such occupied institutional territory presents a setting in which to ask after what might be called the ecological repercussions of pedagogical systems. After all, some classrooms' atmosphere can prove toxic—often unwittingly, but occasionally as part of a bid to maintain order. Long before cancer claimed him, Okada the graduate student tried his best to maneuver amid what felt akin to the intellectual equivalent of slow death. This was decades before the student-led sit-in to hire Asian American faculty and establish Asian American studies at Princeton (Okada 2002), before the Graduate Mentoring Award he received in 2008, or before his turn to ecology, prodded by Miyoshi.

I understand now that Okada had to literally escape the territory of OL and locate other spaces in which to ask the questions that compelled him—regardless of whether or not they had answers, and irrespective of whether or not the prevailing authorities deemed those questions licit. His body in that time and that place was overwhelmingly prone to being apprehended in reductive terms: monitored and misrecognized as a foreign object, if not a native to be domesticated by the Cold War learning machine. He was an object learning to be a subject, but wary of becoming *too* subject—too disproportionately disciplined—in the bargain. Walking the tightrope between affirming subjectivity and enduring subjection is no picnic; Miyoshi undoubtedly helped guide him on this score. I can imagine that Okada's presence might have undermined the very faith in an objective, disembodied scholarship within which the most technocratic notions of disciplinary expertise lodged. In such environs, Theory (imagined if not fetishized with an authorizing, armoring capital *T*) helped him find his footing as a student and pursue both a personhood and an intellectual scope that exceeded any single department, area, or disciplinary perimeter. In short, it lent a fugitive means through which to bypass the insularity of state-sanctioned area study to access worlds more expansive than the sites he'd inherited.

Vital Counterpoint

In some ways, Okada's scholarship was concerned deeply, if not always explicitly, with language's relation to space. His communion with Miyoshi sharpened and ramified this interest. One thing that drove both their work was a determination to articulate the pervasive and often pernicious extent to which space—discursive and otherwise—answered to demands for hierarchy, transparency, and deadened thought. Okada's chosen task as a critic was to examine how textual figuration resisted such demands. Even if that annexed space couldn't be fully reclaimed, its mechanisms had to be confronted, delineated carefully, and somehow countered. Having grown allergic to the strains of disciplinary violence that fostered positivism, he tried to inoculate those of us who'd listen against the hazards of becoming conceptually numbed.

Before he sought refuge with Miyoshi, Okada had been admitted to the program to work under William McCullough and his wife Helen McCullough, a celebrated translator and scholar of classical Japanese literature. Tensions developed between the graduate student committed to exploring the possibilities of classical Japanese literature and the teacher who once wrote, "I do not believe Japan has produced a great literary corpus, or that it can boast a single undisputed literary masterpiece, or that very many works of classical Japanese literature can stand up to sustained, intensive literary criticism."[3] Given her stance, other spaces had to be sought and built to accommodate the "sustained, intensive literary criticism" thought unviable by some.

Okada's graduate seminars were therefore tacitly positioned as the antithesis of the McCullough dungeon: a site which for him epitomized a vacuum of imagination, worldliness, and rigorous critical thinking. Contrapuntal to that other place and time, our seminars were designed to be as capacious as possible. So, anything was fair game as long as it relied on perceptive reading, kept attentive to the conditions under which a text had been produced, and was put forth in a thoughtful manner that opened that text. This tack constitutes a facet of Miyoshi's pedagogical legacy.[4]

Okada's trials in OL annihilated any belief in structure for structure's sake. That territory taught him by negative example how crucial it was to preserve spaces that were more generative and open. Similarly, anything resembling slavish obedience to precedent was scorned, along with faith in the merits of professional apprenticeship. Whatever space and time we graduate students inherited in his seminars slid counter to the strictures that for him had felt most oppressive about OL. In this sense, indiscipline in the classroom became a way to retrospectively redress infractions wrought before our time. Indiscipline held the potential to revise and even resurrect opportunities that had perished decades prior.

Excellence/Theory

Different institutional spaces foster different regimes of assessment or violence, often hosting proprietary attitudes toward expertise as a guarantor of the excellence Bill Readings condemns. For Readings, the notion of excellence as operative within the modern university is especially prized because "excellence has no content to call its own," thus making it uniquely

3. Letter dated July 12, 1978, later released to the Berkeley campus newspaper for publication, quoted in Miyoshi 1991: 12.
4. Miyoshi describes, for example, his free incorporation of a wide variety of "foreign" texts into his courses on Victorian or Japanese literature. See Miyoshi 2010b: 276.

serviceable to limitless, often questionable, aims (Readings 1996: 24). He writes, "However much some of us might think we can resist the logic of consumerism when it comes to tertiary education, everyone still seems to be for excellence. It functions not merely as the standard of external evaluation but also as the unit of value in terms of which the University describes itself to itself" (28). To be sure, departments and factions within them indulge this narcissism as heartily as the larger academy itself does.

Aided by this frame, OL appears to have operated like a bulwark of excellence, especially as demonstrated by linguistic expertise and translation, as factions within it opposed the momentous groundswell of the 1970s. If, as Readings notes about the post-1968 academy, excellence "develops within the University, as the idea around which the University centers itself and through which it becomes comprehensible to the outside world," then we should understand OL's refusal of external critical perspectives and insistence on insularity as ways to center and define itself over and against its perceived outside (22). At its best, OL as Okada experienced it trained scholars to perform advanced research on East Asia. At its worst, it was a colonial outpost: an institutional setting wherein striving for excellent translations could become an alibi for excluding the worldly in favor of a flawless elsewhere that was more manageably and apolitically remote.

Notice, though, that this exclusion of worldly engagement in favor of an area-bound parochialism later finds its counterpart in the more subtle quietism of high theory. In "Ivory Tower in Escrow," Miyoshi notes that "the fear of totality as inevitably totalitarian remains unabated" (Miyoshi 2010c: 232). Such trepidation results in layers of abstraction Miyoshi criticizes as byproducts of the corporatization of the university—subsidized by excellence—and of transnational corporatism's desire to dissimulate the crushing realities of class inequity. Here the atomization of identity under multiculturalism represents "the ideal form of ideology of this global capitalism" (Žižek 1997: 44). These criticisms are valid. However, it is important to mind the gap between the historical function of theory within the heavily corporatized university familiar in 2000 or today and theory's salvific value within the area-centric OL encampment of the 1970s, in which students like Palumbo-Liu and Okada felt starved or silenced by antitheoretical injunctions.

In Okada's case, the issue of incorporating theory into his studies of Heian texts, which metastasized in the OL battle, should be understood as a fight over language: what languages were authorized to be learned and spoken, by whom, under what circumstances, and within what spaces, not to mention who decided what counted as foreign or native. Theory estranged traditional relationships to language, dislodging dominant assumptions about language even as it constituted a lexicon all its own. The idea that this new language would be quarantined from his studies of Japanese literature, that the freedom to explore new worldviews would be barred, was a grievous affront. Furthermore, that the people authorized to teach him Japanese in graduate school had been agents of the same military industrial complex that had displaced his family, confiscated not just property and dignity but also pride in speaking Japanese, moreover, only added insult to injury. Needless to say, the setting was not primed for choruses of John Lennon's "Imagine."

How to frame this conflict? Okada was a subject being maligned as an object of discipline, who was trying to assert his status otherwise. This led him to the harbor outside OL that was Miyoshi and to currents of critical thought that helped him make sense of his historical condition, not to mention his potential to thrive beyond it. Hence, alongside classical Japanese, theory as he encountered it in graduate school became a means of coming to terms with Japanese language that had been not simply lost but stolen, as his parents had been strongly encouraged to abandon speaking Japanese to their son in order to have him assimilate more smoothly into American society and excel in school. As its own language, Theory held the promise of liberating him from a bleak outlook on the world, and on Japan specifically, as rehearsed within an environment in which certain styles of critical thought were deemed foreign contaminants to purportedly valid or rigorous research. That regressive posture for him represented a microcosm of larger structural asymmetries, exploitations of authority, and abuses of power that coated curricula to inculcate expertise. These structural features materialized in efforts to assure excellence through an exclusionary compartmentalization of learning.

No Time for Excellence

But what does this regimentation of space have to do with the times—that historical moment, or time, as measured within the academy? One thing to point out is the way in which asking questions about the disciplinary nature of time in certain institutional contexts, at particular historical moments, can incur harsh marginalization and even expulsion. As it happens, Okada wrote a paper on time—specifically, a seminar paper on time to degree within OL. It was an unprecedented gesture at the time, examining not mere content but rather the very departmental structure within which that content was transmitted and appraised.

As Readings diagnoses, time to degree is a key index of the efficiency coveted within the increasingly corporatized university: "The treatment of pedagogic time as exhaustively accountable is a major feature of the push to excellence. 'Time to completion' is now presented as the universal criterion of quality and efficiency in education" (Readings 1996: 128). Now that those of us teaching in doctoral programs have become accustomed to the incessant administrative refrain of cutting students' time to degree, we might skim past the novelty of raising such an issue nearly forty years ago. It's difficult to imagine the extent to which such a simple question about time could strike so raw a nerve. And yet the swift response to the posing of such a question—a subpar grade and a concomitant withdrawal of funding tantamount to expulsion—exposed an urgent problem with how time was being overseen in that sector of the Ivory Tower.

Michel Foucault's famous work from the same historical moment at which the OL battle took place would emphasize discipline for its role in the production of docile subjects.[5] But even as we recognize intensifications of surveillance and discipline's capillary infiltration into modern life, we still need to reckon with the realities of good old-fashioned punishment. Okada's case highlights how that punishment could be leveled as a delegitimizing blow: a vengeful refusal to grant the seal of disciplinary competence and to thus condemn the student to professional exile.

To ask questions of a certain tenor—about the nature of duration, its institutional mismanagement, and its prejudicial bent—was to probe the unspoken mechanisms by which this engine of discipline sought to reproduce itself indefinitely. Time was out of joint, and to make an analytical object of time to degree punctured the assumption that all was as it should be, running smoothly and equitably. To underscore this tortuous duration was to raise it as a problem and to dispute both its validity and its claims to excellence. To ask in a pointed fashion, "Why so long?" in other words, turned the temporal logic of excellence against itself to expose a hollow core. This simple question trained an icy floodlight on a stark-naked emperor—one whose decrees were scrawled in pencil, no less!

5. Specifically, I have in mind here Michel Foucault's *Surveiller et punir: Naissance de la Prison* (1975), whose English translation, *Discipline and Punish: The Birth of the Prison*, was published in 1977.

Since the guidelines for student performance and disciplinary repercussions were conveniently composed in pencil, the rights of the student
could potentially vanish with an eraser's wobble, at the OL chair's whim. The
precarious nature of traces like these is suspect because in some cases
the very people who were most culpable preferred the transient nature of
the medium. After all, pencil meant malleable parameters that could be
altered to suit the prerogative of those who held the privilege to issue dictates without censure. In "Turn to the Planet" (2001), Miyoshi explains that
as deregulation "create[s] an economic order that not only concentrates
wealth and power among the few, but perpetuates the center against any
future challenge from the fringes," so too do fungible graphite guidelines
similarly serve to undermine opposition by muddling the channels through
which plaintiffs might legitimately plead their case (Miyoshi 2010g: 254).

The very flimsiness of those provisional dictates was what necessitated such violence to disavow the question's threat. Expulsion was the
only answer because to not expel the abject was to poison the system with
a corrosive doubt, not to mention court further risk of insubordinate curi-
osity or loss of departmental sovereignty. For indeed, the question about
time also challenged prevailing arrangements of space within that department: how lines of affiliation and evaluative codes were inscribed, and how
arbitrary demarcations confined or belittled inquiry that failed to reaffirm
prevailing hierarchies. Therefore, indecorous inquiry had to be crushed.
No one in the scenario was naïve, I'm sure. I don't doubt, for instance, that
there was some desire to needle his supervisors that tinted Okada's points
in the essay. But I also don't doubt that the decision to expel the student
who penned that essay struck a retributive extreme. Miyoshi intervened to
set things right.

Locating Justice alongside Humility

As he narrates it in "A Conversation," Miyoshi's attention to justice
was galvanized by his wartime experience: "The Second World War left
me no choice but to search for some basis for fairness and justice, a mod-
est utopian view in which one needs not be ashamed of bigotry and ignorance. . . . Generally speaking, my politics goes way back to the Second
World War and my adolescence, even if its development was slow and tortuous. Justice is a self-evident idea, it seems to me, whether it is about the
Middle East, Africa, Asia, race in America, or gender questions" (Miyoshi
2010b: 280). This quotation makes clear that, like the ideal of planetarian-

ism, for which he advocates in "Turn to the Planet," justice, too, radiates as a total principle for Miyoshi. Both these ideals surpass geographic region or ethnic and gender divisions to address the disproportionate oppression suffered by the have-nots in an exclusionist economy: "Once we accept the planet-based totality, we might for once agree with humility to devise a way to share with all the rest our only true public space and resources" (Miyoshi 2010g: 261).

The mention of "humility" stands out in Miyoshi's appeal: it's not a term that appears much in his writing, and frankly, likely isn't a term many who knew him would associate with his professional persona. The near-insurmountable nature of planetary deterioration summons the term here, as the looming inevitability of environmental collapse and human extinction eclipses the deficiencies of multiculturalism or disciplinary boundaries. Indeed, turning to face the planet meant embracing a humility with regard to the institutional hierarchies and disciplinary esteem we habitually preserve. It entailed, moreover, an acute sensitivity to inequalities coupled with a deep willingness to let the exigencies of dispossession guide one's work, regardless of what fields that work trespassed on.

As it abets an intellectual trespassing, this humility helps haul expertise out from its fiercely guarded academic crannies and back into the realm of an authority unafraid to venture universal visions of humanity or justice. If, "as seen in the context of the theorists in the United States, there is an undeniable common proclivity among them to fundamentally reject such totalizing concepts as humanity, civilization, history, and justice," he writes in "Ivory Tower in Escrow," then we should view this proclivity as not just cowardice but as an indication of entrenched institutional structures of organization, evaluation, and promotion that can actively disincentivize notions of justice and humanity—within the humanities especially (Miyoshi 2010c: 232). To practice such a humility means to forgo the "cynicism that conceals a moral and political failure behind an elaborate intellectual sophistry," not to mention the layers of abstraction and equivocation that subsume it (233).

In tying this moment in Miyoshi's writing back to our primary scenario, we notice that, while the condition of intellectual sophistry as a barrier to justice might span eras, its scale and historical texture shifts. For whereas Miyoshi rails in 2000 against the extent to which theoretical and multiculturalist discourse subsidizes corporatization of the university, circa 1975 the moral failures and denials of justice he witnessed were situated firmly within Berkeley's OL Department, where the stakes were more localized but no less dire for those involved. In fact, the Okada incident alerts us to the ways in which the brute fact of injustice suffered within the academy could be shrouded by the question of expertise, often laced with vacant slogans lauding excellence. In this case, the professorial experts preferred to treat his case as a mere matter of academic merit, severed from matters of official protocol or potential discrimination, and hence ultimately subject to their local departmental—if not individual—jurisdiction. And here we recall Readings's assertion that "to say that excellence is a criterion is to say absolutely nothing other than that the committee will not reveal the criteria used to judge applications" (Readings 1996: 24).

Miyoshi adopted numerous thesis advisees who either defected from OL or were banished from it for their alleged insubordination to its commanding officers. This generosity speaks to his willingness to challenge the limits of his own knowledge to support student learning that outstripped the mandates of department-sanctioned expertise. In this sense, we might say that a desire to advocate on students' behalf and to make sure they were looked after beyond the doors of his classroom carried him outside of Victorian literature. While detractors might have deemed this propensity arrogant in its disregard for disciplinary borders, we might more charitably view it as evidence of a form of humility toward student interests and needs—intellectually, but also in the material sense of their having to survive in the academy and secure employment within it.

These students' paths could dictate where Miyoshi went and could permeate his own research, without reductive assumptions about the sharing of learning needing to proceed in a hierarchical vector from teacher to student. One such example of this exchange is Miyoshi's foray into *Genji* criticism with his review of Edward Seidensticker's translation. In "*The Tale of Genji*: Translation as Interpretation" (1979), his emphatic claim rings allegorically given our trajectory thus far: "The original *Genji*, I repeat, flows and drifts. At every turn, the stream of narrative opens up an unexpected perspective which also revises what has come before . . . the narrator blends with characters, who also subtly intermingle with each other and with their environments" (Miyoshi 2010f: 80–81). This essay was a by-product of a willingness to let Okada's research suffuse his own, to the mutual benefit of both. More significantly, though, the review also staged a public display of solidarity that, through the medium of criticism, legitimized Okada's own approach at the moment it was being disparaged within his home department's domain.

Authority, Expertise, and the Politics of Placement

As a Japanese scholar employed in Berkeley's English Department, Miyoshi's presence was anomalous within the context of postwar American academia. In "'Bunburying' in the Japan Field" (1997), he points out that "when I became an assistant professor of English at Berkeley, I was probably the only Japanese-born faculty in English at any major university in the United States" (Miyoshi 2010a: 163). This was long before the discourse of multicultural diversity or policies designed to institutionalize its presence in the academy took hold. In a time when the regime of area studies dominated the research of cultures within the postwar American university, Miyoshi says, "I felt so unencumbered by segregation either by race or by specialty that I thought nothing of expanding my studies to Japanese literature" (164). However, he also notes that "there was no disapproval of my training at first, until I began to defy the power hierarchy in Japanese studies in Berkeley and, in time, in the United States, Japan and other places. (This is a saga in itself, involving actual students, faculty, administrators, and scholars, inside and outside of the Japan field, which, however, must be told elsewhere.)" (164).

Miyoshi's account suggests that the expansion of study he pursued and the precise location of his disciplinary "home" became problematic only when questions of power, fairness, and the nature of discipline itself surfaced. The moment he resolved to intercede on behalf of students he felt were being crushed between the gears of Berkeley's Japanese studies machine, his credentials suddenly became just as suspect as his motives. That disapproval toward him and efforts to undermine his credibility as an expert in Japanese literature spiked as a consequence of his advocacy underscores the stakes of crossing certain boundaries, not of field or area, necessarily, but of *territory*. That the very same OL Department that had formerly invited this Japanese, tenured literature scholar to teach courses on Japanese literature now impugned his authority on matters of student assessment within that field indicates a capricious, expedient recourse to the rhetoric of expertise to suit the interests of those unwilling to expose their dubious rationales to scrutiny. Once his hegemony as OL chair was threatened, it was, in fact, William McCullough's effort to evade regulation that retrospectively redefined Miyoshi the welcome native authority as Miyoshi the unwelcome interloper.

To be sure, the upper administration's decision to place the department in receivership attested to more egregious inconsistencies in OL's policies and deeper-seated problems besides. The department chair and his wife resented Miyoshi's meddlesome involvement in their affairs. So much so, in fact, that where they could not deflect or harm him, due to his tenured immunity, they went after those students who had expressed interest in figuring out how to improve conditions in the department and who had met with Miyoshi, such as the young woman to whom Helen McCullough wrote to charge with a disloyalty worthy of severed support.

And yet it was the very resistance to appeals for procedural transparency and fairness that catalyzed Miyoshi's pursuit of justice for students—whether they were technically "his" or not. While this demonstration of solidarity with the students no doubt read as an encroachment on academic turf from the McCulloughs' perspective—and indeed resulted in an actual loss of autonomy once the OL Department entered receivership—Miyoshi's advocacy also had the effect of eroding a notion of expertise in favor of a less narrow notion of authority. In criticizing growing trends such as mercenary careerism among faculty and the appropriation of higher education by the market, Miyoshi explains in "Literary Elaborations" that "we are now experts rather than authorities. This difference is hardly trivial: an authority knows not only her/his specialty but also understands its place in the scheme of learning. An expert, on the other hand, is trained only in the field of specialization, and refuses to take even a step beyond it" (Miyoshi 2010e: 3).

What Miyoshi calls his extended "fight" against OL can be understood in part as a conflict waged over the value of authority versus expertise. At the time of the upheaval, several students themselves sought unwittingly to become authorities, not merely experts, but had to confront the harsh reality that to follow such a path smacked of disloyalty to the superiors who administered one's assigned area and could terminate students' departmental support. What the Okada incident accents is the ugly reality that "the scheme of learning" needn't keep students' best interests—or learning—in mind. That scheme can, moreover, aim to amplify their institutional vulnerability and compromise their life prospects through withdrawal of material support. This can force the student to *learn their place* as inferiors and to rehearse a timidity which ensures that neither the field of specialization nor those who police its perimeter are disturbed. Consequently, the question of the field's placement and function within broader hegemonic configurations never ends up being raised.

Miyoshi's commitment to justice for students within the academy nourished his abiding skepticism toward academic discipline as a category and his disdain for the subjugating uses to which it could be put. With his status as an expert in Japanese literary studies now officially under fire from those whose preserves he'd allegedly invaded, Miyoshi had both to imagine otherwise regarding his position within the university complex and to strategize the most sound route by which to protect those students being mistreated. This challenge necessitated interdisciplinary conversations and a degree of coalition building across departments in order to ensure the students were taken care of and awarded their degrees.

Whereas Miyoshi had by that point made connections with colleagues throughout the humanities, this situation pressed him to think pragmatically about how to activate those ties and convert them into effective alliances. His friendship with Earl Miner was one such alliance. Miyoshi's expertise in English literature helped kindle a rapport with Miner, who was situated between the Departments of English, East Asian Studies, and Comparative Literature at Princeton. This personal and professional relationship could be leveraged in helping Okada secure a tenure-track position when traditional channels had been blocked. Without Miyoshi's ardent support, Okada never would have earned the position or tenure. I daresay he might not have survived the academy at all.

Conclusion: Fostering Futures

Miyoshi's trenchant writings about the predations of neoliberal capitalism, or the erosion of political courage in the face of the university's burgeoning disinterest in opposing global inequality, serve as a powerful testament to his intellectual breadth and his investment in exposing and opposing exploitation. But as anyone who has spent time in the academy knows well, talk is cheap. Therefore, what moves me more than any of Miyoshi's probing criticisms of the academy are the stories Okada shared inside and outside the context of graduate seminars about how Miyoshi's active presence enriched his life. Unfortunately, but understandably, many of these stories were never recorded or set down in print. For indeed, many of the most heartening anecdotes Okada shared were beset by a thicket of bitter remembrances that routinely kept him reticent about his graduate school experience. And the quotations I've included here, even as they accrue to suggest something of the contour of those harsh days, still only scratch the surface of a deeper history that has yet to be excavated amply.

Yet there are traces that lend a sense of the fuller story. In the first paragraph of the acknowledgments for his dissertation, for example, Okada writes this:

> The most rewarding experience a student can have is to find himself in the presence of a genuine teacher. I feel fortunate to have been taught by several in my life, but none has left as enduring a mark as my committee chairman, Professor Masao Miyoshi. His extraordinary blend of compassion tempered by a vigorous and insightful critical sense, as well as an ongoing commitment to real world issues, has been a constant source of encouragement and inspiration. It is a debt of gratitude I can repay only by trying to teach my own students in a similar manner. (Okada 1985: i)

We should pause at the term "compassion," which juts like "humility" did. For as cheap as talk could be in the university of 1975 or that of 2015, this term underscores that Miyoshi did far more than merely offer words of support: he dug into the long grind of affirming solidarity through meeting with students and deans, writing open letters, engaging with *Genji* and its secondary scholarship, nurturing alliances across departments and institutions, calling in favors, and just telephoning to ask how things were going and discuss a new book on oceanic pollution. Taken together, all these actions foreground Miyoshi's compassion as manifested through his pedagogical commitment—even as they sketch a legacy less legible than that which his writing leaves us. His hustle in the trenches points to his desire to make the academy more livable and navigable for students trying to orient themselves within the expansive world that the academy's dim corridors sought to deny.

This goal of *supporting humanity in practice*, not just "The Humanities" in theory, is what Miyoshi's broad-spectrum pedagogy, advocacy, and solidarity pursued. Viewed from this vantage, his work does far more than just parse area and discipline, expertise and authority. With tenacious vitality, Miyoshi cherished an indiscipline that drove his pedagogical commitment. This abiding commitment not only spurred him to imagine alternative futures beyond the university. More than this, it led him to foster—for his students, especially—futures askew of the university's most demoralizing routes.

References

Fujii, James. 2014. "From Deconstructing Genji to Deep Ecology: Remembering Richard Okada." In *Proceedings of the Association for Japanese Literary Studies*, edited by Michael Bourdaghs, Reginald Jackson, and Hoyt Long. Vol. 15: 195–202.

Jackson, Reginald. 2014. "In Lieu of Eulogies: Post-Mortem on the Hideki Richard Okada Critical Pedagogies Panel." In *Proceedings of the Association for Japanese Literary Studies*, edited by Michael Bourdaghs, Reginald Jackson, and Hoyt Long. Vol. 15: 203–219.

Krogh, David, ed. 1998. *1998, University of California: In Memoriam*. Oakland, CA: University of California (System) Academic Senate.

McNaughton, James C. 2006. *Nisei Linguists: Japanese Americans in the Military Intelligence Service during World War II*. Washington, DC: Department of the Army.

Mercado, Stephen C. 2010. Review of Roger Dingman's *Deciphering the Rising Sun: Navy and Marine Corps Codebreakers, Translators, and Interpreters in the Pacific War. Studies in Intelligence* 54, no. 2: 1–3.

Miyoshi, Masao. 1979. *As We Saw Them: The First Japanese Embassy to the United States (1860)*. Berkeley, CA: University of California Press.

———. 1991. *Off Center: Power and Culture Relations between Japan and the United States*. Cambridge, MA: Harvard University Press.

———. 2010a. "'Bunburying' in the Japan Field: A Reply to Jeff Humphries." In *Trespasses: Selected Writings*, edited by Eric Cazdyn, 159–74. Durham, NC: Duke University Press.

———. 2010b. "A Conversation with Masao Miyoshi." Interview conducted by Kuan-Hsing Chen and transcribed and edited by Steve Bradbury. In *Trespasses*, 263–84.

———. 2010c. "Ivory Tower in Escrow: Ex Uno Plures." In *Trespasses*, 205–42.

———. 2010d. "Japan Is Not Interesting." In *Trespasses*, 189–204.

———. 2010e. "Literary Elaborations." In *Trespasses*, 1–48.

———. 2010f. "*The Tale of Genji*: Translation as Interpretation." In *Trespasses*, 77–82.

———. 2010g. "Turn to the Planet: Literature and Diversity, Ecology and Totality." In *Trespasses*, 243–62.

Okada, Richard Hideki. 1985. "Unbound Texts: Narrative Discourse in Heian Japan." PhD diss., University of California, Berkeley.

———. 2002. "Areas, Disciplines, and Ethnicity." In *Learning Places: The Afterlives of Area Studies*, edited by Harry Haroutoonian and Masao Miyoshi, 190–205. Durham, NC: Duke University Press.

Palumbo-Liu, David. 2012. "Crossing the Lines: Masao Miyoshi's *Trespasses*." *Criticism* 54, no. 2: 343–51.

Readings, Bill. 1996. *The University in Ruins*. Cambridge, MA: Harvard University Press.

Žižek, Slavoj. 1997. "Multiculturalism, or, the Cultural Logic of Multinational Capitalism." *New Left Review* 225: 28–51.

Transpacific Asymmetries: Masao Miyoshi and Asian American Studies

Chih-ming Wang

> No one today is purely *one* thing. . . . Imperialism consolidated the mixture of cultures and identities on a global scale. But its worst and most paradoxical gift was to allow people to believe that they were only, mainly, exclusively, white, or Black, or Western, or Oriental.
> —Edward Said, *Culture and Imperialism*

> My consistent preoccupation has been this question of borders, in both my personal and professional life: how do we make adjustments when we move across borders?
> —Masao Miyoshi, *Trespasses: Selected Writings*

I begin with these two epigraphs not only because Edward Said and Masao Miyoshi were close friends and allies in life and spirit, but rather

An abridged version of this essay was presented at the English Language and Literature Association of Korea (ELLAK) Conference in Busan, Korea, in 2015. I am grateful for the invitation by Professor Min-jung Kim and the comments made at the gathering. I also thank Professor Guy Beauregard for his incisive suggestions on earlier drafts and Professor Rob Wilson for his encouragement and support of this essay.

boundary 2 46:3 (2019) DOI 10.1215/01903659-7614159 © 2019 by Duke University Press

because they can provide a useful lens for understanding why Eric Caz-dyn characterized Miyoshi as a "trespasser" and "enlivenor" (Cazdyn 2010: xxxiii). A border-crossing intellectual in many of the fields he has engaged, Miyoshi, despite his influences, would stand as an outsider looking in, won-dering why there was a line or fence to begin with, and what that line or fence would tell us about the asymmetry of power. It is thus noteworthy to remember Miyoshi's offhanded remark in an interview with Kuan-Hsing Chen (2000) that, although he "did sponsor a few Asian ethnic studies courses," he does not "believe in any biological animal called the Asian American" (Miyoshi 2010b: 273). Because for him, identity does not stand by itself but always exists in power relations. While it may serve as a power-ful vehicle for struggle, identity is best regarded as a "paradoxical gift" of imperialism that one ought to critically engage rather than readily accept. In *Off Center*, a book that aims to "restore asymmetry in our perception" and dismantle "national and regional borders" for thinking about the "prob-lems and events in global history" (Miyoshi 1991: 2), Miyoshi reminds us that "ethnic consciousness and pride are understood to be vital and indis-pensable instruments only until the day of decolonization, autonomy, and equality—and not a single day longer" (245n4). Miyoshi always engaged with specific historical imperatives and never succumbed to choices or pri-orities in reified and abstract fashion. His strategic negation of identity, both personal and professional, suggests not only a diasporic trajectory that stipulates his intellectual biography—as a Japanese and (Asian) American working "off center" from the fields of Victorian literature, modern Japa-nese literature, as well as cultural studies—but also a transpacific vision, in which historicizations and analyses of asymmetrical relations are indis-pensable to the understanding of East-West cultural contacts and the sub-sequent ethnic and cultural formations. "Who decides, and who speaks" in the transpacific engagement are, for Miyoshi, more central questions than what one is and what one represents.

The above is, of course, a sketchy—if not reductive—summary of Miyoshi's vision and politics, but it may serve as a convenient departure point for reconsidering the linkage, or the lack thereof, between Masao Miyoshi and Asian American studies. Miyoshi's analyses of *shutaisei*/sub-jectivity, the invention of disciplines, and global capitalism as understood through East-West comparisons trailblazed a form of transpacific critique evolving out of Asian studies since the 1980s with an anchor on the spatial metaphor of the Pacific Rim as a space for articulating indigenous, anti-colonial desires within and against US imperial imaginaries that transpired in the transpacific flow of ideas and peoples. Though less recognized, this critique—as evinced in the anthologies he coedited with Harry Harootunian (1989, 1993, 2002) and Fredric James (1998), along with the works by his students and associates (Wilson and Dirlik 1995; Wilson and Dissanayaka 1996; Sakai 1997; Dirlik 1998; Cumings 2002, to name a few)[1]—has left us a rich legacy for addressing the intersectionality of race, nation, gender, and empire, and for rearticulating the linkage between Asian American studies and Asian studies in their respective transnational phases of multilateral attachments and deconstructed subjectivities. This critical approach to the interactive dynamic between Asia and America, and the formations of Asian ethnicity, indigenous Pacific, and diaspora, is transnational and comparative in scope and design. In particular, Miyoshi's comparativism should be understood not in the reductive sense of comparison—of simply pitting one thing against another—but in what Rob Wilson calls a "Blakean" poetics with "visionary reach and planetary politics" that seeks to unsettle and transform the field of comparison (2004: 387).

By situating Miyoshi's work and vision as a strategic negation of identity politics and an analysis of the historical structuration of a transpacific dynamic at a key center of Asian American studies—the University of California, Berkeley, in the 1970s—I hope to demonstrate in this essay that his work has laid the foundation for a form of transpacific critique that exposes US-Japan relations as asymmetrical in power yet as complicit in imperialism since their first encounters in the late nineteenth century. His work and vision could also transnationalize Asian American studies for more critical ends by foregrounding the transpacific as a traumatic site of domination and resistance. In light of the Obama administration's 2011 declaration to "pivot to Asia"—a policy aiming to shape up the transpacific into a militarized front and a free trade zone against the rising China— and the current Abe government's attempts of late to remilitarize Japan and retain US military bases in Okinawa,[2] Miyoshi's insights have dawned

1. These works, moreover, have paved the way for the turn in the late 1990s to the transpacific as a field of inquiry and methodology. See Hoskins and Ngueyn 2014; Suzuki 2014.
2. On October 11, 2011, Hillary Clinton, then US secretary of state, published an article entitled "America's Pacific Century" in *Foreign Policy*, in which the idea of "pivot to Asia" was first proposed to assert the US national interest in Asia. This idea was later developed as the US's "rebalancing strategy," about which Asian countries have aired strong concerns. Across the ocean, on the sixtieth anniversary of the establishment of the Japanese Self-Defense Force, Japanese Prime Minister Shinzo Abe changed the government's long-standing interpretation of the Constitution to allow Japan to deploy its military abroad. The decision effectively undermines the Constitution's war-renouncing Article 9

on us as prescient, critical, and even prophetic. And his attention to how US-Japanese asymmetrical relations—epitomized in Japan's desire for the West, defeat, and postwar dependence on the United States for development and security—enabled and shaped a transpacific complicity in imperialism is especially worthy of our attention. As he pointed out in an essay titled "Out of Agreement," the problem with US-Japan relations is that it is so much about agreement—the agreements to forget the past, to keep the emperor, and to embrace "the universality of Christmas and the hegemony of the West" (1991: 188).

Resistance to such complicity marks the inception of Asian American as an analytic category emerging out of the straitjackets of racism and imperialism, and as a culture participating in minority and imperial formations. Victor Bascara asserts that "Asian American culture functions as both a manifestation and critique of US global hegemony" (2006: xxiv–xxv). Janet Hoskins and Viet Nguyen point out that the domestic focus of Asian American studies since the 1970s on the claims of US citizenship and multicultural inclusion tends to neglect the transpacific dimensions of the community's growth, and its critique of American inequality is "possibly even complicit with even the most exceptionalist versions of American Studies," therefore risking affirming some kind of US-centrism (2014: 19). My discussion of Ruth Ozeki's *A Tale for the Time Being*, a timely and significant novel, joins this line of critique by showing how Miyoshi's emphasis on asymmetry can serve as a critical optic for reexamining the transpacific histories and perspectives that shaped Asian American literature—especially its *immigrant narration*—and for exploring the role Asian Americans played in forging and morphing transpacific ties. How an understanding of transpacific asymmetries as relations of power and affect can help us recapture the politics of a US-Asian dynamic is the question I wish to pursue here.

This essay thus consists of two parts: the first part explores the idea of transpacific asymmetry in Miyoshi's work, and the second part focuses on Ozeki's novel, especially the issue of immigrant narration as a sign of such asymmetry. It attempts to explain how Miyoshi's work performs and theorizes a double critique of Western imperialism and Japanese nationalism through transpacific comparisons and by redirecting our preoccupation with identity to the envisioning of an inclusive totality. Moreover, by critically

---

and caused concerns in neighboring countries. These are not isolated incidents but constitutive of the shifting dynamic in transpacific and inter-Asian relations, which seem to veer toward another round of containment.

engaging with Ozeki's important novel, I hope to reconsider some of the assumptions of Asian American literature as it takes a postidentity, transnational, and even global turn (Nguyen 2005; Ty 2010; Song 2013). At a time when globalization is imagined to have made the world flat, and when Asian American writers, like Ozeki, have come to grapple with the tremors of the planet, it is time that we honor and reclaim Miyoshi's off-centered approach and planetary vision that boldly imagine a world "in which parts and margins are seen on their own terms, in their relations not to the center of power but to a world that has no ordering center at all" (1991: 5), and be vigilant of the transpacific trajectory that is perhaps taken for granted in Asian American studies.

Transpacific Critique: Asymmetrical Formations of the *Shosetsu and Shutaisei*

Without widespread literacy and printing, there would have been no novel; and literacy, printing, and the novel were produced only in certain societies deeply engaged in expansions and colonialism. (Miyoshi 1991: 56)

Do nations, races, classes, sexes, and groups benefit from the unceasing assertion of individual interests and self-concerns? Doesn't brute power always lurk behind the rule of *shutaisei*? (Miyoshi 1991: 123)

It is difficult not to think about Miyoshi's life and work as *transpacific*, a term that seeks to theorize the dynamic flow of ideas, people, culture, and capital across the Pacific and within and to gesture to a mode of travel and dwelling that is not just jet-setting elite and cosmopolitan but no less mobile and glaring in its experience of dispossession and displacement. Miyoshi observes in "A Borderless World?" (1993), an essay well-cited in transpacific studies, that "post-Fordist production methods enable[d] TNCs to move their factories to any sites that can offer trained and trainable cheap labor forces. . . . Low civil rights consciousness, too, including underdeveloped unionism and feminism is crucial: although female labor is abused everywhere, the wage difference between the sexes is still greater in the third world" (2010a: 139). This observation, then as now, offers a diagnosis of the transpacific as complex negotiations between transnational capital, Asian states, and third-world gendered subjects. The transpacific can therefore be understood as a space of interaction formed by networks of

power and domination, and of longings and belongings that are complicated by unruly alliances, unlikely affinities, and even outright resistance.
It names a way of understanding intercultural and transregional exchange
structured by colonial modernity and capitalist globalization. As he has indicated in the above-mentioned interview, "The reasons for living at any particular locality are disappearing except that there are a huge majority of
people who are left behind and cannot dream of leaving for any place else.
They are stuck, often trapped for good. In our era of so-called globalization,
globalization is reserved for the lucky few. I am obviously one of them, and
so I feel an obligation to constantly think about those trapped behind with
little hope" (Miyoshi 2010b: 283).

For Miyoshi, globalization created glaring unevenness in mobility
and quality of life. It also produced asymmetrical relations to capital and
state between the mobile minority and the immobile majority. How such
inequality was first created and how it has manifested in different settings
and moments are concerns running throughout his oeuvre. His three books
on US-Japan relations—*Accomplices of Silence* (1974), *As We Saw Them*
([1979] 1994), and *Off Center* (1991)—eloquently articulate a view of the
transpacific as the asymmetrical formations of knowledge and power, for
which the discussion of the *shosetsu* (the novel) and *shutaisei* (subjectivity) are cases in point. While these works have been read mostly in the
Japan studies context, his emphasis on asymmetry in transpacific contact
is also relevant to Asian American studies because asymmetry can not
only explain why people or things move but can also compel us to rethink
Asian American as a transpacific culture, traversing and linking, however
unevenly, Asia, the Pacific, and America.

Miyoshi's three monographs represent a critical comparative
approach to the question of Japanese (literary) modernity evolving around
the invention of the *shosetsu* and the discussion of *shutaisei* that emerged
in the asymmetrical economy of modernity and translation since the late
nineteenth century. Rather than treating these terms merely as translations of the novel and subjectivity in the West, Miyoshi provides a thick
description of how the genesis of these concepts, while subjected to Western influences, is irreducible to such translations. He writes, "While it is
true that Japanese writers would not have conceived the *shosetsu* without
having fairly close acquaintance with Western literature, this is not to say
that in developing the *shosetsu* they totally abandoned their own tradition"
(1974: iv). Similarly, it is impossible to translate *shutaisei* as subjectivity
without losing sight of the entangled and vexing histories in which *shu-*

taisei—covering issues of individuality, autonomy, responsibility, independence, and self-identity—emerged as a response to the West, especially in
the postwar order of crime and punishment, where Japan found itself both
as an aggressor and a victim.[3]

Not only the linguistic correspondences between the novel and the
shosetsu—and between subjectivity and *shutaisei*—are products of specific histories; their incompatibility in semantics also implies an asymmetrical relation that is constitutive of their meanings. As Naoki Sakai argues,
shutai (the subject) is "that which cannot be contained in the economy
of equivalence in a transnational translational exchange," because it is
"a hybrid from the outset" (1997: 119). Perceptive of the delicate intercultural
circuit that created such terms in the first place, Sakai moreover asserts
that "*shutai* itself is of hybridity that is inevitable in the process in which
the subject is constituted," yet, at the same time, it is also "erased and disavowed in the subject thus constituted" to the point of becoming unrepre-
sentable (119). Sakai's rendition indicates two critical dimensions of *shutaisei* and the *shosetsu* that help explain and highlight Miyoshi's concern
with asymmetry: the repressed hybridity and assumption of individualistic
selfhood in the problematic formation of Japanese identity and modernity.

Like his Japanese colleague Kojin Karatani, Miyoshi, in *Accomplices of Silence*, also traces the origin of modern Japanese literature to
the *gembun'itchi* movement of the late nineteenth century. A state-initiated
project to standardize correspondences between written and spoken languages, the *gembun'itchi* movement represents an early phase of Japan's
cultural modernization where writing in the vernacular—opposed to writing
in traditional *kambun* (Chinese character)—was regarded as pioneering a
new literary form that would be a breath of fresh air in Japanese literature.
The rise of *gembun'itchi* as a vernacular turn connoted a new conception
of literature informed by the Western novel, which for Miyoshi represents
both a new relationship between the writer and his objects and readers,
and Japan's long cultural entanglement with the West. What *gembun'itchi*
enabled was the literary projection of a new Japanese self, which at its origin denies its hybridity as both the resistance to Chinese influences and
the embrace of Western literary norms.[4] Though this new Japanese self

3. For the debate on *shutaisei*/subjectivity as it has evolved in postwar Japanese political
contexts, see also Koschmann 1981–82; Sakai 1997.
4. Karatani calls it the "discovery of landscape." Referring to Soseki's understanding of
literature and using the metaphor of landscape painting, Karatani contends that "literature makes the objectification of *kanbungaku* [Chinese learning] possible. In this sense to

may assume the form of diverse characters in literature, as Miyoshi discovered in the works of such writers as Futabatei Shimei, Mori Ogai, Natsume Soseki, and the like, its identity is not so much rooted in its liveliness in language and sentiment as in the struggle over representation and individuality, for which the *shosetsu* can be regarded as palimpsests of cultural negotiations that have internalized the West as their own.

Citing Roland Barthes's discussion of the Western novel, Miyoshi argues that the *shosetsu* is "the reverse of the novel: rather than a 'credible fabrication which is yet constantly held up as false,' the *shosetsu* is an incredible fabrication that is nonetheless constantly held up as truthful. . . . What makes the *shosetsu* fascinating is this complex negotiation between the formal insistence of the 'I' and the ideological suppression of the self" (1991: 23). Such a comparison brings into view different novelistic techniques between East and West and discrepant conceptions of the self that the *gembun'itchi* movement intended to equalize but at which it failed. Instead, what the vernacular turn achieved was to represent Japanese life and society by incorporating the Western terms and lenses with which modern Japanese writers found themselves struggling. As a result, while the characters these writers created are interesting and absorbing, they appear more as "abstracts finally, markers of the plot-logic, and not portraits of real people" (Miyoshi 1974: xi–xii). Furthermore, the autobiographical fiction called the *shishosetsu* (I-fiction) only intensifies this ironic separation between representation and reality. The works of both Dazai Osamu and Mishima Yukio, two notable writers in Miyoshi's view, demonstrate how the dramatization of individuality ironically relies not on the narrative but on the way that writers act out their suicidal instincts to fulfill their stories' promises of individuality and authenticity. The expectation of the *gembun'itchi* movement to make written language correspond to life and develop individuality through the discovery of interiority therefore ends up achieving the opposite.

Here Miyoshi has detected the oxymoron: the writers' attempts at representing individuality through retelling autobiographical tales result only in the rehearsal of the collectivist culture where novelistic languages remain aloof from real life. As Karatani contends, while *gembun'itchi* may have created an "interiority," the vernacular could not be a purely "inner"

---

compare *kanbungaku* and English literature is to ignore the historicity of literature itself— of 'literature' as a kind of 'landscape'" (1993: 19). Specifically, Karatani regards literature and landscape as mechanisms of inversion through which the structure of perception is transformed. The discovery of interiority is likewise tied to this change of perception.

speech; furthermore, the "inner self" is not an a priori existence waiting for the vernacular to discover it and bring it to life. Rather, it signifies a historical process, a dominant "modern system" of cultural relations into which Japan has been incorporated but has been forgotten (Karatani 1993: 40). Therefore, rather than looking at the *shosetsu* as the Japanese equivalent to the Western novel, Miyoshi proposes to regard it as the Westernization of Japanese literature, with an emphasis on the dynamic processes of transformation within the hegemonic world order of colonial modernity. This distance between representation and real life hence leaves us a trace to the origins of Japanese modernity as the dramatic transformation of self-perception, a hybridizing process that is curated by a Western frame of mind, as Ruth Benedict's *Chrysanthemum and Sword* tellingly reveals (Yoneyama 1999).

That is why for Miyoshi, *shutaisei* is fundamentally a hegemonic program, one which "was from the beginning deliberately, and hopelessly, severed from the world [that modern Japanese writers and intellectuals] in fact inhabit" (1991: 122). In reference to the postwar debate on war responsibility in US-occupied Japan, Miyoshi in *Off Center* moreover argues that though the debate represented an attempt at soul-searching for Japanese to understand what had caused the war and their suffering, it evaded confronting the postwar international frame of justice designed by the United States and the history of Western colonialism that opened Japan's door and dashed its hopes. Such evasion, he believes, exemplifies Japan's "long-standing deference to the West" and its unceasing effort to catch up to it (113). Such a structure of feeling as intensified in the wake of US Occupation made postwar Japanese writers reframe *shutaisei* as "a stoic determination to live on despite poverty and iniquity" for Shiina Rinzo, as an experiment with the flesh for Tamura Taijiro, and as a deliberate act of defiance against social norms for Mishima Yukio (116–21), all of which represented struggles over the torment of war and defeat. Yet, Miyoshi reminds us, despite their apparent defiance and independence, these I-fiction writers only confirmed the tight grip the society had on them: "I-fiction can be looked at not as evidence of *shutaisei* (self-searching, self-determination, self-identity) but as exactly the opposite, the public disclosure of the work's composition" (121).

Here, Miyoshi points out that such *shutaisei* as thus imagined and pursued by postwar Japanese writers was from the beginning alien to the land where it was quested, and that *shutaisei*, understood in terms of subjectivity, independence, and individuality, is "not a universal value" (122) but rather a historical and culture-specific notion arising in the West in the modern period. Similarly, the novel is a product of European expansionism and colonialism, and the notions of individualism and subjectivity that have come with it are Western imports, attached to this expansionist and colonial history. Miyoshi's point is not to lament Japan's failure in obtaining *shutaisei* but to interrogate its fundamental assumption as universal and desirable, and to ask what it has cost Japan. Yet in problematizing *shutaisei*, he also does not simply fall back to a cultural nationalist position to defend conformism and collectivism, as if these are indisputably Japanese cultural traits. Instead, he cautions us against such a danger, articulating a double critique of both the West and Japan by reminding us that an intensified and accelerated form of consumerism is driving *shutaisei* into a global hegemonic program with far wider and deeper implications and consequences (125). Like the *shosetsu* that is Western and Japanese, *shutaisei* and the lack thereof in Japan demonstrates an off-centered approach to the asymmetry of power that created ideas and affects in transpacific motion.

The idea of asymmetry is the keystone of Miyoshi's critique of US-Japan encounters. In *As We Saw Them*, he reexamines the records of the first Japanese embassy to the United States in 1860 to carefully tease out the cultural and political implications of such first encounters. He describes the Japanese delegation's strange perceptions of their journey to America as a sequence of ironies, in which Japanese and Americans misunderstood each other despite their endeavors to harness each other through diplomatic protocols. He also maintains a critical consciousness of incommensurability when comparing the travelogues of early Japanese and American travelers. Juxtaposing Japanese and American travel accounts produced around the same time, he finds that whereas the American travelogues are abundant in details and personal reflections, the Japanese counterparts are instead drab and impersonal, almost in the fashion of technical manuals. However, instead of jumping to conclusions, he emphasizes that these travelogues, or "diaries," while comparable, reflect incompatible cultural conceptions of the self. In particular, he ponders the absence of first-person narratives in the Japanese travelogues—a feature key to the genre of diary in the West. He argues that perhaps this lack of the first person not only indicates the cultural conditioning of the Japanese language in writing—such as the centrality of the honorifics as indications of social relations—but also connotes that the Japanese travelers had consciously kept a distance from the foreign land, and an indifference to their own feelings about it, as if they were only machines to document, not subjects to experience. If the Japanese travelers' perceptions somehow read strange to us, Miyoshi argues, it is because our perception of them already assumes a universalist position: In Japan,

> the "I" tended not to detach itself from the other "I's" and thus stayed immersed in the world. There was neither the joy nor the misery of the lonely self; instead, with the ambiguity of the subject allowing his action and being to be collective, man in Japan retained the security of community. . . . [The Japanese culture] has chosen to forgo universalist knowledge, skeptical observation, and individual reflection in order to sustain a close and coherent community inherited from the long past. (Miyoshi [1979] 1994: 123–24)

For Miyoshi, these Japanese and American travelogues represent two conceptions of selfhood, and neither is superior nor inferior to the other until the late nineteenth century, when the West ascended, through war and conquest, to the universalist position. But Miyoshi's analysis does not end here. He further explains how Japanese traditions and late nineteenth-century contacts conditioned the morphing of the Japanese self—namely, how and why Japan, despite its initial resistance, adopted the Western modernization program and internalized the expansionist and colonialist ethos in the end. As in the discussion of *shutaisei*, the issue at stake is not why Japanese did not produce first-person accounts of their voyages abroad but how colonialism and modernity by default had established an asymmetrical framework for comparison, in which the Japanese conception of selfhood would appear oddly and awkwardly collectivist, a stereotypical image that ushered Japan into the modern.

In "The Invention of English Literature in Japan" (1993) and "Japan Is Not Interesting" (2000), two essays collected in *Trespasses* (2010), Miyoshi takes a step further into the scrutiny of the repressed hybridity in Japanese identity where asymmetry matters. In the former essay, he explains how English literature began in Japan as one of the consequences of the one-sided rendezvous between Japan and the West, and how this asymmetry in power was reinforced by the pedagogical practices of late nineteenth-century Japan, where students of English literature, such as Natsume Soseki, had to learn by memorizing facts about authors, texts, and periods. Miyoshi explains that students were "expected to swallow the teachings whole, without being told what it was that they were ingesting," and were discouraged from thinking about what literature is or can do (2010c:

120). Such pedagogy ran parallel to the Japanese efforts to render equivalences between Japanese and English, not only for communication across cultures but for asserting equality and aspiration, because the fact "that an English text could be translated into Japanese, and vice versa, was seen at least partially as an act of demonstrating Japan's cultural compatibility with Britain at a time when the British Empire ruled the world" (116–17). Such uncritical and imperializing imitation was a problematic aspect of Japan's modernization program through which Japan emerged a reticent but diligent student fixated on catching up with the West and acting like a Western power.[5] Miyoshi notes that even in the 1980s, when Japanese fervor of translating and absorbing critical theory from the West, what was missing "is any indication of the awareness of meaning of these critics and theorists in the context of both English Studies in Japan and Japanese society/culture itself" (124). In the asymmetry of knowledge, the desire for the West superseded the urgency for reflection, turning learning into a superficial performance and *shutaisei* into a mark of struggle for subjectivity.

Similarly, by making a provocative claim that "Japan is not interesting," Miyoshi challenged this uncritical imitation model that has resulted in the silencing of dissent and protest in Japan in the 1990s. He criticized Japan for concentrating on the economy so much that it seemed to have lost interest in the outside world, even at a time when "internationalization" was adopted as a national policy and the discourse of *nihonjin ron* (on Japaneseness) was running rampant.[6] Though he does not address the latter directly in this essay, he contends that "an obsession with the idea of Japan among its people" is an indication of the "absence of critical discourse," which made Japan "an empty signifier" (2010d: 196). Miyoshi believed that because of its role in World War II as both aggressor and victim, Japan withdrew itself to a space of isolation, protected by the United States and thus disconnected from the world at large. It was this psychological withdrawal from historical trauma, to the extent of revising history textbooks and neglecting the misery it had inflicted on neighboring countries, that caused Japan to zoom in on the claim of homogeneity and conceal its heterogeneous formations in history. Most ironically, the introverted gaze, crystallized in the belief in the emperor system, was actually proposed by the

---

5. Miyazaki Hayo's recent anime film *When the Wind Rises* finely recaptures this mindset through the romantic epic of Horikoshi Jiro, the Japanese engineer who designed the Zero fighter jet that was used in the late phase of World War II for *kamikaze* (suicide) bombing.

6. On *nihonjin ron*, see Iwabuchi 1994.

United States as early as 1942, as documented in Edwin O. Reischauer's "Memorandum on Policy towards Japan" to the US War Department.[7]

The emperor system as the cornerstone of the Japanese national body (*kokutai*) and self-identity is not a transhistorical given but a US imperialist design to retain Japan within the Cold War orbit as a "client state." As Sakai has observed, the insistence on Japanese nationality as a homogeneous ethnicity diachronically connected prewar Japanese colonialism with postwar US imperialism in "trans-Pacific complicity," which has turned "Japanese nationalism into an instrument for colonial governmentality" (2012: 293). The postwar discussions of *kokutai, nihonjin,* and *shutaisei* as articulations of Japan's cultural and national differences consequently became forms of disavowal and disengagement, facilitated by the US dominance in Japan. That is why the claim "Japan is not interesting" was actually Miyoshi's call to his compatriots to break out of the inertia of cultural narcissism and to forge alternative alliances—"the alliance of all the exploited" (2010d: 204)—to shake up and shatter the transpacific imperial structure of Pax Americana. What matters is not difference as a coherent identity codified by race or nation, but dissent and the will to challenge and break free from the agreement to the hegemonic world order.

Although the discussion above by no means offers a comprehensive summary of Miyoshi's work, I hope it has demonstrated the centrality of asymmetry in his politics and vision as a double critique against US imperialism and Japanese modernity. For Miyoshi, transpacific asymmetry was never just about the imbalance of power and skewed interplay between America and Japan; more crucially, it was also a structural dynamic that put things in motion. Not only were the contexts for Japan's first contact with the West asymmetrical; the spell of colonial modernity also prompted uncritical imitation before and after Japan's defeat, creating a one-sided flow of immigrants, ideas, military bases, and tourists. The US Occupation policies and security pacts further entrenched this asymmetry as Japan rose to become an economic powerhouse, resulting in a bashing game and trade war in the 1980s and 1990s. Meanwhile, histories of Chinese exclusion and Japanese American internment remind us that transpacific immigration was not always smooth. The US's twisted view of Japan, and of Asia more generally, as both enemy to resist and victim to rescue, has fashioned Asian America's relationship with Asia in the dual models of diasporic displacement and transnational linkage. The decision to manage otherness at

7. On the significance of Reischauer's memorandum, see Sakai 2012.

the border showed how racism and imperialism were actively at work shaping the transpacific passage into asymmetrical relations that alternately take the form of antagonism, market expansion, and even sympathy.

In this view, transpacific asymmetries are better understood as the manifestation of colonial modernity and the structuration of affect that is specific to such border-crossing, racialized subjects as Asian Americans. Their strivings for recognition, equality, and fair treatment represent a potent challenge to the hegemonic world order centering the United States, although their rise in the racial order and beyond is also configured by US global hegemony. Transpacific asymmetry coded in the East-West encounter, in other words, is both the historical condition in which Asian American emerged as an identity and community and the problem its arrival seeks to overcome. As a spatial metaphor, transpacific asymmetry identifies Asian American in a passage to modernity to reckon with the chronopolitics of equality. Almost prophetically, Miyoshi argued in the context of the 1980s trade war between Japan and the United States that "the Western demand for fairness and reciprocity is both desperate and understandable, but it must be acknowledged once and for all that there has never been fair trade or an open market. And if they are going to exist now and in the future, it is because the meaning of geopolitics and chronopolitics is radically changing on this enclosed and endangered globe" (1991: 94).[8] What the optics of asymmetry promises to offer, therefore, is a diagnosis of the global condition that is often veiled by the rhetoric of free trade and fair play, and reified by identity politics within liberal multiculturalism. Miyoshi shows us how to scratch the surface to reach the core of the global system—racist, imperialist, and capitalist—where the asymmetries of resource and power have tipped the globe off balance.

Parallel Universes: Asian/American Entanglements in *A Tale for the Time Being*

Ruth Ozeki's novel *A Tale for the Time Being* is a great text for thinking about transpacific asymmetries. An intriguing and powerful novel built around such global issues as ecological crisis, bubble economy, memory loss, and the cultures of bullying and suicide, and commenting on the trau-

8. For Miyoshi, geopolitics follows chronopolitics, because "'progress' as an imaginary was a brilliantly effective instrument for the justification of a global mission of expansion, which offered civilization, meaning conquest. Geopolitics was thus always legitimated by chronopolitics" (1991: 93–94).

matic histories of World War II, the terrorist bombing of 9/11, as well as the compounded disaster of 3/11 in northeastern Japan, *A Tale for the Time Being* has not only garnered international recognition in the form of literary prize and translation[9] but has also broken new ground for Asian American literature, in both form and content. It is an exemplar of what Asian Canadian scholar Eleanor Ty calls "Asian global" narratives because these stories "arise out of and are contingent on globalization . . . and because they are no longer located just in North America or Britain" (2010: 133). The authors of these texts have moved beyond the identity concerns that previously defined Asian American literature to imagine a more fluid subjectivity and engage with global issues formerly reserved for white writers. Although "globalization has both constrained and empowered" these writers, it has also refashioned them from being merely ethnic or immigrant writers to becoming "travelers, explorers, and the subject of quest narratives," charting the world as white writers do (Ty 2010: xxviii).

Although the novel is filled with autobiographical allusions, it is not an autobiography per se but rather a transpacific interweaving of I-fictions that stages an accidental—but fated—encounter between a Japanese Canadian writer named Ruth and a sixteen-year-old Japanese schoolgirl called Nao, all mixed up and tossed around in a drama of the now, fittingly embodied by the act of reading as imagining.[10] Set in motion by the feeling of compassion, the novel exemplifies how literature functions as what David Palumbo-Liu calls a "delivery system" to engender "a space for imagining *our relation to others* and thinking through why and how that relation exists," which in turn could create *"new forms of narration and representation"* (2012: 14; emphases in original). By portraying different kinds of transpacific passage, from accidentally picking up debris washed ashore, or active researching and dreaming, to the more typical acts of migration, this novel—by delivering otherness (Japan) as relatable to (Asian) American readers—demonstrates how Asian Americans begin to find new mean-

9. By the time I completed this essay, *A Tale for the Time Being* had received the Yasnaya Polyana Literary Award for Foreign Literature in 2015 (Moscow), and both the Kitchie Award (London) and the *LA Times* Book Prize in Fiction (Los Angeles) in 2014; it has also been translated into sixteen languages, including Chinese, Japanese, Hebrew, and Turkish.

10. The novel is also a translingual and transcultural tribute to Marcel Proust's *Remembrance of Things of Past* and to quantum physicist Hugh Everett, whose many-worlds theory of 1957 offered the novel a theoretical backbone and whose personal tragedy inspired the character Haruki II.

ings and knowledge in their ties to Asia, and thus projects Asia as a parallel universe which is coeval with, related to, yet also detached from, North America. As Ozeki herself claims, this novel is about "the black holes in our knowledge and memory" and how they "can be created by political will but also just by neglecting to tell the tale" (Ty 2013: 170). These black holes of memory and knowledge can also tellingly reveal how the transpacific is spatially experienced and imagined—as a subterranean "superposition" that holds America and Asia together as distinctly separate and discrepantly connected spaces, as an "ocean of feeling," so to speak, informed by history, memory, politics, and as the determination to love, save, and care for one another.

A Tale for the Time Being ends with a series of appendices, the last of which is dedicated to Hugh Everett, whose "many-worlds interpretation" provides a theoretical ground for the novel's imagination, and whose personal tragedy (his early death and suicidal daughter) echoes that of a character in the novel, Haruki II, Nao's father. Everett's many-worlds theory, published in 1957, is an interpretation of quantum mechanics that affirms the objective reality of the "universal wave function" (the possible states of being that have yet ossified into a space-time coordinate) and denies the actuality of "wave function collapse" (that the potentiality of multiple universes, once observed, will ossify into a specific space-time coordinate). In short, this theory implies that all possible alternate histories and futures are real, each representing an actual "world," parallel to ours but remaining unknown to us. Astrophysicist Santhosh Mathew explains, "The proponents of parallel universes believe that there are vibrations of different universes everywhere. Probably, we are missing that subtle message, as we're just not in tune with the vibrations" (2014: 19).[11]

The novel is indeed all about being in tune with the vibrations. Beginning with an excerpt from Japanese Zen master Dogen Zenji, the novel immediately challenges the reader to imagine the time being not as a choice between two or more entities but as the potentiality of being all, at once embracing "the entire earth and the boundless sky" (Ozeki 2013: 1), suggesting that in Zen philosophy and practices, there are visions of and methods for accessing parallel universes. The novel evolves around two main characters: Nao, writing her diary in a French maid café in downtown Tokyo, to recount her troubles of being bullied in school and involved in

---

11. For more comprehensive but non-physicist-friendly discussions of the many-worlds thesis in quantum physics and cosmology, see Kaku 2005; Wolf 1988.

illicit sex, dealing with her suicidal father and broken family, and planning to commit suicide—with the hope that someone somewhere will read her diary; and Ruth, a writer of Japanese ancestry who happened to find Nao's diary—along with a watch and letters in French—in a pink Hello Kitty lunch-box that floated across the Pacific in a plastic bag and washed up on the shores of Cortes Island, Canada, where she lives. While Nao's diary hails the reader to be the witness to her struggle, Ruth's voice sets the tone for the novel as a transpacific I-fiction and rescue narrative in which Nao and Ruth are tied together—through the act of reading—as one. In other words, by the magic of the Pacific currents and language, Ruth is able to get in tune with Nao's vibrations, which are now shared by the text in our hands.

Yet, whereas Nao intends the diary to be "something real," proof that she lived and has something important to leave behind, her diary is in fact part of Ruth's meditation on time and memory—the subject of the novel she claims to be writing—and proof of the transpacific linkage in the wake of 3/11, where the name Fukushima (lucky island) has become an irony. Through Ruth's reading of the diary in installments, debating with her loving husband Oliver, searching on the internet about Nao's where-abouts, and reaching out to rescue her in dreams, Nao's and her family's stories are readily unveiled before us as imminently perilous and histori-cally important. In contrast, although we also learn about Ruth—about her reaction to the diary, her life in an isolated community on Cortes Island, and her worry about her Alzheimer's-afflicted mother—this exchange is one-sided and only reciprocal in a magical realist fashion. In this transpacific plural I-fiction about living in perilous times, writer Ruth—on behalf of the reader—plays the role of listener, witness, researcher, and, better yet, res-cuer, who, by the power of dream and words, can affect the lives of Nao and her father (Ruth prevents them from committing suicide and shows Nao that her father is not the loser she thinks he is), only to realize in the end that Nao may not have survived the disaster of 3/11. If the Pacific gyre brought Nao's story into Ruth's hands, the same force could also sever her ties with Nao, leaving only stories and memories in a tale for the time being.

Ozeki's magical realist approach (saving Nao and her father through Ruth's dreams and words) suggests another critical aspect of the many-worlds thesis, namely, the hypothesis of universal wave function collapse. This hypothesis claims that as soon as we try to observe multiple universes, we risk turning all possible states of being into a singular, either/or choice. Ozeki explains this by way of Schrodinger's Cat, a thought experiment in which a cat, being caged in a glass flask of hydrocyanic acid, may either live or die depending on whether the acid becomes radioactive. With an equal probability, this experiment illustrates the "measurement problem" in quantum mechanics: "what happens to entangled particles in a quantum system when they are observed and measured" (Ozeki 2013: 413), namely, how do we keep the parallel universe alive when we begin to access, observe, or narrate it? To put it another way, even though many worlds are possible in the horizon of imagination, wouldn't the space-time coordinate of our presence, as the point of observation and narration, inevitably reduce the possibility of that horizon and subdue it to our command or wish? The novel challenges this hypothesis by making a crow fly from Tokyo to Cortes Island, from Ruth's dream to Nao's reality, to suggest that parallel universes do exist. But that still does not rule out the fact that the crow, like Nao, exists only in Ruth's imagination. What is more important to the novel, though, is that the purpose of time travel is not to remedy past wrongs but to save the future. While the universal wave function is destined to collapse, the novel acts with the power of imagination to suspend reality and return the reader to the moment of potentiality before fate was sealed and history written. In trying to keep abreast of multiple worlds, the novel poses a critical question of ethics: how would we react to the moment of crisis when human lives are at stake? Are we willing to do what we can to stop the wheel of time?

By focusing on the moment of now as transient, fragile, elusive, and yet rich in the possibilities for change through imagination, Ozeki's novel invites the reader to ponder the relationship between fiction, memory, and history. Now, as the novel suggests, is made of parallel universes (Japan and Canada), harking back in time and reaching out to the future. In the novel, there are two versions of now, and they coexist in the act of reading. Whereas Nao's now is one of fragmentation, slipperiness, chaos, and peril, Ruth's is one of certainty, safety, and knowledge, warmly accompanied by a loving husband and cat. While Nao's now evolves in constant danger of expiration, Ruth's rests in assured stability and tranquility, one that may flow and extend beyond infinity. These parallel worlds exist in two different temporalities: Japan is governed by a sense of transience and urgency; in contrast, Canada is anchored in the calmness of modernity—quiet but certain, parochial yet progressive. Multiple and intersected, now functions as a "string of currents" (Ozeki 2013: 13), piecing together relics from the past and bringing ashore diverse memories as lessons and resources so that Nao and her father can find reasons and courage to live. Nao's now is therefore about being formed by time and getting involved in time, a historical practice that translates and rethinks the past for the survival and rebirth of memory. As Nao's diary is fittingly written on the blank pages of a note-book with Marcel Proust's *Remembrance of Things Past* as its cover, now, personified as Nao, is all about recovering lost times and memories, and renewing our time with them. Depicting how now/Nao exists and morphs in the delicate and unruly coordination of time and space, the novel exempli-fies how the transpacific is asymmetrically structured and shared, as part of the delivery system that inevitably renders otherness into our sameness.

Memory and Agency

As a metaphor and crypt that comment on the culture of violence across time and space, Nao's story offers an entry point to access the larger transpacific history. Of importance here are the parallel stories of the two Harukis: Nao's great uncle, Haruki I, was a kamikaze pilot, but he resisted the imperial command to bomb and kill, and Nao's father, Haruki II, was a successful software designer in Silicon Valley who was fired for installing an interface in simulated war games to trigger the player's conscience. Haruki I was a philosophy major at Tokyo Imperial University in the 1940s, a gentle and loving person who was bullied in the military and forced to fight a war not of his choosing. So he resisted, though futilely, by steering his jet away from the target. Similarly, Haruki II, though a computer programmer by pro-fession, was also interested in philosophy. He felt a strong sense of respon-sibility to prevent war, and at least wanted to "make killing not so much fun" (Ozeki 2013: 309), because the interfaces he created were used to design US military weapons for the war against Iraq after 9/11. Both Harukis are tragic, heroic figures, two tormented souls forced into war, but their persis-tent defiance provides the redeeming hope of courage.

These stories, however, were silenced and buried: whereas Haruki I's story, written in French to avoid wartime censorship, must be translated for Ruth and Nao to understand it, Haruki II's story, otherwise lost and unknowable, likewise is recorded only in the memory and emails of a psy-chology professor at Stanford University. The pasts are sealed and kept off-shore; Nao and Ruth must strive to retrieve them. Regaining these stories makes Nao realize that her experience of being bullied is essentially of the same structure of violence (though differing in degrees) as that of the two Haruki's and that their resistance was a quest for survival and free-dom. It also enables Ruth to reflect on the violence unleashed by 9/11 in relation to World War II, and how her mother's loss of memory may have been a symptomatic response to the endless wars in human history. These regretful stories of time—and of being lost in time—recommend a different form of transpacific knowledge about the significance of violence and agency that remain subterranean to the official histories—American, Canadian, and Japanese—of war and peace. They remind us that the menace of war is not only present but also connected to a larger web of forces that haunted the memories of transpacific migration.

If Haruki I's story indexes a period of US-Japanese conflict that subjected innocent Japanese youths to violence and death in the name of the emperor, Haruki II's conscientious revolt is a loud reminder of the transpacific complicity that ropes Asian immigrants into the US war machine, as victims, compatriots, and allies. As Sakai contends, through the preservation of the emperor system, occupation, and security treaties in postwar years, the United States and Japan formed the "trans-Pacific complicity" that facilitated the revival of Japanese jingoism and its imagination of monoracial nationality within the orbits of US empire. Sakai alerts us that "trans-Pacific complicity" is "a sort of colonial relationship"; it is not just an extension of colonial domination but rather "a product of the arduous intellectual, political, and administrative maneuvers" that "transformed and reconstituted national sovereignty in the vocabulary of nineteenth century Liberalism" (2012: 309).[12] Sakai's formulation encourages us to dig further into the two Harukis' stories of defiance and see them as demands for freedom that are deeply entangled in the complicity and continuity of Japanese and US imperialisms. They moreover point to the black holes in our knowledge and memory about transpacific conflict in history, reminding us how Japanese were crushed by nuclear weapons as enemies of war and accepted as allies for the transpacific military containment that still upholds the world as its target. Bullying in this context becomes a fitting metaphor of the transpacific violence that made possible and clear the asymmetrical place imaginations linked by migration across the Pacific, where California is depicted (in Nao's memory) as gleeful and sunny; Canada, full of hope and safety; and Tokyo, in contrast, always dismal, freaky, and deviously dangerous. These distinct, even stereotypical, place imaginations unwittingly attest to the menace of war and reveal a vision of freedom that explains and propels transpacific migration as an East-West passage. It

12. In particular, regarding Shinzo Abe's return to power and recent policies, Sakai argues that he "symbolically represented the complicity of the United States imperial presence with the remnants of pre-war Japanese Imperialism, an eerie shadow of the Cold War that has haunted Japan's postwar democracy" (2012: 300).

can even be read as a contemporary footnote to Lisa Lowe's important thesis that "modern liberal humanism is a formalism that translates the world through an economy of affirmation and forgetting within a regime of desiring freedom" (2015: 39).

Indeed, the magical realist moment—when Nao decides to end her life, and Ruth discovers that the diary she has been reading is beginning to lose pages, that is, the pages written with words start receding to blankness (a fitting and clever comment on Alzheimer's and historical amnesia)—is all about memory and agency. The moment of suspense suspends the diegetic reality of the novel and puts "our [including the reader's] existence into question" (Ozeki 2013: 344). By thrusting the now (the moment of reading) and the reader's subjectivity attached to it into an ontological crisis, Ozeki is testing the dependability of our reality and its basis of knowledge. As Ruth herself ponders: "Was she the dream? Was Nao the one writing her into being?" (392). Truly, had Nao decided to end her life *here and now*, it would mean that all the historical knowledge and memories we learned from her are but illusions, and the reality based on this knowledge that we hold dear and true would also vanish. This magical realist solution, the dream work as the deus ex machina to save and continue life, is not some playful, clever, postmodernist move but an "immigrant narration" that seeks to save *Nao/Now from History* and rescue the past for the present.

Immigrant Narration

Yet this magical realist solution cannot resolve the "observer paradox"—that is, many worlds collapse into one as we begin to access and narrate them. A text seeking to connect 3/11 with 9/11 through the transpacific vibrations of memory and calamity, the novel must also confront itself as a point of observation where many worlds are collapsed and suspended by its narration. In the end, neither Ruth nor the reader knows if Nao survives the 3/11 disaster. While not knowing where Nao is can be read as a sign of her death, counterintuitively it also entails that she perhaps is still alive, living elsewhere with a new identity. That is how Ruth comforts herself—by imagining that Nao might be in Paris or Canada, studying history in graduate school or working on the biography of her great grandmother, Jiko Yasutani. Such an imagination seems plausible, and natural, but it reveals more of Ruth's wish than Nao's fate. Furthermore, it underlines how the immigrant narration—an enunciation that embodies or projects immigration as its telos—can harness the transpacific multiverse of resistance and survival, and subject it to the Asian American frame of otherness and sameness, where Ruth has the final word.

If Nao's diary from Japan is the key to the transpacific history of violence and subjugation, to retrieving fugitive, resistant memories beneath nationalism and imperialism, the *now* of Ruth (incorporating Nao's diary into this novel we read as an Asian North American global narrative) contains and domesticates it in the immigrant mode, displacing and resettling the transpacific within the Asian North American frame. Put differently, if Nao's story potentially opens up a temporal dimension to our transpacific imagination, calling into question Japan's prosperity and security fostered under the wings of US military empire, Ruth's story again encloses the temporal dynamic in the transpacific passage to survival and freedom, where North America is deemed the end point of history. The possibility that, post-3/11, Nao might become Asian American again (for she grew up in California, after all) reduces the urgency of Nao's stories—for their function as the onset of Ruth's writing has been fulfilled and can thus dissolve into the Asian American memory, as part of the "now" of immigrant modernity, waiting to be washed ashore, recognized, and then suspended and set aside. As Ruth finishes reading Nao's diary, and finally "close[s] it," the diary inevitably becomes a mere object with worn fabric and a dark spot on the back, now "cold to her touch" (Ozeki 2013: 391–93). This immigrant narration enables Asian American literature to function as a repository of transpacific memories on the one hand and as a synecdoche of North America's asymmetrical relation to Asia—based on amnesia, sympathy, and complicity—on the other.

While the novel is about remembering and reading the traces of memory, it too has its own moments of amnesia and forgetting. Indeed, though casting Nao as an "Asian/American" figure in danger, recognizable by the discourses of trauma, memory, and human rights, allows Ozeki to work through the deep connections between World War II and 9/11, Ozeki has ignored or suspended the other, but also crucial, connection inherent in the nuclear meltdown between Japan and the United States. For instance, Muto Ichiyo reminds us how the nuclear meltdown in Fukushima is intimately linked to Japan's postwar state and its development of nuclear power. He argues that the slogan of "atoms for peace," arising in 1960s Japan, was in fact a US imposition in the structure of the transpacific complicity that Sakai criticizes. For Muto, Japan's postwar development, fueled by nuclear energy and safeguarded by the US military, posited a view that nuclearization and militarization are two sides of the same coin. He observes that nuclear power generation in Japan is, in fact, "a military presence in non-military form" (2013: 191), since it is convertible to nuclear weapons and hence has links to Okinawa, which shoulders the burden of US military bases. He also contends that the years between 1965 and 1972 constituted a formative period in postwar Japanese society because "the three strategic elements of the postwar state—Anpo [the protests against the US-Japanese security treaties in the 1960s], Okinawa, and nuclear power—were organically combined under overwhelming American hegemonic influence and integrated by strategic cover-up into the fabric of the Japanese 'national security' setup while still retaining their inherent mutual contradictions" (198–99). Hence, Japan's reinitiation of nuclear power plants just a few years after the Fukushima nuclear meltdown, complicated by the US-Japanese "consent" to maintain US military bases in Okinawa—despite repeated protests on the ground—not only reveals how this transpacific complicity continues to exact damage on people and the environment but also suggests that the vibrations of suffering, memory, and resistance between Fukushima and Okinawa are real, poignant, and active. While boldly taking Fukushima as an opening to hold present the memories of both 9/11 and World War II, the immigrant narration of A Tale for the Time Being regretfully overlooks the Fukushima-Okinawa resonance inherent in its own critique of transpacific violence. Instead, it rearticulates the transpacific in the asymmetry of relations, power, and affect, and projects Asia and America as discrepantly connected but distinctly separate spaces.

In other words, if Ruth's Alzheimer's-afflicted mother is confused about whom the United States is at war with now, thirteen years after September 11, 2001, such confusion is not so much a pathological symptom as a statement on how the war has dragged on for the United States and how it has shifted its targets from Iraq and Afghanistan to the Islamic State of Iraq and the Levant as I drafted this essay in 2015. If 9/11 unleashed an unholy chain of global connections through terrorist bombing and warfare, in which Haruki I and II resisted being complicit, then the tragedy of 3/11 should also occasion a reflection on transpacific tsunami and nuclear meltdown—not to arouse sympathy but to critique transpacific complicity, as Muto suggested. My point is not to fault Ozeki for not doing enough, or for missing the point, but simply to suggest that our imagination and knowledge of transpacific movement is not evenly shared or, worse, may have been siphoned off by the thinking of sameness with which the immigrant figure is simultaneously interpellated as physically visible and excluded as dispensable. In the history of modernity that indeed holds parallel worlds, transpacific relations are hardly ever symmetrical, and the turn to globality without a sense of structural totality may risk falling into the trap of imperialism. What matters is not who becomes transnational but instead how and why transnationality is invoked. Similarly, the significance of Asian American literature does not reside so much in its claims of identity or transnational visions as in its engagements with world history by holding parallel universes present: as the voice of immigrants, refugees, laborers, entrepreneurs, travelers, students, and writers who can render clear the transpacific linkage as inescapably overdetermined and yet open to the future.

Conclusion: Toward Inclusive Totality

In "Turn to the Planet" (2001), a lecture on the decline and hope of literature, Miyoshi argued that "literature is now nearly always considered in relation to extraliterary events and situations in history" and applied to the analysis of "the interrelationship of social groups" (2010e: 251). He thought that such a tendency toward difference in the spirit of multiculturalism "avoided, distrusted, and ignored" the idea of totality because it is divisive, self-indulgent, and characteristic of the globalization logic (251). He proposed the idea of "inclusive totality," based on humanitarian and environmental concerns, to counter the hegemony of globalization: "Particularity without totality is, by now we know, nonsense, deadening, and useless. Literary and cultural critics must look out at the world and interconnect all the workings of political economy and artistic and cultural productions. We must keep reminding ourselves that the 'global' economy is not global at all, but an exclusionist economy. We must discover the sense of true totality that includes everyone in the world" (260).

Echoing his discontent with identity politics, Miyoshi's proposal here links the cultural with the political to hold off the global economy that connects as much as divides humanity. Literary studies, he believes, must be a critical enterprise, to read and map the world in interaction, because fiction is as much a product as a response to history. Fiction is an alternate reality, constituting a parallel universe that draws commentaries on our world while it remains open to other vibrations. Fiction is the dynamic, albeit uneven, negotiations between texts and worlds.

If we follow Miyoshi's idea of "inclusive totality" to chart the transpacific as depicted in *A Tale for the Time Being*, we will see that the transpacific is never a smooth, flat, or open space but rather opaque, oblique, and uneven; moreover, it is always oriented toward North America, even though the desire for and interest in Asia has been increasing. The problem again lies in the mode of narration I call "immigrant," which holds the transpacific in a specific trajectory and manner, as implied in the novel's rescue narrative and the attending human rights discourses. The challenge before us, therefore, is not just how to hold present parallel universes in one narrative, as Ozeki achieved with grace and wit, but how to "restore asymmetry in our perception . . . so that history may be read in its fullness undisturbed by borders and boundaries that have been constructed as colonialism progressed," as Miyoshi suggested (1991: 2–3). To take asymmetries as the heart of the transpacific, therefore, suggests that we must also examine Asian American literature not as a separate category located in its own universe of ethnicity but in relation to the structural totality of global political economy that enables its immigrant narration in the first place. That is, we must resist the comfort of imagining Nao as an immigrant or refugee, or even as an international student that figures assimilable otherness, and instead point to the intersected asymmetries inscribed in her and the ellipses in her story, where memories are discordant, security a fiction of fear and debt, and nationalism a strange bedfellow of imperialism. Conceptualizing the transpacific as asymmetrical demands us to rearticulate Asian American literature, and our study of it, not as an end to itself but as a means to radical political imaginings beyond the Pacific.

References

Bascara, Victor. 2006. *Model-Minority Imperialism*. Minneapolis: University of Minnesota Press.

Cazdyn, Eric. 2010. "Trespasser: An Introduction to the Life and Work of Masao Miyoshi." In *Trespasses: Selected Writings*, edited by Eric Cazdyn, xv–xxxiii. Durham, NC: Duke University Press.

Cumings, Bruce. 2002. *Parallax Visions: Making Sense of American–East Asian Relations at the End of the Century*. Durham, NC: Duke University Press.

Dirlik, Arif, ed. 1998. *What Is in a Rim? Critical Perspectives on the Pacific Region Idea*. Lanham, MD: Rowman and Littlefield.

Hoskins, Janet, and Viet Nguyen, eds. 2014. *Transpacific Studies: Framing an Emergent Field*. Honolulu: University of Hawai'i Press.

Iwabuchi, Koichi. 1994. "Complicit Exoticism: Japan and Its Other." *Continuum* 8, no. 2: 49–82.

Jameson, Fredric, and Masao Miyoshi, eds. 1998. *The Cultures of Globalization*. Durham, NC: Duke University Press.

Kaku, Michio. 2005. *Parallel Worlds: A Journey through Creation, Higher Dimensions, and the Future of the Cosmos*. New York: Doubleday.

Karatani, Kojin. 1993. *Origins of Modern Japanese Literature*. Durham, NC: Duke University Press.

Koschmann, J. Victor. 1981–82. "The Debate on Subjectivity in Postwar Japan: Foundations of Modernism as a Political Critique." *Pacific Affairs* 54, no. 4: 609–31.

Lowe, Lisa. 2015. *The Intimacies of Four Continents*. Durham, NC: Duke University Press.

Mathew, Santhosh. 2014. *Essays on the Frontiers of Modern Astrophysics and Cosmology*. London: Springer.

Miyoshi, Masao. 1974. *Accomplices of Silence: The Modern Japanese Novel*. Ann Arbor: University of Michigan Center of Japanese Studies.

———. (1979) 1994. *As We Saw Them: The First Japanese Embassy to the United States (1860)*. New York: Kodansha.

———. 1991. *Off Center: Power and Culture Relations between Japan and the United States*. Cambridge, MA: Harvard University Press.

———. 2010a. "A Borderless World? From Colonialism to Transnationalism and the Decline of the Nation-State." In *Trespasses: Selected Writings*, edited by Eric Cazdyn, 127–50. Durham, NC: Duke University Press.

———. 2010b. "A Conversation with Masao Miyoshi." Interview conducted by Kuan-Hsing Chen and transcribed and edited by Steve Bradbury. In *Trespasses*, 263–84.

———. 2010c. "The Invention of English Literature in Japan." In *Trespasses*, 111–26.

———. 2010d. "Japan Is Not Interesting." In *Trespasses*, 189–204.

———. 2010e. "Turn to the Planet: Literature and Diversity, Ecology and Totality." In *Trespasses*, 243–62.

Miyoshi, Masao, and Harry Harootunian, eds. 1989. *Postmodernism and Japan*. Durham, NC: Duke University Press.

———. 1993. *Japan in the World*. Durham, NC: Duke University Press.

———. 2002. *Learning Places: The Afterlives of Area Studies*. Durham, NC: Duke University Press.

Muto, Ichiyo. 2013. "The Buildup of a Nuclear Armament Capability and the Postwar Statehood of Japan: Fukushima and the Genealogy of Nuclear Bombs and Power Plants." *Inter-Asia Cultural Studies* 14, no. 2: 171–212.

Nguyen, Viet. 2005. "Review of Don Lee's *Yellow*." *Amerasia Journal* 31, no. 2: 190–93.

Ozeki, Ruth. 2013. *A Tale for the Time Being*. New York: Viking.

Palumbo-Liu, David. 2012. *The Deliverance of Others: Reading Literature in a Global Age*. Durham, NC: Duke University Press.

Said, Edward. 1993. *Culture and Imperialism*. New York: Vintage.

Sakai, Naoki. 1997. *Translation and Subjectivity*. Minneapolis: University of Minnesota Press.

———. 2012. "Trans-Pacific Studies and the US-Japan Complicity." In *The Trans-Pacific Imagination: Rethinking Boundary, Culture and Society*, edited by Naoki Sakai and Hyon Yoo Joo, 279–315. Singapore: New Scientific Publishing.

Song, Min Hyoung. 2013. *The Children of 1965: On Writing, and Not Writing, as an Asian American*. Durham, NC: Duke University Press.

Suzuki, Erin. 2014. "Transpacific." In *The Routledge Companion to Asian American and Pacific Islander Literatures*, edited by Rachel C. Lee, 352–64. New York: Routledge.

Ty, Eleanor. 2010. *Unfastened: Globality and Asian North American Narratives*. Minneapolis: University of Minnesota Press.

———. 2013. "'A Universe of Many Worlds': An Interview with Ruth Ozeki." *MELUS* 38, no. 3: 160–71.

Wilson, Rob. 2004. "'Hirelings in the Camp, the Court & the University': Some Figurations of US English Departments, Area Studies and Masao Miyoshi as Blakean Poet." *Comparative American Studies* 2, no. 3: 385–96.

Wilson, Rob, and Arif Dirlik, eds. 1995. *Asia/Pacific as Space of Cultural Production*. Durham, NC: Duke University Press.

Wilson, Rob, and Wimal Dissanayaka, eds. 1996. *Global/Local: Cultural Production and the Transnational Imaginary*. Durham, NC: Duke University Press.

Wolf, Fred Alan. 1988. *Parallel Universes: The Search for Other Worlds*. New York: Simon and Schuster.

Yoneyama, Lisa. 1999. "Habits of Knowing Cultural Differences: *Chrysanthemum and the Sword* in the U.S. Liberal Multiculturalism." *Topoi* 18, no. 1: 71–80.

Looking Back at the Phenomenocene: On the Road, Again, with Masao Miyoshi's Photography

Keijiro Suga

I never met Masao Miyoshi. Belonging to the first generation of Japanese academics after World War II to be trained in the United States, he was a legendary and interesting figure to me since my undergraduate days in the 1980s. I knew, of course, about his critical works, but I didn't know about his photography, or "anti-photography," as he called it. My first exposure to his work came very late.

Miyoshi's photographic images are interesting in many ways, surprisingly fresh and often eloquent. But what is essential about photography is the fact that it is never controllable. Ethically, it is anti-ethics. A photographic image can serve any purpose, regardless of what you want out of it. Aesthetically, it is anti-aesthetics. What is represented within a photographic image is always largely dependent on the subject photographed. Isn't it too easy to call it "aesthetics" when the part of your judgment is so laughably small?

"My photographs," you may say, but the possessive *my* is too much where photography is concerned. Your images are latent and always already given by this world before you are actually shooting them. It is ludi-

boundary 2 46:3 (2019)   DOI 10.1215/01903659-7614171   © 2019 by Duke University Press

crous to call them "my" images. They only belong to the world—they don't really belong to you or to your camera's man-machine system.

Images are given, and your perception of the world is given, too. It's the world of phenomena, appearances, and bodiless ghosts. They come in a thousand layers around the surface of the globe to allow you to inhabit within this shapeless realm, or a realm with too many shapes. Just like a geological upheaval, this regime of images offers a new era that might be called the *phenomenocene*. In this period, images logically and ontologically precede and guide human actions. Each human action materially shapes the world we live in, and each new change is immediately incorporated into the ever-renewing amalgamated body of images.

Now, looking at Masao's photographs, nearly all of them are depictions from his many trips. Quite aptly, he titles his book of photographs *This Is Not Here*. Photography as a powerful time- and space-canceling machine works nicely to bring them together all at once *hic et nunc*. And here we are again, confused to the point that we never know which experience belongs to us, and which does not.

Let me tell you. I think I was with Masao all through his travels on this planet. Like a ghostly, faithful dog. These photographs testify to it. They cover places and times that I've never been to. So how did it happen that I know all his images like the palm of my hand?

© Keijiro Suga

© Keijiro Suga

© Keijiro Suga

© Keijiro Suga

Born in Translation: "China" in the Making of "*Zhongguo*"

Arif Dirlik

From the perspective of nationalist historiography and Orientalist mystification alike, it might seem objectionable if not shocking to suggest that China/*Zhongguo* as we know it today owes not only its name but its self-identification to "the Western" notion of "China." For good historical reasons, as each has informed the other, the development of China/ *Zhongguo* appears in these perspectives as a sui generis process from mythical origins to contemporary realization. Nationalist historians see the developmental success of the People's Republic of China (PRC) as proof of a cultural exceptionalism with its roots in the distant past. The perception derives confirmation from and in turn reaffirms Orientalist discourses that long have upheld the cultural exceptionality of the so-called "Middle Kingdom."

I would like to express my appreciation to David Bartel, Chris Connery, Yige Dong, Harry Harootunian, Ruth Hung, John Lagerwey, Lydia Liu, Kam Louie, Sheldon Lu, Ashis Nandy, Roxann Prazniak, Tim Summers, QS Tong, Wang Gungwu, Wang Guo, Rob Wilson, Zhao Yuezhi, and participants in the seminar at St. John's College, University of British Columbia (February 24, 2016), for their comments and suggestions on this essay. They are not responsible for the views I express. Unless otherwise noted, all translations are my own.

boundary 2 46:3 (2019)   DOI 10.1215/01903659-7614183   © 2019 by Duke University Press

The problematic relationship of China/*Zhongguo* to its imperial and even more distant pasts is most eloquently evident, however, in the ongoing efforts of nationalist historians in the PRC to reconnect the present to a past from which it has been driven apart by more than a century of revolutionary transformation. That transformation began in the last years of the Qing dynasty (1644–1911), when late Qing thinkers settled on an ancient term, *Zhongguo*, as an appropriate name for the nation-form to supplant the empire that had run its course. The renaming was directly inspired by the "Western" idea of "China," which called for radical re-signification of the idea of *Zhongguo*, the political and cultural space it presupposed, and the identification it demanded of its constituencies. Crucial to its realization was the reimagination of the past and the present's relationship to it.

I will discuss briefly below why late Qing intellectuals felt it necessary to rename the country, the inspiration they drew upon, and the spatial and temporal presuppositions of the new idea of China/*Zhongguo*. Their reasoning reveals the modern origins of historical claims that nationalist historiography has endowed with timeless longevity. I will conclude with some thoughts on the implications of such a deconstructive reading for raising questions about the political assumptions justified by the historical claims of China/*Zhongguo*—especially a resurgent Sinocentrism that has been nourished by the economic and political success of the so-called China Model. This Sinocentrism feeds cultural parochialism as well as spatial claims that are imperial if only because they call upon imperial precedents for their justification.[1]

---

1. Claims to exceptionalism may be characteristic of all nationalism, as a defining feature, in particular, of right-wing nationalism. There is nothing exceptional about Chinese claims to exceptionality, except perhaps its endorsement by others. The United States is, of course, the other prominent example. The two "exceptionalisms" were captured eloquently in one of the earliest encounters between the two polities, when the US Minister Anson Burlingame in 1868 proclaimed the prospect of "the two oldest and youngest nations" in the world marching together hand in hand into the future. Exceptionalism, we may note, easily degenerates into an excuse for assumptions of cultural superiority and imperialism. Under pressure from conservatives, Boards of Education in Texas and Colorado have recently enjoined textbook publishers to stress US exceptionalism in school textbooks. The drift to the right has also been discernible in the PRC since Xi Jingping has assumed the presidency and encouraged attacks on scholars who, in the eyes of Party conservatives, have been "brainwashed" by "Western" influence. For a report on US textbook controversies, see Ganim 2015. To their credit, students in Colorado and Hong Kong high schools have walked out of classes in protest of so-called patriotic education, an option that is not available to the students in the PRC—even if they were aware of the biases in their school textbooks.

Naming China/*Zhongguo*

My concern with the question of naming began with an increasing sense of discomfort I have felt for some time now with the words "China" and "Chinese" that not only define a field of study but are also common-places of everyday language of communication. The fundamental question these terms throw up is: If, as we well know, the region has been the site for ongoing conflicts over power and control between peoples of different origins, and varied over time in geographical scope and demographic com-position, which also left their mark on the many differences within, what does it mean to speak of China (or *Zhongguo*) or Chinese (*Zhongguo ren* or *huaren*), or write the history of the region as "Chinese" history (*Zhong-guo lishi*)?[2]

The discomfort is not idiosyncratic. These terms and the translin-gual exchanges in their signification have been the subject of considerable scholarly scrutiny in recent years.[3] "China," a term of obscure origins traced to ancient Persian and Sanskrit sources, since the sixteenth century has been the most widely used name for the region among foreigners, due pos-sibly to the pervasive influence of the Jesuits who "manufactured" "China" as they did much else about it.[4] The term refers variously to the region

2. *Zhongguo* refers throughout to the pre–nation-state usage in Chinese literature. China/*Zhongguo* is a translation marker. "*Zhongguo*" signifies the nation-state remake of the term *Zhongguo*, including a reimagination of the past. "China" and "Chinese" are modern-era historical constructs, as is "*Zhongguo*." "China" and "Chinese" were devised at the hands of Europeans in the sixteenth century; "*Zhongguo*" was absorbed eventually into Qing political thought.

3. Some recent examples are Liu 2004; Wang 1992; Shin 2006; Zhao 2006; Eshe-rick 2006; Dirlik 2011b, 2013; Bol 2009; Yongtao and McClain 2015; Brown 2004; Hsieh et al. 2005; Lin 2015; Shi 2014; Ge 2011, 2014; Ren 1998. For an important early study, see Wang 1982. The bibliographies of all these works refer to a much broader range of studies. Duara 1997 offers an extended critique of nationalism in history writing with refer-ence to the twentieth century. I am grateful to Leo Douw for bringing Ge 2014 to my atten-tion and Stephen Chu for helping me acquire it at short notice.

4. I am referring here to the important argument put forward by Lionel Jensen (1998) that Jesuits "manufactured" Confucianism as the cultural essence of "China," which was equally a product of their manufacture. For the confusion of names in both Chinese and European languages that confronted the Jesuits, see Ricci and Trigault 1953: 6–7. Ricci and Trigault write prophetically, "The Chinese themselves in the past have given many different names to their country and perhaps will impose others in the future" (6). The Jesuits also undertook a mission to make sure that the name popularized by Marco Polo, Cathay, was the same as "China" (312–13, 500–501). A thorough discussion of scholarly discussions and speculations on the origin of the word "China," with a plausible explana-tion, is offered in Wade 2009.

(geography), the state ruling the region (politics), and the civilization occupying it (society and culture), which in their bundling abolish the spatial, temporal, and social complexity of the region. Similarly, "Chinese" as either noun or predicate suggests demographic and cultural homogeneity among the inhabitants of the region, their politics, society, language, culture, and religion. It refers sometimes to all who dwell in the region or hail from it, and at other times to a particular ethnic group, as in "Chinese" and "Tibetans," both of whom are technically parts of one nation called "China" and, therefore, "Chinese" in a political sense. The term is identified tacitly in most usage with the majority Han, who themselves are homogenized in the process in the erasure of significant intra-Han local differences that have all the marks of ethnic difference.[5] Homogenization easily slips into racialization when the term is applied to populations—as with "Chinese Overseas"— who may have no more in common than origins in the region, where local differences matter a great deal, and their phenotypical attributes, which are themselves subject to variation across the population so named.[6] Equally pernicious is the identification of "China" with the state in daily reporting in

5. The term *minzu* absorbs ethnicity into "nationality." From that perspective, there could be no intra-Han ethnicity. See Brown 2004 and Honig 1992. For the establishment of the fifty-six nationalities of the PRC, which also dissolve local differences into a number of nationalities recognized officially, see Mullaney 2011. Ironically, these classifications were inspired by the work of Henry Rudolph Davies, a British military official who first classified the prolific ethnicities of Yunnan around the turn of the twentieth century.

6. The racist homogenization of the Han (not to speak of "Chinese") population is contradicted by studies of genetic variation. There is still much uncertainty about these studies, but not about the heterogeneity of the population, which has been found to correspond to regional and linguistic variation: "Interestingly, the study found that genetic divergence among the Han Chinese was closely linked with the geographical map of China. When comparisons were made, an individual's genome tended to cluster with others from the same province, and in one particular province, Guangdong, it was even found that genetic variation was correlated with language dialect group. Both findings suggest the persistence of local coancestry in the country. When looking at the bigger picture, the GIS [Genome Institute of Singapore] scientists noticed there was no significant genetic variation when looking across China from east to west, but they identified a 'gradient' of genetic patterns that varied from south to north, which is consistent with the Han Chinese's historical migration pattern. The findings from the study also suggested that Han Chinese individuals in Singapore are generally more closely related to people from Southern China, while people from Japan were more closely related to those from Northern China. Unsurprisingly, individuals from Beijing and Shanghai had a wide range of 'north-south' genetic patterns, reflecting the modern phenomenon of migration away from rural provinces to cities in order to find employment" (see Fletcher 2009). For a discussion of racism directed at minority populations, see Tuttle 2015.

headlines that proclaim "China" doing or being all kinds of things, anthropo-
morphizing "China" into a historical subject abstracted from the social and
political relations that constitute it.

The reification of "China" and "Chinese" has temporal implications
as well.[7] "Chinese" history constructed around these ideas recognizes the
ethnic and demographic complexity in the making of the region but still
assumes history in "China" to be the same as history *of* "Chinese," which
in a retroactive teleology is extended back to Paleolithic origins. Others
appear in the story only to disappear from it without a trace. The paradigm
of "Sinicization" (*Hanhua, tonghua*) serves as alibi to evolutionary fictions
of a "five-thousand-year-old" "Chinese" civilization and, even more egre-
giously, a "Chinese" nation, identified with the Han nationality descended
from mythical emperors of old of whom the most familiar to Europeans and
Americans would be the Yellow Emperor.

One of the most important consequences of the reification of "China"
and "Chineseness" was its impact on the identification of the region and the
self-identification of its dominant Han nationality. Until the twentieth century,
these terms did not have native equivalents. The area was identified with
successive ruling dynasties, which also determined the self-identification
of its people (as well as identification by neighboring peoples). Available
transdynastic appellations referred to ethnic, political, and cultural legacies
that had shaped the civilizational process in the region but suggested little
by way of the national consciousness that subsequently has been read into
them. As Lydia Liu has observed, "the English terms 'China' and 'Chinese'
do not translate the indigenous terms *hua, xia, han*, or even *zhongguo* now
or at any given point in history" (Liu 2004: 80).[8]

Contemporary names for "China," *Zhongguo*, or *Zhonghua* have a
history of over two thousand years, but they were neither used consistently
nor had the same referents at all times. During the Warring States Period
(ca. 5th–3rd centuries BC), the terms referred to the states that occupied
the central plains of the Yellow River basin that one historian/philologist has

7. It is noteworthy that the reification of "China" has a parallel in the use of "the West"
(*xifang*) by both Chinese and Euro-Americans, which similarly ignores all the complexities
of that term, including its very location. The commonly encountered juxtaposition, China/
West (*Zhongguo/xifang*), is often deployed in comparisons that are quite misleading in
their obliviousness to the temporalities and spatialities indicated by either term.
8. Endymion Wilkinson tells us that there were more than a dozen ways of referring to
"what we now call 'China.'" For a discussion of some of the names and their origins,
including "China," see Wilkinson 2000: 132.

described as the "East Asian Heartland" (Mair 2005). During the 8th to the 15th centuries, according to Peter Bol, "*Zhong guo* was a vehicle for both a spatial claim—that there was a spatial area that had a continuous history going back to the 'central states' (the *zhong guo* of the central plain during the Eastern Zhou)—and a cultural claim—that there was a continuous culture that had emerged in that place that its inhabitant ought to, but might not, continue, and should be translated preferably as 'the Central Country'" (Bol 2009: 2; see also Dardess 2003, esp. 112–22).[9]

Bol's statement is confirmed by contemporaries of the Ming and the Qing in neighboring states. Even the "centrality" of the Central Country was not necessarily accepted at all times. The Chosŏn dynasty in Korea, which ruled for almost five hundred years (equaling the Ming and Qing put together), long has been viewed as the state most clearly modeled on Confucian principles (and the closest tributary state of the Ming and the Qing). It is worth quoting at some length from a recent study which writes with reference to seventeenth-century Chosŏn Confucian Song Si-yol, resentful of the Qing conquest of the Ming, that,

9. An interesting argument has been offered by the Japanese historian Okada Hidehiro, who suggests that in the most important comprehensive history written during the imperial period, *Zizhi tongjjian* (*A Comprehensive Mirror for Aid in Government*), Sima Guang shifted the historical center from the emperor and *zhong guo* to Han ethnicity. During the Northern-Southern dynasties, when there were two rulers simultaneously, and both "*zhongguo*" and real power lay with the Toba Wei ruler in the north, according to Hidehiro, Sima Guang nevertheless traced "orthodox" descent (*zhengtong*) through the relatively powerless Southern Han ruler. Sima's own time paralleled the earlier period in the coexistence of the Song with the Qitan. See Hidehiro 2016: 208–13. Ge Zhaoguang and Zhao Gang have also found evidence of broader uses of *Zhong Guo*. Ge is particularly insistent on the existence of Zhongguo from the late Zhou to the present, with something akin to consciousness of "nationhood" (*ziguo*, literally "self-state") emerging from the seventeenth century, not only in Zhongguo (under the Qing) but also in neighboring Japan and Korea. The consequence was a shift from Under-Heaven (*tianxia*) consciousness to something resembling an interstate system (*guoji zhixu*) (Ge 2014: 9). Ge's argument is sustained ultimately by Zhongguo exceptionalism that defies "Western" categories. At the latest from the Song dynasty, he writes, "this Zhongguo had the characteristics of 'the traditional imperial state,' but also came close to the idea of 'the modern nation-state" (25). That China is not an ordinary "nation" but a "civilization-state" is popular with sympathetic prognostications of its "rise," such as Jacques 2012 and chauvinistic apologetics like Zhang 2012. Highly problematic in ignoring the racialized nationalism that drives domestic and international policy, such arguments at their worst mystify PRC imperial expansionism. There are, of course, responsible dissenting historians who risk their careers to call the "Party line" into question. For one example, Ge Jianxiong of Fudan University, see Vembu 2007.

For Song, disrecognition of Qing China was fundamentally linked to the question of civilization, and as adamant a Ming loyalist as he was, he also made it quite clear that civilization was not permanently tied to place or people. Both Confucius and Mencius, for example, were born in states where previously the region and its people had been considered foreign, or barbaric (*tongyi*), and Song argued vigorously that it was the duty of learned men in Chosŏn Korea to continue the civilizational legacy that began with the sage kings Yao and Shun, a precious legacy that had been cultivated and transmitted by Confucius, Mencius and Zhu Xi, and taken up by Yi Hwang (Toegye) and Yi I (Yulgok) of Chosŏn Korea. . . . To reclaim its authority over rituals and discourse on the state of Chosŏn Korea's civilization, and even as it performed rituals of submission to the Qing, the Chosŏn court took the dramatic step of also establishing a shrine to the Ming. . . . This high-stakes politics over ritual practice helped establish a potent narrative of Chosŏn Korea as *soChunghwa*, a lesser civilization compared to Ming China, but after the Manchu conquest of China, the last bastion of civilization. (Em 2013: 28–29)[10]

I will say more below on the idea of "Under Heaven" (*tianxia*) in the ordering of state relations in Eastern Asia. Suffice it to say here that these relations were based not on fealty to "China" (or *Zhongguo* understood as "China") but to a civilizational ideal embedded in Zhou dynasty classics. Even *Zhonghua*, one of the names for "China" in the twentieth century, was portable. It should be evident also that where Chosŏn Confucians were concerned, the sages who laid the foundations for civilization were not "Chinese" but Zhou dynasty sages, whose legacies could be claimed by others against the "Central Country" itself. Indeed, both the Chosŏn in Korea and the Nguyen dynasty in Vietnam claimed those legacies even as they fought "Central Country" dominion (Woodside 1971).

The term *Zhongguo* (or *Zhonghua*) assumed its modern meaning as the name for the nation in the late nineteenth century (used in international treaties, beginning with the Treaty of Nerchinsk with Russia in 1689). Its use "presupposed the existence of a translingual signified 'China' and the fabulation of a super-sign *Zhongguo/China*" (Liu 2004: 77). As Bol puts it more directly,

10. It is noteworthy that as Confucianism enjoyed a revival in the PRC in the late 1980s, Korean Confucians sent a delegation to the PRC to offer advice on rituals that had been forgotten during revolutionary years.

In the twentieth century "China/*Zhongguo*" has become an officially mandated term for this country as a continuous historical entity from antiquity to the present. . . . This modern term, which I shall transcribe as *Zhongguo*, was deployed in new ways, as the equivalent of the Western term "China." In other words the use of "China" and "Chinese" began as a Western usage; they were then adopted by the government of the people the West called the "Chinese" to identify their own country, its culture, language, and population. This took place in the context of establishing the equality of the country in international relations and creating a Western-style nation-state, a "China" to which the "Chinese" could be loyal. (Bol 2009: 4; see also Hsieh et al. 2005: 31)[11]

The idea of *Zhongguo* as a fiction based on a "Western" invention obviously goes against the claims of a positivist nationalist historiography that would extend it, anachronistically, to the origins of human habitation in the region and claim both the region's territory and history as its own.[12] Properly speaking, *Zhongguo* (or *Zhonghua*) as the name of the country should be restricted to the political formation(s) that succeeded the last imperial dynasty, the Qing. Even if the modern sense of the term could be read into its historical antecedents, it does not follow that the sense was universally shared in the past or was transmitted through generations to render it into a political or ideological tradition or part of popular political consciousness. A recent study by Shi Aidong offers an illuminating (and amusing) account of the translingual and transcultural ironies in the deployment of terms such as "China," "Chinese," or *Zhongguo*. The author writes with reference to the early sixteenth-century Portuguese soldier-merchant Galeoto Pereira, who had the privilege of doing time in a Ming jail and subsequently related his experiences in one of the earliest seminal accounts of southern China:

> Pereira found strangest that Chinese [*Zhongguoren*] did not know that they were Chinese [*Zhongguoren*]. He says: "We are accus-

11. We might add that the celebrated "Sinocentrism" of "Chinese," based on this vocabulary, is a mirror image of the "Eurocentrism" that has been internalized in native discourses.
12. European (including Russian) Orientalist scholarship provided important resources in the formulation of national historical identity in other states, e.g., Turkey. For a seminal theoretical discussion, with reference to India, see Chatterjee 1986. With respect to the importance of global politics in the conception of "China," we might recall here the Shanghai Communique (1972) issued by the US and the PRC. The Communique overnight shifted the "real China" from the Republic of China on Taiwan to the PRC.

tomed to calling this country **China** and its inhabitants **Chins**, but when you ask Chinese [*Zhongguoren*] why they are called this, they say "[We] don't have this name, never had." Pereira was very intrigued, and asked again: "What is your entire country called? When someone from another nation asks you what country you are from, what do you answer?"

The Chinese [*Zhongguoren*] thought this a very odd question. In the end, they answered: "In earlier times there were many kingdoms. By now there is only one ruler. But each state still uses its ancient name. These states are the presentday provinces (*sheng*). The state as a whole is called the Great Ming (Da Ming), its inhabitants are called Great Ming people (Da Ming ren). (Shi 2014: 8–9; emphasis in the original)[13]

Nearly four centuries later, a late Qing official objected to the use of terms such as "China," in the process offering a revealing use of *"Zhongguo"* as little more than a location. The official, Zhang Deyi, complained about the names for China used by Euro-Americans, "who, after decades of East and West diplomatic and commercial interactions, know very well that *Zhongguo* is called Da Qing Guo [literally, "the Great Qing State"] or Zhonghua [the Central Efflorescent States] but insist on calling it Zhaina (China), Qina (China), Shiyin (La Chine), Zhina (Shina), Qita (Cathay), etc. *Zhongguo* has not been called by such a name over four thousand years of history. I do not know on what basis Westerners call it by these names?" (Zhang 1982: 182).

13. For the original reference in Pereira, see Boxer 1953: 28–29. Da Ming and Da Ming ren appear in the text as Tamen and Tamenjins. Interestingly, the account by de Rada in the same volume states that "The natives of these islands [the Philippines] call China 'Sangley', and the Chinese merchants themselves call it Tunsua, however its proper name these days is Taibin" (260). According to the note by the editor, Tunsua and Taibin are, respectively, Zhong hua and Da Ming from the Amoy (Xiamen) Tiong-hoa and Tai-bin. Shi recognizes that "the invention of the Chinese dragon" presupposed "the invention of China," which is also the title of a study by Catalan scholar, Olle Manel, *La Invencion de China: Perceciones et estrategias filipinas respecto China durante el siglo XVI* (*The Invention of China: Phillipine China Perceptions and Strategies during the 16th Century*) (Wiesbaden: Otto Harrassowitz Publishers, 2000). Jonathan Spence credits Pereira with having introduced lasting themes into European Images of China (1998: 20–24). In a similar vein to Pereira's, Matteo Ricci wrote at the end of the century, "It does not appear strange to us that the Chinese should never have heard of the variety of names given to their country by outsiders and that they should be entirely unaware of their existence" (Ricci and Trigault 1953: 6).

The official, Zhang Deyi, was right on the mark concerning the discrepancy between the names used by foreigners and Qing subjects. Even more striking is his juxtaposition of Qing and *Zhongguo*. Only a few years later, the distinguished Hakka scholar-diplomat Huang Zunxian would write that, "if we examine the countries (or states, *guo*) of the globe, such as England or France, we find that they all have names for the whole country. Only *Zhongguo* does not" (quoted in Wang 1982: 451). Liang Qichao added two decades later (in 1900) that "hundreds of millions of people have maintained this country in the world for several thousand years, and yet to this day they have not got a name for their country" (quoted in Fitzgerald 1996: 117). *Zhongguo* was not a name of the country; it waited itself to be named.

What, then, was *Zhongguo*? A mere "geographical expression," as Japanese imperialism would claim in the 1930s to justify its invasion of the country? And how would it come to be the name of the country only a decade after Liang wrote of the nameless country where the people's preference for dynastic affiliation over identification with the country was a fatal weakness that followed from an inability to name where they lived?

By the time late Qing intellectuals took up the issue around the turn of the twentieth century, diplomatic practice already had established modern notions of China and Chinese, with *Zhongguo* and *Zhongguoren* as Chinese-language equivalents. More research is necessary before it is possible to say why *Zhongguo* had come to be used as the equivalent of China in these practices and how Qing officials conceived of its relationship to the name of the dynasty. It is quite conceivable that there should have been some slippage over the centuries between *Zhong guo* as Central State and *Zhong guo* as the name for the realm, which would also explain earlier instances scholars have discovered of the use of the term in the latter sense. There is evidence of such slippage in Jesuit maps dating back to the early seventeenth century. It does not necessarily follow that the practice of using *Zhongguo* or *Zhonghua* alongside dynastic names originated with the Jesuits, or that their practice was adopted by Ming and Qing cartographers. There is tantalizing evidence nevertheless that however hesitant initially, the equivalence between "China" and *Zhongguo* suggested in Jesuit cartographic practice was directly responsible for the dyadic relationship these terms assumed in subsequent years, beginning with the treaties between the Qing and various Euro-American powers.[14]

14. For a discussion of problems in the reception of Jesuit maps by Ming/Qing cartographers, see Yee 1994.

Matteo Ricci's famous Map of the World (*Imago Mundi*) in Han characters (*Hanzi*) from 1602 provides an interesting and perplexing example. The map designates the area south of the Great Wall ("China proper") as "the Unified Realm of the Great Ming" (*Da Ming yitong*).[15] At the same time, the annotation on Chaoxian (Korea) written into the map notes that during the Han and the Tang, the country has been "a prefecture of *Zhongguo*," which could refer to either the state or the realm as a whole—or both as an administrative abstraction—which is likely, as the realm as such is named after the dynasty.[16] It is also not clear if Ricci owed a debt to his Ming collaborators for the annotation, where he stated that the historical predecessors of the contemporary Joseon State had been part of *Zhongguo*, which explained the close tributary relationship between the Ming and the Joseon.[17] Four centuries later, PRC historical claims to the Goguryeo Kingdom, situated on the present-day borderlands between the two countries for six centuries from the Han to the Tang, would trigger controversy between PRC and South Korean historians over national ownership both of territory and history.

Jesuits who followed in Ricci's footsteps were even more direct in applying *Zhongguo* or *Zhonghua* to dynastic territories. According to a study of Francesco Sambiasi, who arrived in the Ming shortly after Ricci's death in 1610, on his own map of the world,

> Sambiasi calls China Zhonghua 中華, which is what [Giulio] Aleni uses in his *Zhifang waiji*, rather than Ricci's term Da Ming 大明. Aleni, however, is far from consistent. On the map of Asia in his *Zhifang waiji* he has Da Ming yitong 大明一統, "Country of the Great Ming [dynasty]," for China, and he uses the same name on his map of the world preserved in the Bibliotheca Ambrosiana. On another copy in the Biblioteca Nazionale di Brera, he uses yet another name

15. This term, literally "unified under one rule," was the term Mongols used when the Yuan dynasty unified the realm that had been divided for nearly two centuries between the Song, Liao, Jin, and Xi Xia. Brook explains that the Ming took over the term to claim "identical achievement for themselves" (2013: 134). For a close analysis of this period, see Rossabi 1983.

16. Various versions of the map are available at https://www.google.com/search?q=matteo+ricci+world+map&safe=off&biw=1113&bih=637&site=webhp&tbm=isch&tbo=u&source=univ&sa=X&ei=LmL2VKjWJ5C1ogSroII4&ved=0CB0QsAQ&dpr=1.

17. For Ricci's own account of the production of the map, and the different hands it passed through, see Ricci and Trigault 1953: 168, 331.

for China, Da Qing yitong 大清一統, "Country of the Great Qing [dynasty]." (Heirman et al. 2009: 39)[18]

It was in the nineteenth century, in the midst of an emergent international order and under pressure from it, that *Zhongguo* in the singular acquired an unequivocal meaning, referring to a country with a definite territory but also a Chinese nation on the emergence.[19] The new sense of the term was the product, in Lydia Liu's fecund concept, of "translingual encounter." Already by the 1860s, the new usage had entered the language of Qing diplomacy. The conjoining of China/*Zhongguo* in international treaties in translation established equivalence between the two terms, which now referred both to a territory and the state established over that territory.[20] Zhongguo appeared in official documents with increasing frequency, almost interchangeably with *Da Qing Guo*, and most probably in response to references in foreign documents to China. It no longer referred to a "Central State." Historical referents for the term were displaced (and "forgotten") as it came to denote a single sovereign entity, China. It is not farfetched to suggest, as Liu has, that it was translation that ultimately rendered *Zhongguo* into the name of the nation that long had been known internationally by one or another variant of China.

A few illustrations will suffice here. The world map printed in the first Chinese edition of Henry Wheaton's *Elements of International Law* in 1864 used the Han characters for *Zhongguo* to identify the region we know as China (Liu 2004: 126). *Da Qing Guo* remained in use as the official appellation for the Qing. For instance, the nineteenth article of the Chinese-Peruvian Trade Agreement (ZhongBi tongshang tiaoyue) in 1869 referred to the signatories as "Da Qing Guo" and "Da Bi Guo" (Chen 1984: 3:1015).

---

18. It is quite significant that Aleni's map, first published in 1623, toward the end of the Ming, was widely available during the Qing and found its way into the Imperial Encyclopedia compiled under the Qianlong Emperor in the late eighteenth century.

19. In this sense, the Qing case is a classic example of the Giddens-Robertson thesis that the international order preceded, and is a condition for, the formation of the nation-state, especially but not exclusively in non-Euro-American societies (Robertson 1994).

20. It may be worth mentioning here that in spite of this equivalence, the English term is much more reductionist and, therefore, abstract. Chinese has a multiplicity of terms for "China": *Zhongguo, Zhonghua, Xia, HuaXia, Han, Tang*, etc. The term "Chinese" is even more confusing, as it refers at once to a people, to a "race," to members of a state that goes by the name of China, as well as the majority Han people who claim real Chineseness, creating a contradiction with the multiethnic state. Once again, Chinese offers a greater variety, from *huaren, huamin, huayi, Tangren, Hanzu*, to *Zhongguoren*, etc.

Without more thorough and systematic analysis, it is difficult to say what determined choice. It seems perhaps that where reference was to agency, *Da Qing Guo* was the preferred usage, but this is only an impressionistic observation. More significant for purposes here may be the use of *Da Qing Guo* and *Zhongguo* in the very same location and, even more interestingly, the reference further down in the article to *Zhongguo ren*, or Chinese people.

The extension of *Zhongguo* to the Hua people abroad is especially significant. *Zhongguo* in this sense overflows its territorial boundaries, which in later years would be evident in the use of such terms as *"Da Zhongguo"* (Greater China) or *"Wenhua Zhongguo"* (Cultural China). Even more revealing than the proliferating use of *Zhongguo* in official documents and memoranda may be the references to "Chinese." In the documents of the 1860s, *Huaren* and *Huamin* are still the most common ways of referring to Chinese abroad and at home (as in Guangdong *Huamin*).[21] However, the documents are also replete with references to *Zhongguo ren* (Chinese), *Zhongguo gongren* (Chinese workers), and, on at least one occasion, to "Biluzhi *Zhongguo ren*," literally, "the Chinese of Peru," which indicates a deterritorialized notion of China on the emergence, which demands recognition and responsibility from the "Chinese" state beyond its boundaries.[22]

In its overlap with Hua people, primarily an ethnic category, *Zhongguo ren* from the beginning assumed a multiplicity of meanings—from ethnic and national to political identity, paralleling some of the same ambiguities characteristic of terms like China and Chinese. Foreign pressure in these treaties—especially US pressure embodied in the Burlingame mission of 1868—played a major part in enjoining the Qing government to take responsibility for Hua populations abroad. The confounding of ethnic, national, and political identities confirmed the racialization of Hua popula-

21. "Zongli yamen fu zhuHua Meishi qing dui Bilu Huagong yu yi yuanshou han" ("Zongli yamen Letter to the American Ambassador's Request for Help to Chinese Workers in Peru") (April 18, 1869), in Chen 1984: 966. The Zongli Yamen (literally, "the general office for managing relations with other countries"), established as part of the Tongzhi Reforms of the 1860s, served as the Qing Foreign Office until the governmental reorganization after 1908.
22. "Zongli yamen wei wuyue guo buxu zai Hua sheju zhaogong bing bujun Huaren qianwang Aomen gei Ying, Fa, E, Mei Ri guo zhaaohui" ("Zongli yamen on the Prohibition of Labor Recruitment by Non-Treaty Countries and on Chinese Subjects Communicating with England, France, Russia, United States, and Japan in Macao"), in Chen 1984: 968–69, esp. 968.

tions that already was a reality in these foreign contexts by bringing under one collective umbrella people with different national belongings and his-torical/cultural trajectories.

Late Qing intellectuals such as Liang Qichao and Zhang Taiyan, who played a seminal part in the formulation of modern Chinese nationalism, were quick to point out shortcomings of the term *Zhongguo* as a name for the nation. Liang Qichao offered pragmatic reasons for their choice: since neither the inherited practice of dynastic organization nor the foreign under-standing (China, Cathay, etc.) offered appropriate alternatives, the use of "*Zhongguo*" made some sense, as most people were familiar with the term. Nearly three decades later, the historian Liu Yizheng would offer a similar argument for the use of *Zhongguo* (Wang 1982: 452, 456).[23] One historian recently has described the change in the meaning of *Zhongguo* as both a break with the past and continuous with it (Chen 1994: 96–97). The contra-diction captures the ambivalent relationship of modern China to its past.

Naming the nation was only the first step in "the invention of China." The next, even more challenging, step was to Sinicize, or, more appropri-ately, make Chinese (*Zhongguohua*), the land, the people, and the past. Liang Qichao's 1902 essay, "The New History," appears in this perspective as a program to accomplish this end. As the new idea of "China/*Zhong-guo*" was a product of the encounter with Euromodernity, the latter also provided the tools for achieving this goal. The new discipline of history was one such tool. Others were geography, ethnology, and archaeology. History education in the making of "new citizens" was already underway before the Qing was replaced by the Republic, and it has retained its significance to this day. So has geography, intended to bring about a new consciousness of "Chinese" spaces. Archaeology, meanwhile, has taken "Chinese" origins ever farther into the past. And ethnology has occupied a special place in the new disciplines of sociology and anthropology because of its relevance to the task of national construction out of ethnic diversity.[24]

It was twentieth-century nationalist reformulation of the past that

23. See also Cheng 2008. I am grateful to Peter Kang for bringing this work to my attention.
24. For history, geography, and archaeology, in the late Qing and early Republic, see the essays by Zarrow, Hon, and Leibold in Moloughney and Zarrow 2011. See also Chen 2008. For ethnology and sociology, see Wang 1997 and Dirlik 2012. See also Wang 2001; Leibold 2006; Hon 2007. A recent study provides a comprehensive account of the trans-formation of historical consciousness, practice, and education during this period through the growth of journalism (see Liu 2007).

would invent a tradition and a nation out of an ambiguous and discontinuous textual lineage. It is noteworthy that despite the most voluminous collection of writing on the past in the whole world, there was no such genre before the twentieth century as *Zhongguo lishi* (the equivalent of "Chinese" history)—some like Liang Qichao blamed the lack of national consciousness among "Chinese" to the absence of national history. The appearance of the new genre testified to the appearance of a new idea of *Zhongguo* and the transformation of historical consciousness it inspired. In the new vision of the past, the rise and fall of dynasties of different ethnic affinity, longevity, spatial scope, power, and achievement was contained in a linear temporality of national emergence and unfolding (Kwong 2001). The new history would be crucial in making the past "Chinese"—and, tautologically, would legitimize the new national formation.[25]

Especially important in constructing national history were the new "comprehensive histories" (*tongshi*), covering the history of China/*Zhongguo* from its origins (usually beginning with the Yellow Emperor, whose existence is still very much in doubt) to the present (Zhao 2007). What distinguished the new "comprehensive histories" from their imperial antecedents was their linear, evolutionary account of the nation as a whole that rendered the earlier dynastic histories into building blocks of a progressive narrative construction of the nation. The first such accounts available to Qing intellectuals were histories composed by Japanese historians. Not surprisingly, the first "comprehensive histories" composed by Qing historians were school textbooks. It is worth quoting at length the conclusion to a 1920 *New Style History Textbook* that concisely sums up the goals of nationalist historiography from its Qing origins to its present manifestations with Xi Jinping's "China Dream":

> The history of China is a most glorious history. Since the Yellow
> Emperor, all the things we rely on—from articles of daily use to the
> highest forms of culture—have progressed with time. Since the Qin
> and Han Dynasties created unity on a vast scale, the basis of the
> state has become ever more stable, displaying China's prominence

25. For further discussion, see Dirlik 2011b: 173–80. Shi Aidong's study of "the invention of the Chinese dragon" offers an amusing illustration of how the dragon, rendered into a symbol of "China" by Westerners, has been appropriated into the Chinese self-image and extended back to the origins of "Chinese" civilization. It is not that the dragon figure did not exist in the past, but that a symbol that had been reserved exclusively for the emperor (and aspirants to that status) has been made into the symbol of the nation.

in East Asia. Although there have been periods of discord and disunity, and occasions when outside forces have oppressed the country, restoration always soon followed. And precisely because the frontiers were absorbed into the unity of China, foreign groups were assimilated. Does not the constant development of the frontiers show how the beneficence bequeathed us from our ancestors exemplifies the glory of our history? It is a matter of regret that foreign insults have mounted over the last several decades, and records of China's humiliation are numerous. However, that which is not forgotten from the past, may teach us for the future. Only if all the people living in China love and respect our past history and do their utmost to maintain its honor, will the nation be formed out of adversity, as we have seen numerous times in the past. Readers of history know that their responsibility lies here.[26]

This statement does not call for much comment, as it illustrates cogently issues that have been raised above, especially the rendering of "Chinese" history into a sui generis narrative of development, where "outside forces" appear not as contributors to but "disturbances" in the region's development, and imperial conquests of "the frontiers" a beneficent absorption into a history that was always "Chinese." Ironically, while Marxist historiography in the 1930s (and until its repudiation for all practical purposes in the 1980s) condemned most of this past as "feudal," it also provided "scientific" support to its autonomous unfolding through "modes of production" that of necessity followed the internal dialectics of development.[27]

A noteworthy question raised by this statement concerns the translation's use of "China," presumably for *Zhongguo* in the original, which returns us to the perennial question of naming in our disciplinary practices. How to name the new "comprehensive histories" was an issue raised by

26. Quoted (as an epigraph) in Zarrow 2011: 169. We may note that the notion of "China" going back to legendary emperors resonated with orientalist notions of "China" as a timeless civilization. It is inscribed in the appendices of most dictionaries, which means it reaches most people interested in "China" and "Chinese."

27. For further discussion, see Dirlik 2011a. Marxist historiography took a strong nationalist turn during the War of Resistance against Japan (1937–45). The rise of "cultural nationalism" among Marxists and non-Marxists alike during this period is explored in Tian 2005. Possibly the most influential product of this period well into the post-1949 years was *Zhongguo tongshi jianbian* (*A Condensed Comprehensive History of Zhongguo*), sponsored by the Zhongguo Historical Research Association and compiled under the chief editorship of the prominent historian Fan Wenlan (1st ed. 1947).

Liang Qichao from the beginning. In a section of his essay "Discussion of *Zhongguo* History" (1901) entitled "Naming *Zhongguo* History," he wrote,

> Of all the things I am ashamed of, none equals my country not having a name. It is commonly called *ZhuXia* [all the Xia], or Han people, or Tang people, which are all names of dynasties. Foreigners call it *Zhendan* [Khitan] or *Zhina* [Japanese for China], which are names that we have not named. If we use Xia, Han or Tang to name our history, it will pervert the goal of respect for the *guomin* [citizens]. If we use Zhendan, Zhina, etc., it is to lose our name to follow the master's universal law [*gongli*]. Calling it *Zhongguo* or *Zhonghua* is pretentious in its exaggerated self-esteem and self-importance; it will draw the ridicule of others. To name it after a dynasty that bears the name of one family is to defile our *guomin*. It cannot be done. To use foreigners' suppositions is to insult our *guomin*. That is even worse. None of the three options is satisfactory. We might as well use what has become customary. It may sound arrogant, but respect for one's country is the way of the contemporary world. (Liang 1960: 3:3)

Liang was far more open-minded than many of his contemporaries and intellectual successors. Interestingly, he also proposed a three-fold periodization of *Zhongguo* history into *Zhongguo*'s *Zhongguo* from the "beginning of history" with the Yellow Emperor (he consigned the period before that to "prehistory") to the beginning of the imperial period, when *Zhongguo* had developed in isolation; Asia's *Zhongguo* (*Yazhou zhi Zhongguo*) from the Qin and Han dynasties to the Qianlong period of the Qing, when *Zhongguo* had developed as part of Asia; and, since the eighteenth century, the world's *Zhongguo* (*shijie zhi Zhongguo*), when *Zhongguo* had become part of the world (Liang 1960: 11–12; see also Tang 1996: chap. 1).

Historicizing "China/*Zhongguo*"

Historicizing terms like China/*Zhongguo* or Chinese/*Zhongguo ren* is most important for disrupting their naturalization in nationalist narratives of national becoming. It is necessary, as Leo Shin has suggested, "to not take for granted the 'Chineseness' of China," and to ask "how China became Chinese" (Shin 2006: xiii).[28] It is equally important, we might add,

---

28. As the above discussion suggests, how "China" became "China" is equally a problem.

to ask how and when *Zhong guo* became *Zhongguo*, to be reimagined under the sign of "China."

Strictly speaking by the terms of their reasoning, *Zhongguo*/China as conceived by late Qing thinkers named the nation-form with which they wished to replace the imperial regime that seemed to have exhausted its historical relevance. The new nation demanded a new history for its substantiation. Containing in a singular continuous *Zhongguo* history the many pasts that had known themselves with other names was the point of departure for a process Edward Wang has described pithily as "inventing China through history" (Wang 2001). The schemes proposed for writing the new idea of *Zhongguo* into the past by the likes of Liang Qichao, Zhang Taiyan, or Xia Zengyou (author of the first "new" history textbook in three volumes published in 1904–6) drew upon the same evolutionary logic that guided the already available histories of "China" by Japanese and Western historians, retailoring them to satisfy the explicitly acknowledged goal of fostering national consciousness. In these "narratives of unfolding," in Melissa Brown's felicitous phrase, the task of history was no longer to chronicle the "transmission of the Way" (*Daotong*), as it had been in Confucian political hagiography, but to bear witness to struggles to achieve the national idea that was already implicit at the origins of historical time (Brown 2004: 28–33).[29] The break with the intellectual premises of native historiography was as radical as the repudiation of the imperial regime in the name of the nation-form that rested its claims to legitimacy not on its consistency with the Way or Heaven's Will but on the will of the people who constituted it, no longer as mere subjects but as "citizens" (*guomin*) with a political voice. From the very beginning, "citizenship" was the attribute centrally if not exclusively of the majority ethnic group that long had self-identified as Han, Hua, or HuaXia—for all practical purposes, the "Chinese" of foreigners. Endowed with the cultural homogeneity, longevity, and resilience that also were the desired attributes of *Zhongguo*, this group has served

---

29. For *Daotong*, see Cai 2003. Cai traces the origins of *Daotong* thinking to the legendary emperors Fuxi, Shennong, and Yellow Emperor, and its formal systematization and establishment to the Tang dynasty Confucian Han Yu, who played an important part in rolling back the influence of Buddhism and Daoism to restore Confucianism to ideological supremacy. He attributes the formulation of *"Daotong* historical outlook" (*Daotong shi guan*) to the Han dynasty thinker Dong Zhongshu, who formulated a cosmology based on Confucian values (239). In this outlook, dynasties changed names, but the *Dao* (the Way) remained constant, and dynasties rose and fell according to their grasp or loss of the *Dao*.

as the defining center of *Zhongguo* history, as it has of "Chinese" history in foreign contexts.

In "What Is a Nation?," a speech delivered at the Sorbonne on March 11, 1882, and celebrated for its democratic approach to the nation, the French philosopher Ernst Renan observed, "Forgetting, I would even say historical error, is an essential factor in the creation of a nation and it is for this reason that the progress of historical studies often poses a threat to nationality. Historical inquiry, in effect, throws light on the violent acts that have taken place at the origin of all political formation, even those that have been the most benevolent in their consequences" (Renan 1992: 3).

The quest for a national history set in motion in the late Qing has likewise been beset by the same struggles over memory and forgetting that have attended the invention of nations in the modern world. Similarly as elsewhere, the same forces that spawned the search for a nation and a national history transformed intellectual life with the introduction of professional disciplines, among them, history (see the essays in Moloughney and Zarrow 2011). The imperial Confucian elite that had monopolized both official and nonofficial historical writing had developed sophisticated techniques of empirical inquiry and criticism that found their way into the new historiography. But the new historians answered to different notions and criteria of "truth" that at least potentially and frequently in actuality made their work "a threat to nationality." From the very beginning, moreover, historians were divided over conceptions of the nation, its constitution, and its ends. These divisions were manifest by the late thirties in conflicts over the interpretation of the national past among conservatives, liberals, and Marxists, to name the most prominent, all of whom also had an ambivalent if not hostile relationship to official or officially sanctioned histories (see Li 2013).

What was no longer questioned, however, was the notion of *Zhongguo* history, which by then already provided the common ground for historical thinking and inquiry, regardless of the fact that the most fundamental contradictions that drove historical inquiry were products of the effort to distill from the past a national history that could contain its complexities. Laurence Schneider has astutely captured by the phrase "great ecumene" the notion of *tianxia* (literally, "Under-Heaven"), which in its Sinocentric version has commonly been rendered into a "Chinese world-order" (Schneider 1971: 261).[30] If *tianxia* had a center, it was *Zhong guo* as Central State, not

---

30. *Ecumene* is understood here in the anthropological sense of "an area of intense and sustained cultural interaction." See, for further discussion and references, Dirlik 2011b:

Zhongguo as "China." Control of the Central State gave legitimate access to resources of the region. And it was not ethnic affiliation that served as the source of legitimacy but compliance by the rules of government established in the Zhou classics and imperial precedents (*daotong*). *Zhongguo*/ China history not only has erased (or marginalized) the part others played in the making of this ecumene (and of the Central State itself) but also has thrown the alluring cover of benevolent "assimilation" upon successive imperial states that controlled much of the space defined by the ecumene not by virtuous gravitation but by material reward and colonial conquest— including the area contained by the Great Wall, so-called China proper. It is rarely questioned if neighboring states that modeled themselves after the Central State did so not out of a desire to emulate the superior *"Chinese"* culture but because of its administrative sophistication and roots in venerated Zhou dynasty classics—or, indeed, when Confucius became "Chinese"—especially as these states were quite wary of the imperialism of the Central State and on occasion at war with it. It is commonly acknowledged by critics and defenders alike, moreover, that the various societies that made up the "great ecumene" at different times were governed by different principles internally and externally than those that govern modern nations. The Han/Hua conquest of "China proper" no doubt brought about a good measure of cultural commonality among the people at large and uniformity for the ruling classes, but it did not erase local cultures, which have persisted in intraethnic differences among the Han. Even more significantly from a contemporary perspective, so-called tributary states and even colonized areas such as Tibet and Xinjiang were independent parts of an imperial tribute system rather than "inherent" properties of a *Zhongguo*/ Chinese nation. Nationalist historiography has not entirely erased these differences, which are recognized in such terms as "five races in unity" (*wuzu gonghe*) under the Guomindang government in the 1930s, and "many origins one body" (*duoyuan yiti*), which is favored by its Communist successors. But these gestures toward multiculturalism has not stopped successive nationalist governments (or the histories they have sponsored) from

157–96, esp. 190–96. For a concise and thoughtful historical discussion of *tianxia* by a foremost anthropologist, see Wang 2012. Rossabi 1983 offers a portrayal of the ecumene. It was only in the late imperial period during the Ming and the Qing dynasties (1368–1911) that the centralized bureaucratic regime emerged that we know as "China." For a portrayal of cosmopolitanism during the Mongol Empire, see Allsen 1997. For a critical discussion of the PRC preference for Sinocentrism over "shared history" in the region, see Rozman 2012.

claiming *tianxia* as their own, or even extending their proprietary claims into the surrounding seas. In Ruth Hung's incisive expression, "Sino-orientalism thrives on the country's expansionism and success on the global stage. It is about present-day China in relation to the world, and in relation to itself—to its past and to its neighbouring peoples in particular. Its critique of external orientalism conceals and masquerades a nationalism; it is an alibi for nationalism and empire" (Hung 2014: 74).

Critical historians have not hesitated to question these claims. The prominent historian Gu Jiegang, known for his "doubting antiquity" (*yigu*) approach to the past, wrote in 1936, in response to officially sponsored claims that Mongols, Manchus, Tibetans, Muslims, et cetera, were all descended from the Yellow Emperor and his mythical cohorts, "If lies are used, what is to keep our people from breaking apart when they discover the truth? Our racial self-confidence must be based on reason. We must break off every kind of unnatural bond and unite on the basis of reality" (quoted in Schneider 1971: 261). His warning was well placed. The contradictions generated by *Zhongguo*/China history continue to defy conservative nationalist efforts to suppress or contain them. Such efforts range from claims to exceptionalism to, at their most virulent, xenophobic fears of contamination by outside forces, usually "the West."[31] Interestingly, attacks on pernicious "Western" influences betray little recognition of the "Western" origins of the idea of "*Zhongguo*" they seek to enforce.

The Politics of Names

Knowing the origins of *Zhongguo* in its translingual relationship to "China" is not likely to make any more difference in scholarly discourse

31. For a recent report on the attack on academics "scornful of China" or their deviations from official narratives, see "China Professors Spied on, Warned to Fall in Line," CBS News, November 21, 2014, http://www.cbsnews.com/news/china-communist-news paper-shames-professors-for-being-scornful-of-china/# (accessed November 22, 2014). It is not only official histories that promote a "five-thousand-year glorious history." The same mythologizing of the past may be found among the population at large, nativist historians, and opponents of the Communist regime, such as the Falun Gong, which serves to unsuspecting spectators the very same falsehoods dressed up as Orientalist exotica. A brochure for the Falun Gong "historical spectacle," Shen Yun, in Eugene, OR, states, "Before the dawn of Western civilization, a divinely inspired culture blossomed in the East. Believed to be bestowed from the heavens, it valued virtue and enlightenment. Embark on an extraordinary journey through 5000 years of glorious Chinese heritage, where legends come alive and good always prevails. Experience the wonder of authentic Chinese culture."

or everyday communication than knowing that words like "China" or "Chinese" are reductionist misrepresentations that reify complex historical relationships. It may be unreasonable to expect that they be placed in quotation marks in writing to indicate their ambiguity, and even less reasonable to qualify their use in everyday speech with irksome gestures of quotation. It should be apparent from the Chinese language names I have used above, however, that I believe we should be able to use a wider range of vocabulary in Chinese even in popular communication to enrich our store of names for the country and for the people related to it one way or another.

Is the concern with names otherwise no more than an esoteric academic exercise? I think not. Three examples should suffice here to illustrate the political significance of naming. First is the case of Taiwan, where proponents of independence insist on the necessity of a Taiwan history distinct from *Zhongguo* history, justified by a deconstruction of *Zhongguo* history that opens up space for differences in trajectories of historical development for different "Chinese" societies, including on the Mainland itself (Hsieh et al. 2005).[32] In the case of Taiwan, these differences were due above all to the presence of an indigenous population before the arrival of the Han and the colonial experience under Japan, which are considered crucial to the development of a local Taiwanese culture (see Dirlik 2014). The colonial experience as a source of historical and cultural difference has also been raised as an issue in recent calls for a Hong Kong history, along with calls for independence. Such calls derive plausibility from proliferating evidence of conflict between local populations in "Chinese" societies such as Hong and Singapore and more recent arrivals from the PRC.[33]

The second example pertains to the seas that are the sites of ongoing contention between the PRC and its various neighbors. In the PRC maps that I am familiar with, these seas are still depicted by traditional directional markers as Southern and Eastern Seas. Their foreign names,

---

32. Former Taiwan president, and proponent of independence, Lee Teng-hui, was involved in the publication of Hsieh, Tai, and Chou's book (2005). The title translates literally as "Taiwan Is Not Zhongguo's"—in other words, Taiwan does not belong to Zhongguo.
33. Conflicts in Hong Kong are quite well known. A theoretically and historically sensitive account is offered in Hung 2014. In 2015, the Hong Kong Federation of Students decided not to attend a Tiananmen vigil: "'Many of us dislike the vigil's underlying notion that we're all Chinese,' explained Sunny Cheung, a 19-year-old leader of the student union of Hong Kong Baptist University, which had voted against attending the vigil. 'We want to build a democratic Hong Kong. It's not our responsibility to build a democratic China'" (Wong 2015). For a thoughtful discussion of conflicts in Singapore that does its best to put a positive spin on the problem, see Yang 2013.

South China Sea and East China Sea, are once again reminders of the part Europeans played in mapping and naming the region, as they did the world at large, with no end of trouble for indigenous inhabitants. The names bring with them suggestions of possession that no doubt create some puzzlement in public opinion if not bias in favor of PRC claims. They also enter diplomatic discourses. In the early 1990s, "ASEAN states called for a name change of the South China Sea to eliminate 'any connotation of Chinese ownership over that body of water'" (Hyer 1995: 41).[34] The Indian author of a news article dated 2012, published interestingly in a PRC official publication, *Global Times*, writes, "While China has been arguing that, despite the name, the Indian Ocean does not belong to India alone, India and other countries can equally contend that South China Sea too does not belong to China alone" (Sharma 2012; see also Poon 2015). A recent petition sponsored by a Vietnamese foundation located in Irvine, California, addressed to Southeast Asian heads of state, proposes that the South China Sea be renamed the Southeast Asian Sea, a practice I myself have been following for over a year now.[35] In a related change not directly pertinent to the PRC, Korean Americans in the state of Virginia recently pressured the state government successfully to add the Korean name "East Sea" in school textbook maps alongside what hitherto had been the "Sea of Japan."

Names obviously matter, as do maps, not only defining identities but also their claims on time and space. Histories of colonialism offer ample evidence that mapping and naming was part and parcel of colonization. It is no coincidence that decolonization has been accompanied in many cases by the restoration of precolonial names to maps. Maps are a different matter, as they also have come to serve the nation-states that replaced colonies, again with no end of trouble in irredentist or secessionist claims.

My third example is the idea of "China" itself, the subject of this essay. The reification of "China" finds expression in an ahistorical historicism: the use of history in support of spatial and temporal claims of dubious historicity, projecting upon the remote past possession of territorial spaces that became part of the empire only under the last dynasty, and under a very different notion of sovereignty than that which informs the nation-state. It was

34. The best available and historically informed discussion of the Southeast Asian Sea that I am aware of is Hayton 2015.
35. See Nguyen Thai Hoc Foundation 2015 and Kassim 2017. For a proposal that "South Sea" would be less conflictual than "Southeast Asian Sea," see Frost 2016. See also McLaughlin 2011. Bowring 2016 also provides a useful smattering of names by which the sea had been known in the past.

the Ming (1368–1644) and Qing (1644–1911) dynasties, following Yuan (Mongol) consolidation, that created the coherent and centralized bureaucratic despotism that we have come to know as "China." These dynasties together lasted for a remarkable six centuries (roughly the same as the Ottoman Empire in Western Asia), in contrast to the more than twenty fragmented polities (some of equal duration, like the Han and the Tang) that succeeded one another during the preceding fifteen hundred years of imperial rule. The relatively stable unity achieved under the consolidated bureaucratic monarchy of the last six centuries has cast its shadow over the entire history of the region, which up until the Mongol Yuan dynasty (1275–1368) had witnessed ongoing political fluctuation between dynastic unity and "a multistate polycentric system" (Mancall 1984: 5; see also Dardess 2003).

In his study of Qing expansion into Central Asia, James Millward asks the reader to "think of the different answers a scholar in the late Ming and an educated Chinese at the end of the twentieth century would give to the questions, 'Where is China?' and 'Who are the Chinese?'" and goes on to answer: "We can readily guess how each would respond: The Ming scholar would most likely exclude the lands and peoples of Inner Asia, and today's Chinese include them (along with Taiwan, Hong Kong, and perhaps even overseas Chinese communities). These replies mark either end of the process that has created the ethnically and geographically diverse China of today" (Millward 1998: 18).

In light of the discussion above, Millward goes only part of the distance. Unless he was a close associate of the Jesuits, the late Ming scholar would most likely have scratched his head, as did Pereira's subjects, wondering what "China" might be. Even so, the questions raised by Qing historians like Millward, who advocate "Qing-centered" rather than "China-centered" histories, have prompted some conservative PRC historians to charge them with a "new imperialism" that seeks "to split" China—a favorite charge brought against minorities that seek some measure of autonomy, or those in Hong Kong and Taiwan who would rather be Hong Kongers and Taiwanese rather than "Chinese."[36]

Such jingoistic sentiments aside, it is a matter of historical record that it was Manchu rulers of the Qing that annexed to the empire during

36. "Xuezhe ping 'xin Qing shi': 'xin diguo zhuyi' biaoben" ("Scholar Criticizes 'New Qing History': 'An Emblem of 'New Imperialism'"), *Chinese Social Science Net*, April 20, 2015, http://www.cssn.cn/zx/201504/t20150420_1592588.shtml. Such attacks are most likely intended as warnings to more open-minded historians in the PRC not to fall in with foreign historians, which has become part of a resurgent repressiveness under the Xi Jinping regime.

the eighteenth century approximately half of the territory the PRC commands presently—from Tibet to Xinjiang, Mongolia, Manchuria, and Taiwan—as well as territories occupied by various indigenous groups in the Southwest. Until they were incorporated into the administrative structure in the late nineteenth century, moreover, these territories were "tributary" fiefdoms of the emperor rather than "inherent" (*guyoude*) possessions of a "Chinese" nation, as official historiography would claim. Complex histories are dissolved into a so-called five-thousand-year Chinese history, which has come to serve as the basis for both irredentist claims and imperial suppression of any hint of secessionism on the part of subject peoples. Names and maps figure prominently in these claims, which is evident especially in PRC claims over the Southeast Asian Sea.

The PRC today is plagued by ethnic insurgency internally and boundary disputes with almost all of its neighboring states. It may not bear sole responsibility for these conflicts, as these neighboring states in similar fashion project *their* national claims upon the past. Suffice it to say here that "*Zhongguo*/China," which represented a revolutionary break with the past to its formulators in the early twentieth century, has become a prisoner of the very myths that sustain it. Ahistorical historicism is characteristic of all nationalism. "*Zhongguo*/China" is no exception.

There are no signs indicating any desire to rename the country after one of the ancient names that are frequently invoked these days in gestures to "tradition"—names like Shenzhou, Jiuzhou, et cetera. Those names in their origins referred to much more limited territorial spaces, shared with others, even if they were adjusted over subsequent centuries to accommodate the shifting boundaries of empire. *Zhongguo*/China, as putative heir to two thousand years of empire, claims for the nation imperial territories as well as the surrounding seas at their greatest extent (which was reached, not so incidentally, under the Mongols and Manchus) and at least in imagination relocates them at the origins of historical time. The cosmological order of "all-under-heaven" (*tianxia*), with the emperor at its center (*Zhongguo*) has been rendered into a *Chinese tianxia*. Its re-centering in the nation rules out any conceptualization of it as a shared space in favor of an imperium over which the nation is entitled to preside, which hardly lends credence to assertions by some PRC scholars and others of significant difference from modern imperialism in general.[37] An imperial search for global

37. The foremost contemporary advocate of *tianxia* as a desirable substitute for Westphalian international relations is the philosopher Zhao Tingyan of the Chinese Academy of Sciences. See, for an example, Zhao 2006. Zhao's arguments are often murky and

power is also evident in the effort to remake into *"Chinese"* silk roads the overland and maritime silk roads constructed over the centuries out of the relay of people and commodities across the breadth of Asia.

Names do matter. They also change. I will conclude here by recalling the prophetic words of the Jesuit Matteo Ricci as he encountered "China" in the late sixteenth century: "The Chinese themselves in the past have given many different names to their country and perhaps will impose others in the future" (Ricci and Trigault 1953: 6). Who knows what the future may yet bring?

References

Allsen, Thomas T. 1997. "Ever Closer Encounters: The Appropriation of Culture and the Apportionment of Peoples during the Mongol Empire." *Journal of Early Modern History* 1, no. 1: 2–23.

Baik, Young-seo. 2015. "Implications of Chinese Empire Discourses in East Asia: Critical Studies on China." *Inter-Asia Cultural Studies* 16, no. 22: 206–26.

Bol, Peter K. 2009. "Middle-Period Discourse on the *Zhong guo*: The Central Country." *Hanxue yanjiu*. http://nrs.harvard.edu/urn-3:HUL.InstRepos:3629313.

Bowring, Philip. 2016. "The Misnomer of the South China Sea." *Wall Street Journal*, August 22, 2016. http://www.wsj.com/articles/the-misnomer-of-the-south-china-sea-1471883439.

Boxer, C. R., ed. 1953. "The Report of Galeote Pereira." In *South China in the Sixteenth Century: Being the Narratives of Galeote Pereira, Fr. Gaspar de Cruz, O.P., Fr. Martin de Rada, O.E.S.A.*, 3–43. London: The Hakluyt Society.

Brook, Timothy. 2013. *Mr. Selden's Map of China: Decoding the Secrets of a Vanished Cartographer.* New York: Bloomsbury Press.

Brown, Melissa J. Brown. 2004. *Is Taiwan Chinese? The Impact of Culture, Power, and Migration on Changing Identities.* Berkeley: University of California Press.

Cai Fangli. 2003. *Zhongguo Daotong sixiang fazhan shi* [*History of Zhongguo Daotong Thinking*]. Chengdu: Sichuan Renmin Publishers.

Chatterjee, Partha. 1986. *Nationalist Thought and the Colonial World: A Derivative Discourse?* Minneapolis: University of Minnesota Press.

Chen Baoyun. 2008. *Xueshu yu guojia: "Shidi xuebao" ji qi xue renqun yanjiu* [*Scholarship and the State: The History and Geography Journal and Its Studies of Social Groupings*]. Hefei, Anhui: Anhui Educational Press.

---

ahistorical. He goes so far as to assert that *"tianxia"* declined after the Zhou dynasty because it was "too good" for the post-Zhou imperial regimes, without bothering to explain why it should not be "too good" for the contemporary world! For a historically and theoretically sensitive discussion of *"tianxia,"* see Wang 2012. Possibilities of "sharing" are explored in Ha 2014; Baik 2015.

Chen Hansheng, ed. 1984. *Huagong chuguo shiliao huibian* [*Collection of Historical Materials on Hua Workers Abroad*]. 10 vol. Beijing: Zhonghua shuju.

Chen Yuzheng. 1994. "Zhongguo—cong diyu he wenhua gainian dao guojia mingcheng" ["Zhongguo: From Region and Culture Concept to National Name"]. Chap. 4 in *Zhonghua minzu ningjuli de lishi tansuo* [*Historical Exploration of the Chinese Nation's Power to Come Together*]. Kunming: Yunnan People's Publishing House.

Cheng Ch'in-jen. 2008. "Chung-kuo min-tsu lundi yan-pian" ["Changes in Discourses on the Chinese Nation"]. *Taiwan feng-wu* [*Taiwan Folkways*] 60, no. 4. Separately published by the author as a volume (n.p., 2011).

Dardess, John W. 2003. "Did the Mongols Matter? Territory, Power, and the Intelligentsia in China from the Northern Song to the Early Ming." In *The Song-Yuan-Ming Transition in Chinese History*, ed. Paul Jakov Smith and Richard von Glahn, 111–34. Cambridge, MA: Harvard University Press.

Dirlik, Arif. 2011a. "Marxism and Social History." In *Transforming History: The Making of a Modern Academic Discipline in Twentieth-Century China*, edited by Brian Moloughney and Peter Zarrow, 375–401. Hong Kong: Chinese University of Hong Kong Press.

———. 2011b. "Timespace, Social Space and the Question of Chinese Culture." In *Culture and History in Postrevolutionary China*, 157–96. Hong Kong: Chinese University of Hong Kong Press.

———, ed. 2012. *Sociology and Anthropology in Twentieth-Century China: Between Universalism and Indigenism*. Hong Kong: Chinese University of Hong Kong Press.

———. 2013. "Literary Identity/Cultural Identity: Being Chinese in the Contemporary World." *Modern Chinese Literature and Culture*. Columbus, OH: MCLC Resource Center Publication. http://u.osu.edu/mclc/book-reviews/literary-identity/.

———. 2014. "Taiwan: The Land Colonialisms Made." Keynote address at the Conference on Taiwan, the Land Colonialisms Made, College of Hakka Studies, National Chiao Tung University, Taiwan, December 18–19, 2014.

Duara, Prasenjit. 1997. *Rescuing History from the Nation: Questioning Narratives of Modern China*. Chicago: University of Chicago Press.

Em, Henry H. 2013. *The Great Enterprise: Sovereignty and Historiography in Modern Korea*. Durham, NC: Duke University Press.

Esherick, Joseph W. 2006. "How the Qing Became China." In *Empire to Nation: Historical Perspectives on the Making of the Modern World*, edited by Joseph W. Esherick, Hasan Kayali, and Eric Van Young, 229–59. Lanham, MD: Rowman and Littlefield.

Fitzgerald, John. 1996. *Awakening China: Politics, Culture, and Class in the Nationalist Revolution*. Stanford, CA: Stanford University Press.

Fletcher, Will. 2009. "Thousands of Genomes Sequenced to Map Han Chinese

Genetic Variation." *Bionews* 596 (November 30, 2009). Accessed December 5, 2014. https://www.bionews.org.uk/page_92019.

Frost, Ellen. 2016. "Re-naming the Waters: 'Southeast Asian Sea' or 'South Sea'?" *RSIS Commentary*, January 28, 2016. https://www.rsis.edu.sg/rsis-publica tion/rsis/co16021-re-naming-the-waters-southeast-asia-sea-or-south-sea /#.XG2jiKB7n3g.

Ganim, Sara. 2015. "Making History: Battles Brew over Alleged Bias in Advanced Placement Standards." CNN.com. February 24, 2015. Accessed March 8, 2015. https://www.cnn.com/2015/02/20/us/ap-history-framework-fight/index .html.

Ge Zhaozhuang. 2011. *Zhai zi Zhong guo: zhongjian youguan 'Zhong guo' de lishi lunshu* [*Dwelling in This Zhongguo: Renarrating the History of 'Zhongguo'*]. Beijing: Zhonghua Publishers.

———. 2014. *He wei Zhongguo: jiangyu, minzu, wenhua yu lishi* [*What Is Zhongguo: Frontiers, Nationalities, Culture, and History*]. Hong Kong: Oxford University Press.

Ha, Young-sun. 2014. "Building a New Coevolutionary Order in Asia." East Asia Institute (EAI) Commentary, No. 35, July 10, 2014.

Hayton, Bill. 2015. *The South China Sea: The Struggle for Power in Asia*. New Haven, CT: Yale University Press.

Heirman, Ann, Paolo De Troia, and Jan Parmentier. 2009. "Francesco Sambiai, a Missing Link in European Map Making in China?" *Imago Mundi* 61, no. 1: 29–46.

Hidehiro, Okada. 2016. *Shijie shide tansheng: Menggu diguo yu dong/xiyang shiguande zhongjie* [*Birth of World History: The Mongol Empire and the End of East/West Historical Outlook*]. Translated from the Japanese original by Chen Xinhui. New Taipei City, Taiwan: Gusa Publishing.

Hon, Tze-Ki. 2007. "Educating the Citizens: Visions of China in Late Qing History Textbooks." In *The Politics of Historical Production in Late Qing and Republican China*, edited by Tze-Ki Hon and Robert J. Culp, 79–105. Leiden: Brill.

Honig, Emily. 1992. *Creating Chinese Ethnicity: Subei People in Shanghai, 1580–1980*. New Haven, CT: Yale University Press.

Hsieh Hua-yuan, Tai Pao-ts'un, and Chou Mei-li. 2005. *Taiwan pu shih Chung-kuo te: Taiwan kuo-min te li-shih* [*Taiwan Is Not Zhongguo's: A History of Taiwanese Citizens*]. Taipei: Ts'ai-t'uan fa-jen ch'un-ts'e hui.

Hung, Ruth Y. Y. 2014. "What Melts in the 'Melting Pot' of Hong Kong?" *Asiatic* 8, no. 2: 57–87.

Hyer, Eric. 1995. "The South China Sea Disputes: Implications of China's Earlier Territorial Settlements." *Pacific Affairs* 68, no. 1: 34–54.

Jacques, Martin. 2012. *When China Rules the World: The End of the Western World and the Birth of a New Global Order*. London: Penguin Books.

Jensen, Lionel. 1998. *Manufacturing Confucianism: Chinese Traditions and Universal Civilization.* Durham, NC: Duke University Press.

Kassim, Yang Razali. 2017. "South China Sea: Time to Change the Name." In *The South China Sea Disputes: Flashpoints, Turning Points and Trajectories*, edited by Yang Razali Kassim, chap. 5.11. Singapore: World Scientific Publishing Co. Pte. Ltd.

Kwong, Luke S. K. 2001. "The Rise of the Linear Perspective in History and Time in Late Qing China, c. 1860–1911." *Past and Present* 173: 157–90.

Leibold, James. 2006. "Competing Narratives of National Unity in Republican China: From the Yellow Emperor to Peking Man." *Modern China* 32, no. 2: 181–220.

Li Huaiyin. 2013. *Reinventing Modern China: Imagination and Authenticity in Chinese Historical Writing.* Honolulu: University of Hawaii Press.

Liang Qichao. 1960. "Zhongguo shi Xulun" ["Discussion of Zhongguo History"] (1901). In *Yinping shi wenji* [*Collected Essays from Ice-Drinker's Studio*], #6, vol. 3, 1–12. 16 vols. Taipei: Zhonghua Shuju.

Lin Jianliang. 2015. "The Taiwanese Are Not Han Chinese." *Society for the Dissemination of Historical Fact.* Newsletter No. 96 (June 6, 2015). http://www.sdh-fact.com/essay-article/418.

Liu Lanxiao. 2007. *Wan Qing baokan yu jindai shixue* [*Late Qing Newspapers and Journals and Modern Historiography*]. Beijing: People's University.

Liu, Lydia H. 2004. *The Clash of Empires: The Invention of China in Modern World Making.* Cambridge, MA: Harvard University Press.

Mair, Victor. 2005. "The North(western) Peoples and the Recurrent Origins of the 'Chinese' State." In *The Teleology of the Nation-State: Japan and China*, edited by Joshua A. Fogel, 46–84. Philadelphia: University of Pennsylvania Press.

Mancall, Mark. 1984. *China at the Center: 300 Years of Foreign Policy.* New York: Free Press.

McLaughlin, Kathleen E. 2011. "Rivals Push to Rename the South China Sea." CNN.com. June 14, 2011. http://globalpublicsquare.blogs.cnn.com/2011/06/14/rivals-push-to-rename-the-south-china-sea-2/.

Millward, James A. 1998. *Beyond the Pass: Economy, Ethnicity and Empire in Qing Central Asia, 1759–1864.* Stanford, CA: Stanford University Press.

Moloughney, Brian, and Peter Zarrow, eds. 2011. *Transforming History: The Making of a Modern Academic Discipline in Twentieth-Century China.* Hong Kong: Chinese University of Hong Kong Press.

Mullaney, Thomas S. 2011. *Coming to Terms with the Nation: Ethnic Classification in Modern China.* Berkeley: University of California Press.

Nguyen Thai Hoc Foundation. n.d. "Change the Name 'South China Sea' to 'Southeast Asia Sea.'" https://www.change.org/p/change-the-name-south-china-sea-to-southeast-asia-sea.

Poon, Linda. 2015. "China Cracks Down on Politically Incorrect Maps." *Citylab*, December 17, 2015. http://www.citylab.com/politics/2015/12/china-cracks -down-on-politcally-incorrect-maps/421032/.

Ren Jifang. 1998. "'HuaXia' kaoyuan" ["On the Origins of 'HuaXia'"]. *Chuantong wenhua yu xiandaihua [Traditional Culture and Modernization]*, no. 4.

Renan, Ernest. 1992. "What Is a Nation?" In *Qu'est-ce qu'une nation?*, translated by Ethan Rundell. Paris: Presses-Pocket.

Ricci, Matteo, and Nicholas Trigault. 1953. *China in the Sixteenth Century: The Journals of Matteo Ricci, 1583–1610*. Translated from the Latin by Louis Gallagher, S.J. New York: Random House.

Robertson, Roland. 1994. *Globalization: Social Theory and Global Culture*. Thousand Oaks, CA: Sage.

Rossabi, Morris. 1983. *China among Equals: The Middle Kingdom and Its Neighbors, 10th–14th Centuries*. Berkeley: University of California Press.

Rozman, Gilbert. 2012. "Invocations of Chinese Traditions in International Relations." *Journal of Chinese Political Science* 17, no. 2: 111–24.

Schneider, Laurence A. 1971. *Ku Chieh-kang and China's New History: Nationalism and the Quest for Alternative Traditions*. Berkeley, CA: University of California Press.

Sharma, Rajeev. 2012. "China and India Jostle in Indian Ocean." *Global Times*, October 18, 2012. http://www.globaltimes.cn/content/739276.shtml.

Shi Aidong. 2014. *Zhongguo longde faming: shijide long zhengzhi yu Zhongguo xingxiang [The Invention of the Chinese Dragon: Dragon Politics during the 16–20th Centuries and the Image of China]*. Beijing: Joint Publishing Company.

Shin, Leo. 2006. *The Making of the Chinese State: Ethnicity and Expansion on the Ming Borderlands*. New York: Cambridge University Press.

Spence, Jonathan. 1998. *The Chan's Great Continent: China in Western Minds*. New York: W. W. Norton.

Tang, Xiaobing. 1996. *Global Space and the Nationalist Discourse of Modernity: The Historical Thinking of Liang Qichao*. Stanford, CA: Stanford University Press.

Tian Liang. 2005. *Kangzhan shiqishixue yanjiu. [Historiography during the War of Resistance]*. Beijing: Renmin Publishers.

Tuttle, Gray. 2015. "China's Race Problem: How Beijing Represses Minorities." *Foreign Affairs* 94, no. 3 (May/June 2015).

Vembu, Venkatesan. 2007. "Tibet Wasn't Ours, Says Chinese Scholar." *Daily News & Analysis*, February 22, 2007. http://www.dnaindia.com/world/report-tibet -wasn-t-ours-says-chinese-scholar-1081523.

Wade, Geoff. 2009. "The Polity of Yelang and the Origins of the Name 'China.'" *Sino-Platonic Papers*, no. 188, May 1990.

Wang Ermin. 1982. "'Chung-kuo' ming-cheng su-yuan chi ch'I chin-tai ch'uan-shih" ["The Origins of the Name 'Chung-kuo' and Its Modern Interpretations"]. In

Chung-kuo chin-tai si-hsiang shih lun [*Essays on Modern Chinese Thought*], 441–80. Taipei: Hushi Publishers.

Wang Gungwu. 1992. *China and the Chinese Overseas*. Singapore: Academic Press.

Wang Jianmin. 1997. *Zhongguo minzuxue shi* [*History of Chinese Ethnology*]. Vol. 1. Kunming: Yunnan Educational Publishers.

Wang Mingming. 2012. "All under Heaven (*tianxia*): Cosmological Perspectives and Political Ontologies in Pre-modern China." *HAU: Journal of Ethnographic Theory* 2, no. 1: 337–83.

Wang, Q. Edward. 2001. *Inventing China through History: The May Fourth Approach to Historiography*. Albany: State University of New York Press.

Wilkinson, Endymion. 2000. *Chinese History: A Manual*. Cambridge, MA: Harvard University Asia Center.

Wong, Alan. 2015. "Hong Kong Student Organization Says It Won't Attend Tiananmen Vigil." *New York Times*, April 29, 2015. http://sinosphere.blogs.nytimes .com/2015/04/29/hong-kong-student-organization-says-it-wont-attend -tiananmen-vigil/?_r=0.

Woodside, Alexander. 1971. *Vietnam and the Chinese Model: A Comparative Study of Nguyen and Ching Civil Government in the First Half of the Nineteenth Century*. Cambridge, MA: Harvard University Press.

Yang, Peidong. 2013. "Why Chinese Nationals and S'poreans Don't Always Get Along." *Singapolitics*, April 11, 2013. Available at https://www.academia.edu /3263103/_commentary_article_2013_Why_Chinese_nationals_and_Singa poreans_dont_always_get_along_2_.

Yee, Cordell D. K. 1994. "Traditional Chinese Cartography and the Myth of Westernization." In *The History of Cartography, Volume 2, Book 2: Cartography in the Traditional East and Southeast Asian Societies*, edited by J. B. Harley and David Woodward, 170–202. Chicago: University of Chicago Press.

Yongtao Du, and Jeff Kyong McClain, eds. 2015. *Chinese History in Geographical Perspective*. Lanham, MD: Lexington Books.

Zarrow, Peter. 2011. "Discipline and Narrative: Chinese History Textbooks in the Early Twentieth Century." In *Transforming History: The Making of a Modern Academic Discipline in Twentieth-Century China*, edited by Brian Moloughney and Peter Zarrow, 169–207. Hong Kong: Chinese University of Hong Kong Press.

Zhang Deyi. 1982. *Suishi Faguo ji* [*Random Notes on France*]. Hunan: Renmin chuban she.

Zhang Weiwei. 2012. *The China Wave: Rise of a Civilizational State*. Hackensack, NJ: World Century.

Zhao Gang. 2006. "Reinventing China: Imperial Ideology and the Rise of Modern Chinese National Identity in the Early Twentieth Century." *Modern China* 32, no. 1: 3–30.

Zhao Meichun. 2007. *Ershi shiji Zhongguo tongshi bianzuan yanjiu [Research into the Compilation of Comprehensive Histories in Twentieth-Century China].* Beijing: Chinese Social Science Publications Press.

Zhao Tingyan. 2006. "Rethinking Empire from a Chinese Concept 'All-under-Heaven' (Tianxia)." *Social Identities* 12, no. 1: 29–41.

Dialectics of Sovereignty, Compromise, and Equality in the Discourse on the "Tibetan Question"

Tsering Wangmo Dhompa

Introduction

The People's Liberation Army (PLA) of the People's Republic of China (PRC) accomplished their goal in capturing Chamdo, in eastern Tibet, in a total of two weeks in October 1950. Seven months after the invasion, the Tibetan government signed the document known as the Seventeen-Point Agreement in Beijing, which acknowledged Chinese sovereignty for the first time in Tibetan history. Since then, the Chinese government has determined the status and position of Tibetans, although it has not won the battle for Tibetans' hearts and minds. Tibetan popular resistance and the attendant mobilization of diverse expressions of Tibetan identity, desires, and experiences under Chinese rule, both on the rise since the late 1980s, point to serious fissures in the Chinese state's ideological and cultural project of "liberating" Tibet. The March 2008 Tibetan protests against Chinese

I am indebted to Professor Chris Connery for his guidance and support in writing and thinking through this essay. I also thank Professor Christine Hong, Professor Rob Wilson, and Professor Eric Hayot for their comments and suggestions.

boundary 2 46:3 (2019)   DOI 10.1215/01903659-7614195   © 2019 by Duke University Press

rule in and around Lhasa, and thereafter continued in the Tibetan areas of Qinghai, Gansu, and Sichuan, outside the Tibetan Autonomous Region (TAR), is one recent example. The Chinese government responded to the protests by further militarizing the Tibetan plateau.

In this essay, I focus on the chapter "The 'Tibetan Question' East and West: Orientalism, Regional Ethnic Autonomy, and the Politics of Dignity," in *The Politics of Imagining Asia*, by Wang Hui (2011: 136–227), a major Chinese intellectual associated with the "New Left" and a professor at Tsinghua University in Beijing with publications on Chinese intellectual history and the ideology of nation and empire, among other topics. Wang analyzes the March 2008 events in order to understand the impediments to a real solution to the crisis in Tibet and then imagines productive ways of moving beyond them.[1] He shares some similar ideological presuppositions—dialogue, accommodation, and reconciliation—with the Middle Way Approach (MWA) advocated by the Central Tibetan Administration (CTA) in Dharamsala, India, that could indeed form a basis of a productive way forward (2010). I demonstrate, though, that Wang's Sinocentrism, a position he doesn't explicitly recognize but which he implicitly maintains as evident in the nature of his questionable historical and political arguments, remains an impediment to a genuine politics of equality and respect. I conclude with concerns raised by Tibetans, beyond the purview of both sets of discourses, and suggest that all proposals for genuine respect and equality for Tibetans must begin by recognizing the historical consciousness expressed by Tibetans living inside Tibet.

A Brief Summary of Key Concerns Related to the "Liberation" of Tibet

The decision to "liberate" Tibet had deep nationalistic and symbolic meaning for China, the most significant being "the issue of national honor" (Goldstein 2007: 20). The restoration of full sovereignty over territories that were under Qing and Guomindang rule was a step toward reversing past national humiliations. Mao Zedong believed that a peaceful liberation of Tibet afforded the ideal solution for legitimizing the PRC's sovereignty over Tibet and for winning Tibetan trust and loyalty. Mao realized that Tibet had

---

1. Tibetans are more familiar with the report "An Investigative Report into the Social and Economic Causes of the 3.14 Incident in Tibetan Areas," conducted by Li Kun, Huang Li, Li Xiang, and Wang Hongzhe for the Gongmeng Law Research Center (2009). The document was translated and published online by the International Campaign for Tibet.

been independent from China at least since 1911.[2] Consequently, China's military successes in Kham (Eastern Tibet) in 1950 were followed by assurances that traditional Tibetan social and religious systems would not be altered. Mao's dual "carrot and stick" strategy offering "the Dalai Lama very attractive terms to return to the 'motherland'" and, simultaneously, threatening "a full-scale military invasion if he did not" were the context under which Tibetans entered negotiations with the Chinese (Goldstein 2007: 25). On May 23, 1951, a Tibetan negotiating team headed by Ngabo Ngawang Jigme, then Tibetan governor-general, and the Chinese team headed by Li Weihan, the chairman of the National Minorities Commission, signed the Seventeen-Point Agreement.[3] The agreement reassured the traditional Tibetan elite that Tibetans would exercise national regional autonomy under the guidance of the Central People's Government without any changes to the existing political authority of the Dalai Lama. The agreement also stipulated that, regarding "various reforms in Tibet," there would be "no compulsion" from the central government and that the religious beliefs, customs, and habits of the Tibetan people would be protected and respected (103).[4] This agreement and its accommodations set Tibet apart from other Chinese regions.

These arrangements, however, were recast after the uprising by Tibetan peoples in 1959,[5] fundamentally overturned during the Cultural Revolution (1966–76), and further eroded in the 1975 Constitution, which took away the nationalities' rights to maintain their cultural customs, languages, and traditions (He 2006: 75). It was only in the reform period, after 1978, that the Chinese government took steps to reestablish a form of regional autonomy. Meanwhile, the Dalai Lama, living in exile in India, unveiled a proposal for autonomy through the Five-Point Peace Plan in 1987 before the United States Congress, which he explained in greater detail a year later in the 1988 Strasbourg Proposal before the European Parliament. The 1988 proposal asked for a self-governing democratic politi-

2. For details, see Goldstein 2007: 19–41.
3. Ngabo was in favor of modernizing Tibet and is viewed as being in favor of signing the agreement.
4. Point 7 and Point 11 of the agreement are very important to Tibetans. The former assured that the "religious beliefs, customs, habits of the Tibetan People shall be respected, and lama monasteries shall be protected. The central authorities will not effect a change in the income of the monasteries and temples" (Goldstein 2007: 103). Point 11 promised no forced reforms. For more on the Seventeen-Point Agreement, see Goldstein 2007.
5. The Dalai Lama escaped to India in March 1959. He issued a statement renouncing the Seventeen-Point Agreement on April 18, 1959, stating it had been forced on Tibet.

cal body in Tibet for all three regions of Tibet: Kham, Amdo, and the TAR.[6] Tibetan uprisings in March 1989 altered the course of the limited cultural liberalization underway in Tibet in the 1980s, as well as the future of any of the proposals. Since March 1989, Tibet has been under varying degrees of de facto martial law.

The MWA, the third incarnation of the Dalai Lama's earlier policies, continues to appeal to China's morality and to international support. Its significant feature is a concession to respect the territorial integrity of the PRC, while recognizing the uniqueness of the Tibetan situation. The MWA shares the scope and structure of the Seventeen-Point Agreement in seeking the following: respect for the integrity of the Tibetan nationality; the right for Tibetans to govern themselves; the right to the basic need of self-governance, which includes the freedom to practice Tibetan culture, customs, and religion; and the establishment of a single administration for all Tibetans. Chinese leaders accuse the MWA of concealing the exile Tibetan government's true desire for full independence. They also argue that the MWA seeks autonomy for Tibetan regions that fall outside the borders of "political Tibet." Tibetans posit that without autonomy for all Tibetans, China will not be freed from Tibetan desires.

Toward a New Politics of Respect

In the chapter "The 'Tibetan Question' East and West: Orientalism, Regional Ethnic Autonomy, and the Politics of Dignity," Wang presents a distinctive and useful perspective on the present crisis in Tibet that raises questions about the historical category of empire and nation, the nature of sovereignty and suzerainty, and the values of ethnic and religious identity. Wang is inspired by the intensity of two opposing responses—from the Chinese media and the Western public—to the March 14, 2008, "riots" and focuses his argument on three areas: Western attitudes toward Tibet formed by imperialist practices and an orientalizing exoticism; the Tibetan crisis within the context of Chinese market reforms; and the responses from a new generation (of Chinese) at home and abroad. For Wang, the question of Tibetan independence is a product of Western imperialism and politics. Aspirations for Tibetan independence and the concomitant estrangement of

6. The term *Cultural Tibet* is sometimes used to describe Kham and Amdo. This is to differentiate these two regions from *Political Tibet*, which stand for the regions under the Dalai Lama government before 1950 (present-day TAR).

Tibet from the Qing arose when Western imperialist politics of recognition, which he explains as "a system of recognition based on the nation-state as the unit of sovereignty" (2011: 155), was extended to Asia. Wang contrasts the tribute system's many and diverse suzerain relations to suzerain relations under imperialism. Important historical differences were erased when the new, imperialist concept of suzerainty was equated with the various versions of enfeoffment, tribute, and dependency relations that had earlier obtained in the Asian region. This resulted in ignoring "the complex evolution of the relations between Tibet and the central Chinese empire" (156), and in the equating of relations between the Qing dynasty and Tibet with relations between European countries and their colonies. Thus, destabilizing the orientalizing image of utopian Tibet and the totalizing tendencies of Western nation-state discourses becomes an essential step in the reengagement for a new middle ground on the question of Tibet.[7]

In the second half of the article, Wang examines the 2008 revolts inside Tibet as a component of a larger crisis in postsocialist China as well as a crisis of modernity.[8] Wang estimates that changes in Tibet—the dissolution of the egalitarian class politics and social relations of the socialist period, increasing economic and educational inequalities, and crisis in identity due to a religious revival—take place within the context of China's market reform period of economic growth and the consequent social divisions. He sums up these changes under the "'Rubrics of 'depoliticization,'' 'the expansion of the market,' and 'expansion of religion'" (199). He proposes a different position for Tibet within China that could be part of a better, more egalitarian and diverse notion of "Chineseness" and ethnicity in general. Keeping in mind the challenges of respecting simultaneously the two principles of social difference and equality in a diverse society, Wang favors transforming the politics of identity into a "politics of recognition," or a politics of respect. To preempt the politics of recognition from developing into ethnic politics, he suggests that diversity be the basis for coexistence instead of a basis of separate nationalism (223). Wang's proposal aims to reconsider China's developmental logic and create a tolerant public space that allows "the voices of ordinary people fuller expression in that space" (224). The core of his proposal, like the MWA, upholds a need for Tibetans to be able to represent themselves and be protected by the laws of the Chi-

7. Wang writes, "Theosophy created an ideal and surreal image of Tibet" (2011: 148).
8. For Wang, it is a crisis that religious societies have been undergoing since the nineteenth century (2011: 220).

nese state. To achieve that, Wang and the MWA both recommend a spirit of accommodation, dialogue, and a loosening of fixed positions.

Wang's aim to provide a middle ground for initiating conversations on the "Tibetan question" is placed within his larger project in *The Politics of Imagining Asia* to wrest Asia from the hegemonic, self-evident definitions and nation-state discourse originating in Europe. To reconstitute Asia as the agent of its own history, he suggests, requires putting Europe under scrutiny. Any new imagining of Asia has to practice flexibility and pluralism to honor the region's cultural and political heterogeneity. Building on the work of Hamashita Takeshi, Wang's intention is to avoid essentialist and culturalist perspectives and to challenge and transcend, "rather than strengthen the narrative of the nation-state" (78). This entails understanding the historical experiences under European domination girding Asian movements and divisions.

Wang illustrates how the Japanese colonization of the Ryukyu Islands and the first invasion of Taiwan in 1874 changed the norms of interaction in Asia. He contends that Japanese colonial rule justified itself with a dual standard, where "imperialist aggression was seen as liberation, because treaty relationships were taken as links between formally equal agents" (242). In reality, he explains, these were unequal treaties imposed under the guise of formal equality between the parties. He sees the need to observe inequalities and to listen to the demands of ordinary people because sovereignty and its relations do not exist in "isolation and cannot be unilaterally put into effect by a single national entity" (262). The process of working toward the dream of a new Asia is one that can flexibly skirt the traps of both the imperial and the nation-state model.

As Wang notes, Western imperialistic fetishization of Tibet and Tibetan Buddhism is problematic, and it has shaped and contributed to the containment of the "Tibetan question" and expressions of Tibetan selfhood within Western discourses of international law and rights. It is true, too, that current nation-state-based categories do not fit and describe the complexity of relations in imperial-era geopolitical categories, such as those that obtained between Tibet and China. However, little existing scholarship suggests that Western orientalization of Tibet was a significant factor in the politics, either during the period of inter-imperial rivalry or during the Cold War.[9] What has been far more devastating culturally, in fact, is the influence

9. Tsering Woeser addresses Wang Hui's disappointment in Chinese orientalization of Tibet in an essay, "Who Are the Real 'Orientalists'?" She asks, "But does this mean that China usually demonizes Tibet and has now started to cater to the West? Or does it

of a Chinese orientalizing of Tibet since the beginning of the twenty-first century—through popular culture, consumer culture, and tourism (a fact that Wang also criticizes)[10]—that has remained embedded in the discourse of "progress" and "liberation" and consigned Tibetan history to a position of subalternity within a hegemonic Sinocentric worldview.[11] In addition, as Wang insufficiently emphasizes, it is China that has most forcefully applied nation-state logic to justify its sovereignty over Tibet. Despite very useful perspectives, his critique remains within the parameter of the two imperiums (the West and China), and somewhat peculiarly, given his ambivalence about the nation form, he goes to considerable effort to defend the fait accompli of an incontrovertible nationalistic position: that Tibet has always been part of China and that the course of history in Tibet was a process of "social liberation."

Wang's analysis, limited by multiple ideological contradictions, results in repeating some problematic assumptions and elisions:

1. He ignores different modes and periods of autonomy experienced by Tibetan regions and the heterogeneity of the political and social formations practiced by Tibetan nomadic states in Kham and Amdo. Instead, he domesticates China-Tibet relations into the homogenizing narrative of a nation justifying a necessary "peaceful liberation" of Tibet.

2. He presents Chinese policy as applying equal respect to individuals as well as to collective objectives of ethnic minorities. He emphasizes the state's innate largesse, citing that minority cadres have prominent positions (222) and that minorities get preferential treatment (they can have more children). This claim wittingly or unwittingly repeats the orientalist trope that constructs Tibetans as ungrateful citizens, despite the sacrifices of benevolent Han Chinese, and allows for Tibetan attempts to protect their languages, cultures, and religion to be read as the designs of separatists.

3. He mobilizes the tribute system and older forms of relationships as the basis for claims of (modern) sovereignty over Tibet.

---

mean that the West has finally managed to change China's demonizing stance towards Tibet?" (2011).

10. In 2001, the Tibetan town of Zongdian, the capital of Dechen prefecture, was renamed Shangri-La to attract tourists.

11. In "Postcoloniality and the Artifice of History: Who Speaks For 'Indian' Pasts?," Dipesh Chakrabarty problematizes the idea of Indians being seen as representing themselves in history by pointing out that Indian history is itself in a position of subalternity to the master (European) narrative of history (1992: 1). The way to speak back is by speaking polyvocally and from multiple local and collective spaces (23).

4. He presents Tibetan desire for independence as being dreamed up by Western imperialists or manipulated by exiled Tibetans. Tibetan voices are precluded from conversations related to Tibetan history, experiences, or aspirations.

At its core, the "Tibetan question" is about independence. As such, it is also a question tied to the ongoing project of decolonization for Asia. Any (Chinese) narrative that attempts to obscure these anticolonial stakes by calling on the grand narratives of Western imperialism as an obstacle to a new imagining of Asia is itself in danger of reproducing a colonialist logic. It is difficult not to read Wang's position on Tibet as statements of power and authority made from a place that relegates Tibet to a position of "a lack, an absence, or an incompleteness."[12] For all his good intentions, Wang fails to lift Tibet out of the advanced/backward binary that typifies late nineteenth-century orientalism. Instead, the specter of Western imperialism is mobilized to camouflage the real crisis Tibetans endure, which is Chinese occupation and imperialism.

Who Speaks on the Question of Tibet?

On May 14, 1957, the Communist Central Committee issued a document providing reasons why reform in Tibet had to be postponed for as long as six years and then, too, had to be applied only with the consent of Tibetans. Although the document still maintained that Tibet became an inseparable part of China, it captured the historical reality that is no longer admitted by present-day Chinese leaders: that "Tibetans' centrifugal tendencies away from China and their distrust of Han Chinese" is related to Tibet's independent or semi-independent status that "existed for a long period of time in history" (Goldstein 2014: 454).

The question of Tibet is a political and a cultural one, and it becomes crucial to know at the outset who is imposing, shaping, and representing Tibet in this discourse. We can approach this problem through Edward Said's definitions of Orientalism in *Orientalism* (1978): as a way of "coming to terms with the Orient" based on European experience; as a style of thought based on "ontological and epistemological distinction" made between "the Orient" and, quite often, the "Occident"; and as the corporate institutionalizing of dealing with the Orient (2). The last definition

12. See also Chakrabarty referring to colonial British rendering of Indian history and Indian society (1992: 5).

entails "dealing with it by making statements about it, authorizing views of it, describing it, by teaching it, settling it, ruling over it: in short, Orientalism as a Western style for dominating, restructuring, and having authority over the Orient" (3). Given China's strength versus Tibet's relative weakness, we need to ask: What are the political, sociological, military, ideological, and imaginary frameworks within which Tibet is discussed? Who speaks? Who constructs and provides answers to the "Question of Tibet," and to whom is the question directed? Are Tibetans analyzed as citizens, or are they "problems to be solved or confined or—as the colonial powers openly coveted their territory—taken over" (207)?

Dawa Norbu writes in *China's Tibet Policy* (2001) that, in 1950, the PLA "justified their 'liberative' action with a combination of old historical claims, new Marxist mission and age-old security imperatives" (1). The justifications remain the same today: that Tibet has been an integral part of China since the eighth century, or since the Yuan dynasty in the mid-thirteenth century, and that Tibet was liberated from serfdom under the PRC. The promise of economic development and a prosperous future is an additional platform serving to buttress Chinese authority.[13] Tibetans counter that Tibet has always been independent and that Sino-Tibetan relations were no more than that of a patron and priest. Historian Tsering Shakya writes, "Neither the Tibetans nor the Chinese want to allow any complexities to intrude on their firmly held beliefs" (1999: xxviii). This "political myth-making" process has resulted in what Shakya calls "the denial of history" (xxviii). Such an activity involves invoking symbols of the past to legitimate the two opposing positions, making it impossible to arrive at a viable solution.

Dibyesh Anand points out that both Chinese and Tibetan historical arguments "ignore the fact that the very idea of presenting one's case in terms of sovereignty or exclusive national jurisdiction is a feature of modernity—modernity where Western ideas have been more or less hegemonic" (2006: 288). Wang is sensitive to such contradictions. Establishing "a new horizon for reflection and critique and conceiving of new types of regional-global relationships and rules for them," is a recurring idea in *The Politics of Imagining Asia* (2011: 243). It is for this reason, too, that I wish to respond to Wang's own attempt to rationalize Chinese territorial claims for Tibet. While it is not possible for me to provide a comprehensive analysis of contempo-

13. Emily Yeh speaks of how state intervention is justified in the self-cultivation of Tibetans as desiring subjects of development (2007).

rary Tibet, I would like first to present a kaleidoscopic perspective on claims made for the territorial category of the "new China" in the twentieth century by turning briefly to the tribute system, with a focus on its inconsistencies and lacunae. Next, I present Tibetan aspirations for nationhood as a long practice within Inner Asia polities and one that is an evolving construction. Lastly, I contest Wang's determination that the present crisis in Tibet is simply a part of the general crisis in China by presenting the voices and works of Tibetan scholars, activists, and writers who point to a profound suffering and hopelessness in being a Tibetan in China. In my engagement with both the historiographical and polito-economic claims that Wang musters, I aim to show that even an effort as constructively minded as his is will be unavailingly flawed, if it confines itself, as his does, to the Sinocentric perspective. And, ultimately, this reproduces politically more fateful structures of orientalist knowledge production that are among his targets.

The Systems of the Tribute System

The Chinese tribute system does not find equivalent concepts or structures in Western terms, practice, and usage. The very concept of the tribute system, as Mark Mancall points out, "is a descriptive western formulation to explain a complex institutional process within Chinese society" (1968: 64). The premodern Chinese concept of *tianxia* ("All under Heaven") was formed out of a variety of intercultural relations, as well as "cosmopolitical alterity" positions, according to Wang Mingming, who offers a rich, nuanced, conceptual history of the system. *Tianxia*, translated as "the world," comprised "all the realms on earth, and as such, it referred to a kind of polity radically different from the nation" (2012: 340). He examines the features that altered *tianxia* over time: the shift from "a pluralist perspective" of earlier times to a unifying perspective during the Warring States (475–221 BC); the politicization of ritual, cosmology, and society during the Qin and Han periods; and the influence of Daoism and Buddhism in self/other distinctions are a few examples.[14] Wang Mingming points out that the defining characteristic of this Sinocentric "world system" was hierarchy, and the imperial "cosmo-geographies" were remade when needed (such as following the fall or disintegration of power). In the Chinese world, the

---

14. Wang Mingming writes that the orthodox cosmology was altered with respect to the ethnographic other. In contrast to earlier periods where imperial sacrifices were made to the East, orientation of the popular Buddhist religion was made toward the West (India) (2012: 358–62).

kings and sons of heaven were in the center. The system was "projected in a civilizing line departing from the central zone and extending into the zones of the 'savages'" (364). For this manifold system, the Chinese had no single practice in dealing with non-Chinese within or outside the borders; conquest, forced assimilation, or a lord-vassal relationship were all possible options.

Likewise, the function of the tribute system cannot be narrowed to one single factor, according to John Fairbank and Ssu-yu Teng, who surveyed the system under the Qing dynasty of the Manchus (1941: 137). The tribute system was used for self-defense, for commercial exchanges, and as a medium for international relations and diplomacy (Mancall 1968: 78). It was a "framework within which all sorts of interests, personal and imperial, economic and social, found their expression" (Fairbank and Teng 1941: 141). The non-Chinese frontier zone, bounded by the "long walls," demarcated the lands of nomadic peoples from settled cultures. This "liminal space" offered commercial opportunity to the nomads, and these exchanges became bound up with tributary relations (Perdue 2005: 20).[15] The system's "flexibilities" also served as strategies to benefit and secure Chinese ideological hegemony, as well as its imperial ambitions in the frontier regions. Nicola Di Cosmo explains how Qing imperial officials in Kashgar were able, on the one hand, to use the "language and 'structure' of the tribute system" (2003: 351) to provide a political space where economic prospects were opened to the tribes without challenging their internal structure and, on the other hand, to create the "conditions for the nomads' subordination to the Qing dynasty" (352).

The "Lama-patron," or "priest-patron," relationship, beginning with Kublai Khan (r. 1260–1249) and Phagpa Lama Lodro Gyeltsen (1235–1280), which furnished the foundations of the Mongol polity in Tibet, is one feature of the political and cosmological system.[16] Norbu believes this new Lamaist tribute policy used some of the prominent Lamas, recognized and popular in Inner Asian politics and societies, as a way to pacify "Central Asian war-

15. Perdue explains that Central Asia is defined in various ways: for Cyril Black, it includes Iran, Afghanistan, Xinjiang, Tibet, and Outer Mongolia, while Joseph Fletcher (1968) divides the area into steppe regions (Kazakhstan, Zungharia, Amdo, present-day Qinghai), the south Russian steppe, and Mongolia (Perdue 2005).

16. Norbu explains that the "Lamaist form of tribute relations," established by the Yuan, was adopted with modifications by the Ming and Qing dynasties. In this form, Buddhist items such as an image of the Buddha, a stupa, or Buddhist texts replaced the typical Confucian tribute of local products (2001: 31). Norbu also points out that high Lamas did not kowtow to the emperor.

riors who threatened Chinese security for centuries" (2001: 31). In other words, the Lamas became something like instruments of indirect rule. Likewise, James Hevia (1993) describes the importance of Tibetan Buddhism in Inner Asia and its influence on Manchu politics. He writes that Manchu emperors had to address Tibetan Buddhism regardless of their personal beliefs. More importantly, they had to do it in an "idiom that was already well established throughout the region. Their successes at incorporating Inner Asia into their multi-ethnic empire were just as much a result of mastering this idiom, of 'reducing ambiguity' and concentrating power in the form of discursive authority, as it was of their military might and administrative acumen" (245). They did so by drawing on the model of the tribute system.

For Norbu, one of the central problems of the Confucian world order and its tribute relations involved starkly varied understandings of the dynamics of subordination. So while Tibetans understood the Sino-Tibetan relations as Buddhist *Chod-Yon* (priest and patron), the Chinese imperial official might have interpreted it within their own Confucian tributary terms. Both worldviews are valid, or were valid until they were interpreted within the terms of Western suzerainty and protectorship. A number of scholarly monographs chart the flexibility and shifting positions of power through the Yuan, Ming, and Qing dynasties and make clear that the long history of Chinese-Tibetan relations is full of breaks and lacunae.[17] Scholarly consensus suggests that claims for Chinese sovereignty over Tibet can in no way rest on unequivocal claims for imperial-era precedent and that any attempt to fit an often amorphous, fluid, and contradictory relationship into the terms of the modern sovereign state will distort more than it illuminates.

Tibetan Independence and the "Politics of Recognition"

The British invasion of Tibet in 1903–4 played a pivotal role in drawing attention to Tibet's relations with India and Russia, and notably with China.

17. For more on Mongol and Tibetan relations, read Petech 1983, 1980, and Mote 1999; for the new "lamaist form" of tribute system, read Norbu 2001; on Tibet's independence before Ming came into existence, read Wylie 1980; on diminishing Ming interest for Tibet, see Wylie 1980, Petech 1980; on Mongol intertribal conflicts that brought the Qing Emperor Kangxi to Tibet, see Perdue 2005, Van der Kuijp 2013. For more on Qing and Tibetan relations and the miniscule Manchu Chinese influence on Tibet by the mid-nineteenth century, see Gernet 1982, Mote 1999, Suzuki 1968, and Goldstein 1989. For more on the tribute system's historical records, language, and the system's variety read Beckwith 1980, Fletcher 1968, Mote 1999, Perdue 2005, and Wang 1983.

The invasion triggered a new Chinese attitude toward Tibet that sought to bring Tibet and the semiautonomous regions of Kham under direct control through the Chinese military operation in Batang in 1905 and the deployment of Chinese forces to Lhasa in 1910 (Goldstein 1989). Wang justifies the imposition of these "new policies" as being "produced in response to British invasion and attempts at domination" (Wang 2011: 168). Tibetans received these impositions as Chinese intentions to colonize Tibet. In a letter to Lo Ti-t'ai in 1910, the thirteenth Dalai Lama explains Chinese aggression as a shift away from old relations. He writes, "The Manchu Emperors have always shown great care for the welfare of the successive Dalai Lamas, and the Dalai Lamas have reciprocated these feelings of friendship. We have always had each other's best interests at heart" (Goldstein 1989: 54). Not long after this letter was sent, the Qing dynasty was overthrown by the Nationalists; the Dalai Lama returned to Lhasa from exile in 1913 and without delay issued a proclamation that established his rule and his new vision for Tibet. "Now, the Chinese intention of colonizing Tibet under the patron-priest relationship has faded like a rainbow in the sky," he stated (60). He outlined the need to defend the country and protect its independence.

Wang argues that the Dalai Lama's determination to overthrow the emperor and establish a new country was made on the basis of the new model of the "politics of recognition" of nationalism and that this "politics of difference" deviated from the traditional model linked to "religion and the tribute system" (2001: 169). Indeed, the Dalai Lama's letter expresses the new annexationist character of Chinese domination over Tibet as a shift from the traditional model. Perhaps Tibetan national consciousness was developing in response to this new shift, one that might be identified as an imperialist-nationalist relationship. The proclamation of independence made by the thirteenth Dalai Lama in 1913 confirms the view that Tibetans felt no ties to China under the newly evolving geopolitical categories: the Dalai Lama's relationship, attenuated as it was, had been with the Manchus.[18]

Decolonizing movements in the mid-twentieth century sought to transform themselves as well as the world, but first, nations like China and India had to consolidate the nation-state internally and externally. According to Prajensit Duara (2009/2010), the problem for China and India emerged

18. Not much was accomplished, however, to modernize Tibet or protect its independence in meaningful ways after 1913 because the Tibetan elite and traditional monastic powers resisted change.

during the task of defining national territories, precisely because it meant extending the principle of nationality to parts of the old empires. For China, these were the Qing dynasty's peripheral regions of Tibet, Mongolia, and Xinjiang, whose relations to the old empire included multiple and "flexible positions" and whose "incorporation into the empire was often based on patronage of common religious or other cultural symbols, rather than the modern conception of absolute belonging to a territorial nation" (Duara 2009/2010: 24). He points to the difficulties of grasping the historical legacy of the Qing in the modern era because of the "fundamental incommensurability between the principles of the Chinese imperial formation built between elite ruling structures and modern ideas of sovereignty" (2008: 154).

Wang (2011) admits that the traditional Chinese concept of "All under Heaven" cannot explain the features of the political culture and organizations under different dynasties, just as the empire/nation-state binary cannot explain the particularities of Chinese political culture. In fact, Wang states, "In modern times, colonialists often exploited the empire/nation-state binary for their own ends, using the culture of the 'sovereign nation-state' to belittle traditional social relationships and political models" (84). The opposite is true, too. Chinese officials used and continue to use British acknowledgment of Qing suzerainty to claim "Qing sovereignty of Tibet" (Tuttle 2005: 44).[19]

Similarly, the Seventeen-Point Agreement represents the "legal and historical basis for Chinese rule in Tibet" (Shakya 2013: 610) and proves Tibet's special status within the PRC. The agreement gave Mao "everything he wanted" (Goldstein 2007: 104) but allowed Tibetans to feel that their government, religious practices, and social system would not be challenged. The agreement, in reality, was unequal. As Chen Jian clarifies, while Tibetan commitment (accepting Tibet as an integral part of the PRC) was permanent and irreversible, the party's commitment to respect and coexist with Tibet's existing systems "was conditional and provisional" (2007: 157). Chen suggests that in using "liberation" for the exercise of domination, the party had already placed itself in a "superior position to destroy the 'old' Tibet and build a 'new' one. All of this, on another level, formed a crucial component of the party's nation-building project aimed at creating a 'new' China" (158).

19. Zhang Yintang, the first Chinese civil official to Tibet, negotiated the Anglo-Tibetan Convention of 1904 with the British and managed to include a clause that stated China was not a "foreign power" in Tibet. In the 1906 Anglo-Chinese Convention, Zhang inserted Qing sovereignty over Tibet.

The Fiction of Tibet in the Making of a New China

The first significant encounter the Chinese Communist Party (CCP) had with Tibetans was during the "Long March" in 1935–36, when the Red Army and local Tibetans clashed in several areas of Sichuan. Victory over Chiang Kai-shek and the Nationalists left Mao Zedong and his comrades in the CCP with the difficult task of defining and creating a "new China." Up to the 1940s, as Chen points out, the party initially favored giving the outlying regions of Xinjiang, Mongolia, and Tibet full autonomy, after which they would decide according to the principles of national self-determination whether they would form a federation with China and the Han people. This program of China federation disappeared from the party's official discourse in 1949. In its place came "a grand plan of pursuing a unified socialist China incorporating Xinjiang, Inner Mongolia, and Tibet" (Chen 2007: 131). This new plan rested on the myth of the unity of the five nationalities (*wuzu gonghe*—Hans, Manchus, Mongolians, Hui Muslims, and Tibetans) created by the nationalist government. The "new" China did not come about by destroying the "old" but rather by continuing some very salient features of the Nationalists that the CCP had initially repudiated as concealing "its policy of national oppression" (132). This shift from national self-determination to "uniting all nationalities into a big family" (134) seemed to have gone unnoticed by most other party members.[20] The agenda of unifying the country meant defining the territory, and the configuration of the nation was once again found in the historical legacies of the Qing. It was in this context, Chen suggests, that the party leadership "formulated and carried out plans to 'liberate' Tibet" (135). It became important to liberate Tibet to complete China's unification as well as to show the world that "we the Chinese people have stood up" (138). Chen emphasizes, though, that although the party's military strength and political strategy enabled it to "liberate" Tibet, it has to date not been able to settle the question of Tibet.

One of the challenges in the early Republic era was presenting Tibet as an old member of the new nation-state of China to the Chinese, who had previously viewed frontier races as different—and as barbarians. Additionally, the citizens of frontier races had little relationship, direct or indirect, with Chinese rulers.[21] The incommensurability between modern ideas of

20. Cadres who did notice, such as Phunstok Wangay, paid the price by spending years in prison.
21. Duara writes that the nation form relies on a homogenized and a fairly direct relationship between citizen and state (2008: 154).

sovereignty and the foundations of the Chinese imperial structure meant a sharp assessment of control and a reimagining of nation as well as of Chineseness. Such reimaginings brought the hitherto small Tibetan regions of Kham, East Tibet, into prominence as strategic zones of contact, providing access to the more prized central Tibetan territory (Tsomu 2013).

In her study of the kingdom of Nyarong in Kham,[22] Yudru Tsomu shows how the integration strategies (or what might be considered revisionist strategies) adopted by the government of Republican China toward the Kham frontier were shaped by the efforts of the new Chinese intellectuals of the Republican period to reimagine "a new geo-space" where frontier peoples were made "co-nationals" (337).[23] The struggle for writers and officials such as Ren Naiqiang, an influential figure during the Republican era, and regarded today as the "founding father of Kham studies in China," was to create a deep history so that Tibetan culture and tradition was viewed "not as an alien other, but as an integral part of China's past" (333). Tibetan practices were identified as ancient Chinese traditions, so that Kham's local cultural traditions became both primitive and a part of ancient China. "Han culture is the natural condition" (334) against which Kham was read. Through a variety of narrative strategies—narratives of similarity, rhetoric of privation, and rhetoric of primitivism—scholars such as Ren produced new meaning to the region and legitimized the "civilizing mission" (338) sponsored by the state. These narratives contrast those written by Tibetans whose understanding of Tibetan traditions, culture, and history was separate from China.

22. Present-day Sichuan Province. In 1837, the chieftain of Nyarong, Gonpo Namgyel, expanded his domain to a considerable size and brought Qing authorities to a military expedition to curb his growth. Nyarong was contested by Qing China and the Lhasa government. Qing frontier officials saw the repossession of Nyarong as crucial in consolidating Qing rule in Kham. See Tsomu 2013 for more on Nyarong.
23. In the late nineteenth and early twentieth centuries, there was very little information produced on Tibet by Chinese. Ren Naiqiang wrote about his experiences in the Sichuan borderlands, where he worked as an official. Tsomu explains that Ren's work was tied to the nationalist agenda of turning the borderlands into an integral part of the nation-state. For Ren, the people of Kham could be civilized "by means of a historical analogy with many 'barbarians' in Chinese history, who had long been assimilated into the Chinese population" (Tsomu 2013: 336).

A Tibetan Communist Nationalist's
Dream of Tibetan Independence

Tibetans accept the proclamation of independence issued by the thirteenth Dalai Lama in 1913, and his letter to warlord ruler Yuan Shih-k'ai, to be a declaration of independence. Although these documents may not conform to Western norms of declarations of independence, the proclamation can be seen to introduce the notion of individual agency, national independence, and a vision for a greater Tibet in the political framework of the Tibet of that era. Dreams of a Tibet ruled by Tibetans and encompassing all Tibetans in Kham, Amdo, and Tibet proper are not limited to the ruling elite, as Wang suggests; they have been expressed and pursued by ordinary Tibetans since the early 1900s. An unusual perspective on Tibetan (communist) nationalism is found in *A Tibetan Revolutionary*, the story of a strong nationalist and "modern" Tibetan, Bapa Phuntso Wangye, or Phunwang, from Batang, in Kham. Phunwang, a controversial figure for Tibetans, feared both British and Guomindang influence and power over Tibet, as well as the internal disunity among Tibetans from the three regions of Tibet. His nationalism was a response to the oppressive and exploitative treatment of the Chinese warlord Liu Wenhui, who ruled the regions of Batang where Phunwang was born. Phunwang saw a connection between communist ideas and Tibetan independence and took hope in the model of a brief (Tibetan-run) government established by the Red Army in Kham in 1935 during the Long March. The party had convinced Tibetans in Kham that the national liberation movement by Tibetans set the path for achieving genuine independence and liberation from Britain as well as from Nationalist China.

Phunwang formed the first Tibetan Communist Party and was a leading Tibetan cadre as part of the team "liberating" Tibet from 1951 to 1958. He imagined that Tibet would modernize as part of the PRC but still maintain its national identity, language, and culture (Goldstein et al. 2004: 155). Despite Phunwang's role in establishing the CCP's rule in Tibet, he was later accused of local nationalism and arrested for counterrevolutionary acts in 1960. Phunwang spent eighteen years in solitary confinement in the Qingchen Number One Prison in the Beijing environs.

In his biography, Phunwang states that the "original policy of equality of nationalities had been suppressed in favor of what we in the party used to call Great Han Chauvinism, that is to say, the ethnic Chinese (Han) controlling and dominating the minority nationalities, which in turn undermined the local minorities' autonomy and culture" (281). He explains that Chinese and Tibetan relations "had devolved into a master/servant relationship" and that Tibetans were being forced to become like Han Chinese. This was the reason, he writes, "for the anger of Tibetans despite their dislike and rejection of the oppressive traditional feudal system" (281). He believed that national unity required new (Marxist) policies that would provide real equality, not suppression. Phunwang's empirical and pungent analysis of his role in the CCP and his conceptualization of the Tibet-China conflict is valuable for numerous reasons.

First, he shows the disjunctions in China's treatment of Tibetans. He writes that Chinese comrades never progressed beyond "overall concepts in their thinking" (183) in the direction of equality for Tibetans. His view contrasts with Wang's assessment of the contemporary system as a synthesis evolving from "exploration, innovation and praxis based on precepts of equality, development and diversity" (2011: 280). For Wang, the current system is not a recasting of the old but an entirely new creation, born out of "the imperial legacy, the nation-state and socialist values" (180). For Phunwang, it is in fact the recasting of an old repudiated system, and a system whose disregard for principles of equality are glaringly deceptive and problematic.

Second, Phunwang shows how the two sides hold very different perspectives of history and how the Tibetan perspective was not represented in the new Chinese national culture and policies (Goldstein et al. 2004: 162). He holds that PLA officials did not understand Tibetans' view of Tibet and China being two distinct countries and whose only historical connection was as priest-patron.

Third, Phunwang's story is a profoundly persuasive example of an individual Tibetan's desire for a revolution that would separate Tibet from the Chinese (and the British) and build a less oppressive Tibet. His lifelong insistence on a principle of meaningful equality for Tibetans familiarized him with the institutional and ideological impediments that kept Tibetan desires and voices at bay. Ultimately, Phunwang's own life illustrates his critique of the gap between the precepts of equality (toward Tibetans) and its praxis in contemporary China, a gap disavowed to this day.

In the document "An Investigative Report into the Social and Economic Causes of the 3.14 Incident in Tibetan Areas," a report written by Li Kun, Huang Li, Li Xiang, and Wang Hongzhe for the Gongmeng Law Research Center in May 2009, the researchers challenge the official position that the 2008 protests were solely incited by exiled Tibetans. The report

begins by posing a few simple questions: "What is the current state of education and employment in Tibetan areas? What are the lives and thoughts
of ordinary people?" (Li Kun et al. 2009: 5). After conducting a thorough
investigation into how Tibetans understood the protests, the authors arrive
at some honest conclusions. Of Tibet's transition from a "tradition[al] to
modern" world, they write, "This hurried process of modernization and the
path it has taken are not the result of choices made by Tibetans of their own
volition; there were very many powerful external forces at play" (6). They
show that Tibetans receive poor basic education, lack social opportunities, and struggle to compete with non-Tibetans. Tibetans, the researchers
argue, are not equal citizens and do not have the "fundamental ideological identification with the state" (17). The report points out that the process
of modernization has come about by attacking core Tibetan values and
destroying religious and cultural frameworks.[24]

Wang cautions against taking the current crisis as ethnic strife. He
explains the present Tibetan crisis as the effects of the economic night-
mare suffered by all of Chinese society (2011: 211–12). In Tibet, the logic
of market society conflicts with Tibetan religious culture, and it is this pain
Tibetans feel acutely, he believes. While it is true that events in Tibet cannot be isolated from the economic changes sweeping over the whole of
China, and while it is also true that the protest in the late 1980s was triggered by tensions between the monasteries and the Communist Party, the
2008 protest, in contrast, represented groups from all of Tibetan society:
schoolchildren, farmers, nomads, intellectuals, workers, and monks. Additionally, in giving less importance to the active participation of the Chinese
state in the spread of market reforms and wage labor in his discussion on
Tibet, Wang allows the state to be conceived as a benevolent force still
capable of ameliorating the social consequences that were in fact caused
by its own policies.

In the years since Wang's essay, more than 140 Tibetans have self-
immolated and died in Tibet, many of them not too far from the regions
he visited in Sichuan, as recorded in his essay. Most of these Tibetans
were young monks and nuns, but there were students, nomads, and artists among them. Many of them expressed a desire for the Dalai Lama to
be allowed into Tibet. Chinese authorities claim the self-immolators were

24. The report was prepared by a nongovernmental organization formed by lawyers and
law professors. The organization was shut down by Beijing authorities on tax charges
(Veg 2009: 98).

encouraged into action by Tibetans in exile, that they were of unsound mind and character, and that they committed acts of terrorism. Such responses do not seek to listen or understand why Tibetans are seeking death over life; they only confirm the state's biopolitics.

Tsering Woeser seeks to understand and analyze the act of self-immolation in *Tibet on Fire: Self-Immolations against Chinese Rule* (2016). She understands the act as the continuation of a response to the "wake-up call" Tibetans experienced after witnessing the state violence in 2008; she also sees it as the beginning of a new form of protest addressing the deep wound inflicted by the Chinese state on three generations of Tibetans. Everything changed for Woeser in March 2008. In the epilogue to *Voices from Tibet*, a book coauthored by Woeser and Wang Lixiong in 2014, Woeser writes about the silence that followed the violent suppression of Tibetan voices inside Tibet. It was the loudness of the Chinese state's "propaganda machine" drowning Tibetan suffering and voices in the months following the March 2008 protests that compelled Woeser to speak out. She and Wang Lixiong became the daily chroniclers of events in 2008. She declares that writing became her own way to fight against oppression. To write is to "experience," to "pray," and to "bear witness." For her, all three intertwine. To bear witness, she writes, "is to give voice" (epilogue).

Woeser attempts to give voice to the act of self-immolation (2016: 14–18). She believes that self-immolation can be judged only "by its political results" (26). It is precisely because it is a form of protest against a systematic tyrannical government that the protest will not cease till the root causes are addressed. It is the CCP who can halt these protests—not Tibetans, not the Dalai Lama (65). She explains that the present generation, the third generation of Tibetans living under Chinese rule, suffers in five areas of everyday life: their beliefs are suppressed; their ecosystem is decimated and looted; their language is devalued and deemphasized in their own education systems; Han population transfer into Tibetan areas is transforming Tibetan life and livelihood; and Tibetans live under "an Orwellian monitoring system" rendering Tibet a vast prison.

Just as the self-immolations can be understood by turning to the 2008 protests, the 2008 protests are understood by turning to the 1989 protests, or indeed as Woeser points out, to 1959, when Tibetans in Lhasa rose to express their anger against the Chinese.[25] The dead are not for-

---

25. As well as against some of the ruling Tibetan elite, "who they believed, had betrayed their leader" (Shakya 1999: 192).

gotten because almost every Tibetan is impacted by the repressions of 1959 and 1969, having a family member imprisoned or killed. The death of each Tibetan is therefore a "torch" shedding light "on a land trapped in darkness" (26).

Woeser, Phunwang, and the Tibetans who have died from self-immolations are pointing to the memory and history of a long oppression. They insist on addressing what is at the heart of politics: how we live or desire to live as humans. Delinking the social and cultural crisis from its political center is in effect a depoliticization of what it means to live as humans. If death is chosen over life, what does it say about the Tibetan aspiration for life under the Chinese state? If the only response from the state is to ban Tibetans from setting one's body on fire, or to punish the dead by banning Buddhist burial rites, how are Tibetans, who wish to live in China, to reconcile their place within the Chinese state?

"We Have Tomorrow": Diverse Tibetan Voices and Tibetan Desires

The Tibetan Parliament in exile adopted the MWA as a resolution on March 20, 2010. As the middle path between two extreme positions, it does not seek independence nor does it accept the present conditions under Chinese rule. For activists demanding independence, the MWA is a product of the process of the internationalization of the "Tibetan issue." Tibetan independence activist Tenzin Dorjee writes that the Tibetan campaign's use of "Western democracies as a lever" to bring China into negotiations and bring Tibet's story to the larger world was successful largely through a focus on the protection of human rights and a focus on the growing international recognition of the Dalai Lama (2013: 78–80). However, in framing the "Tibetan issue" within the discourse of human rights and not the restoration of sovereignty, Dharamsala is perceived as having given too much without even getting the Chinese to the negotiating table (83). Independence activists feel that while it was crucial to bring Tibet's condition to international attention, and while the CTA's moral approach to politics is unique and admirable, state leaders do not respond adequately. Indeed, state leaders are increasingly succumbing to Chinese pressure to avoid meeting the Dalai Lama in any official capacity.

The ethos of the MWA echoes a Buddhist worldview of interdependence. It can also be received as a radical, or aspirational, inter-nationalism with the relinquishment of nationhood serving as the core of its proposal.

Both its moral features as well as its radical enlightenment are attributed to the Dalai Lama, whose metonymic relationship to Tibet is both a boon and a challenge.[26] It is largely due to the Dalai Lama that the Tibetan struggle has become international. Some Tibetan activists see the tremendous force available to the Dalai Lama, one he has never directly used against the Chinese. "The greatest strength His Holiness the Dalai Lama has at his disposal to save Tibet is not his international stature, nor is it his compassionate overture to the Chinese, but the absolute unshakable faith of his people in him," wrote Tashi Phuntsok more than a decade ago (Phuntsok 2008).

Criticisms against Tibetan decision makers also imply that the leaders do not mobilize their own voices to find their own strengths and come up with creative strategies other than the ones set in motion by the Dalai Lama. Dorjee expresses concern that Tibetan strategies in the late 1980s brought global attention to Tibet but failed to "assign a role to the Tibetan public inside Tibet" (2013: 107). He sees opportunity for the new administration in Dharamsala to fulfill the Dalai Lama's hope for democracy in the Tibetan community. He would like to see the CTA "liberate itself from the religious worldview that had shaped the vision and constrained the action of the previous administration"[27] and "chart a new path firmly rooted in realpolitik" (108). Yet it is also true that "realpolitik" as practiced by China, Great Britain, the United States, and India has not brought Tibet any solution. For the moment, discourse on Tibetan culture, history, or nationalism continues to be tinged with Buddhist aspirations and ethos. This is so even inside Tibet, where monasteries and Tibetan Buddhism are forces fostering a meaningful civic society and identity.

But what if the day comes when Tibetan youth have no access to their language and culture? Bhuchung D. Sonam, a poet and writer who was born in Tibet and now lives in Dharamsala, finds hope in the revolutionary musical explosion inside Tibet and outside Tibet (2012: 169–71). He looks toward music's force in uniting people in resistance to occupation. He insists on ceaseless revolution and stresses the need to compose, sing, and distribute songs as much as possible so that young Tibetans will not forget songs about the mountains and rivers of Tibet. He calls for songs of freedom and resistance that will "not only enrage the CCP but also put its entire propaganda machine on alert to block word after word and phrase

26. Because Tibetan leaders and people defer to his approval for all crucial decisions or use his name to gain the support from Tibetans.
27. Led by Samdhong Rinpoche, a Buddhist Lama and teacher.

after phrase," so that its entire security apparatus is exhausted trying to ban song after song after song (171). "When that day comes," Sonam explains, "Tibetans will be speaking in a language that Beijing cannot and will not understand, and sing songs that the CCP will never comprehend" (171). In other words, it is only when Tibet is ungovernable that China will listen. But does China have the incentive to listen? Since 2008, more than fifty Tibetan writers, artistes, and academics in Tibet have been arrested for representing themselves and expressing their desire to be free to choose their own identity, beliefs, and leaders.[28]

In an interview with the *New York Review of Books* on August 7, 2014, Wang Lixiong and Tsering Woeser address some of the concerns of Tibetans in Tibet. These include the use of Han immigration into Tibetan areas as a strategy to solve the ethnic problems and the everyday restrictions on Tibetan life. Wang Lixiong declares there are two Tibets: "One is the Tibet outside the borders and the other is the Tibet inside the borders. The Tibet inside the borders has no voice and no representatives. Abroad you have a few hundred thousand people but are they really the representatives of the Tibetan people?" (Johnson 2014). This question points to the asymmetrical relationship between the now two branches of the Tibetan nation. For decades, a few hundred Tibetans in exile have been speaking for and representing six million Tibetans, without knowing or understanding fully the everyday travails and desires of Tibetans inside Tibet. No real solution to the question of Tibet can be reached without keeping Tibetans inside Tibet central and visible in all conversations.

Wang Lixiong explains that the Tibetan exile government's policies are inadequate to solve the problem of Tibet. The exile government should have put emphasis "on the people inside Tibet and help[ed] them determine their future" (Johnson 2014). Tibetans need strategies that invite diverse voices to think creatively, variously, and at the grassroots level in addition to the framework of Buddhism. Woeser's voice is one among many in Tibet. She views village self-rule as a path to real regional autonomy. She believes that giving ordinary villagers genuine self-rule will allow them to become active participants of their own lives and bring an end to the "high-stake political games between Beijing and Dharamsala" (Woeser and

---

28. *A "Raging Storm": The Crackdown on Tibetan Writers and Artists after Tibet's Spring 2008 Protests*, a report produced by the International Campaign for Tibet in 2010, has cases about fifty Tibetans in the arts and public service who were/are in prison or who have disappeared (2010).

Wang 2014: 18). Can Tibetan villages take this on? Woeser believes that once a village sets an example, others will follow. "When ten more succeed, the end of the tunnel would be near. When a hundred rise up, a truly autonomous Tibet would become within reach" (18).

Woeser insists on keeping the Tibetan people, their voices, and their humanity central to the future. She helps to reveal what is problematic in existing proposals: a politics of dignity that gives ordinary Tibetans the power to effect the changes they seek. The chances of that succeeding are uncertain, but so is everything else in the present.

What Woeser and various Tibetan voices are also articulating is hope for a world that invites and listens to their existential questions in a genuinely serious and political spirit. The existing frameworks are not equipped to do so. Despite the possibilities in Wang's politics of dignity and the Central Tibetan Administration's MWA, both begin from a position that maintains the status quo of inequality. Ultimately, Wang's essay as well as the MWA address the international audience, not the heterogeneous Tibetans at the heart of this "problem." As such they also do not adequately reflect the participation and desires of ordinary Tibetans for tomorrow's Tibet, not the one they live in today and neither that of the past.

In the song "We have Tomorrow," the popular Tibetan artist Sherten sings,

> We have the snow mind of glittering light
> We have the endurance of pure rivers
> The hopeful youth
> You are the life of the Snowland
> If the ring of unity is not slackened
> We have tomorrow.

Hope for tomorrow is a talisman. Woeser reminds us that the Tibetan people's courage is yet another talisman. She asks a simple question: "If you are not afraid of setting yourself on fire, what else can scare you?" (2014: 18).

References

Anand, Dibyesh. 2006. "The Tibet Question and the West: Issues of Sovereignty, Identity and Representation." In *Contemporary Tibet: Politics, Development, and Society in a Disputed Region*, edited by Barry Sautman and June Teufel Dreyer, 285–304. New York: East Gate.

Beckwith, Christopher. 1980. "The Tibetan Empire in the West." In *Tibetan Studies in Honour of Hugh Richardson*, edited by Michael Aris and Aung San Suu Kyi, 30–38. New Delhi: Vikas Publishing House.

Central Tibetan Administration. 2010. *Middle Way Policy and All Related Documents*. Dharamsala: Department of Information & International Relations (DIIR).

Chakrabarty, Dipesh. 1992. "Postcoloniality and the Artifice of History: Who Speaks for 'Indian' Pasts?" In "Imperial Fantasies and Postcolonial Histories." Special issue, *Representations*, no. 37: 1–26.

Chen, Jian. 2007. "The Chinese Communist 'Liberation' of Tibet, 1949–51." In *Dilemmas of Victory*, edited by Jeremy Brown and Paul G. Pickowicz, 130–59. Cambridge, MA: Harvard University Press.

Di Cosmo, Nicola. 2003. "Kirghiz Nomads on the Qing Frontier: Tribute, Trade, or Gift Exchange?" In *Political Frontiers, Ethnic Boundaries, and Human Geographies in Chinese History*, edited by Nicola Di Cosmo and Don J. Wyatt, 351–72. London: RoutledgeCurzon.

Dorjee, Tenzin. 2013. "Diplomacy or Mobilization: The Tibetan Dilemma in the Struggle with China." In *China's Internal and External Relations and Lessons for Korea and Asia*, edited by Jung-Ho Bae and Jae H. Ku, 63–112. Korea: Korea Institute for National Unification.

Duara, Prasenjit. 2008. "History and Globalization in China's Long Twentieth Century." In "The Nature of the Chinese State: Dialogues among Western and Chinese Scholars." Special issue, *Modern China* 34, no. 1: 152–64.

———. 2009/2010. "Civilization and Realpolitik." In "INDIACHINA Neighbours Strangers." Special issue, *India International Centre Quarterly* 36, no. 3/4: 20–33.

Fairbank, K. John, and Ssu-yu Teng. 1941. "On the Ch'ing Tributary System." *Harvard Journal of Asiatic Studies* 6, no. 2: 135–246.

Fletcher F. Joseph. 1968. "China and Central Asia, 1368–1884." In *The Chinese World Order*, edited by John K. Fairbank, 206–24. Cambridge, MA: Harvard University Press.

Gernet, Jacques. 1982. *A History of Chinese Civilization*. Cambridge: Cambridge University Press.

Goldstein, Melvyn. 1989. *A History of Modern Tibet, 1913–1951: The Demise of the Lamaist State*. Berkeley: University of California Press.

———. 2007. *A History of Modern Tibet. Volume 2: The Calm before the Storm, 1951–1955*. Berkeley: University of California Press.

———. 2014. *A History of Modern Tibet. Volume 3: The Storm Clouds Descend: 1955–1957*. Berkeley: University of California Press.

Goldstein, Melvyn, Sherap Dawei, and William R. Siebenschuh. 2004. *A Tibetan Revolutionary: The Political Life and Times of Bapa Phuntso Wangye*. Berkeley: University of California Press.

He, Baogang. 2006. "The Dalai Lama's Autonomy Proposal: A One-Sided Wish?" In *Contemporary Tibet: Politics, Development, and Society in a Disputed Region*, edited by Barry Sautman and June Teufel Dreyer, 67–84. New York: East Gate.

Hevia, James. 1993. "Lamas, Emperors, and Rituals: Political Implications in Qing Imperial Ceremonies." *Journal of the International Association of Buddhist Studies* 16, no. 2: 243–78.

International Campaign for Tibet. 2010. *A "Raging Storm": The Crackdown on Tibetan Writers and Artists after Tibet's Spring 2008 Protests*. Washington, D.C. International Campaign for Tibet, May 18, 2010. http://www.savetibet.org/a-raging-storm-the-crackdown-on-tibetan-writers-and-artists-after-tibets-spring-2008-protests/#sthash.COg4kvIT.dpuf.

Johnson, Ian. 2014. "Beyond the Dalai Lama: An Interview with Woeser and Wang Lixiong." *New York Review of Books*, August 7, 2014. http://www.nybooks.com/blogs/nyrblog/2014/aug/07/interview-tsering-woeser-wang-lixiong/?insrc=hpbl.

Li Kun, Huang Li, Li Xiang, Wang Hongzhe. 2009. "An Investigative Report into the Social and Economic Causes of the 3.14 Incident in Tibetan Areas." Translated by International Campaign for Tibet. Gongmeng Law Research Center, available at http://blog.foolsmountain.com/2009/06/02/an-investigative-report-into-the-social-and-economic-causes-of-the-314-incident-in-tibetan-areas/all/1/.

Mancall, Mark. 1968. "The Ch'ing Tribute System: An Interpretive Essay." In *The Chinese World Order*, edited by John K. Fairbank, 63–89. Cambridge, MA: Harvard University Press.

Mote, F. W. 1999. *Imperial China: 900–1800*. Cambridge, MA: Harvard University Press.

Norbu, Dawa. 2001. *China's Tibet Policy*. Surrey, UK: Curzon Press.

Perdue, C. Peter. 2005. *China Marches West. The Qing Conquest of Central Eurasia*. Cambridge, MA: Harvard University Press.

Petech, Luciano. 1980. "The Mongol Census in Tibet." In *Tibetan Studies in Honour of Hugh Richardson*, edited by Michael Aris and Aung San Suu Kyi, 233–38. New Delhi: Vikas Publishing House.

———. 1983. "Tibetan Relations with Sung China and with the Mongols." In *China among Equals*, edited by Morris Rossabi, 173–203. Berkeley: University of California Press.

Phunstok, Tashi. 2008. "Why the Middle Way Approach Failed." Phayul.com, November 11, 2008. http://www.phayul.com/news/article.aspx?id=23190.

Said, Edward. 1978. *Orientalism*. New York: Vintage Books.

Shakya, Tsering. 1999. *The Dragon in the Land of Snows: A History of Modern Tibet since 1947*. New York: Penguin Compass.

———. 2013. "The Genesis of the Sino-Tibetan Agreement of 1951." In *The Tibetan*

History Reader, edited by Gray Tuttle and Kurtis R. Schaeffer, 609–32. New York: Columbia University Press.

Sherten. 2014. "We Have Tomorrow." Translated by High Peaks Pure Earth. July 7, 2014. http://highpeakspureearth.com/2014/music-video-we-have-tomorrow -by-sherten/.

Sonam, Bhuchung D. 2012. *Yak Horns: Notes on Contemporary Tibetan Writing, Music, Film & Politics*. Dharamsala: TibetWrites.

Suzuki, Chusei. 1968. "China's Relations with Inner Asia: The Hsiung-Nu, Tibet." In *The Chinese World Order*, edited by John K. Fairbank, 180–97. Cambridge, MA: Harvard University Press.

Tsomu, Yudru. 2013. "Taming the Khampas: The Republican Construction of Eastern Tibet." *Modern China* 39, no. 3: 319–44.

Tuttle, Gray. 2005. *Tibetan Buddhists in the Making of Modern China*. New York: Columbia University Press.

Van der Kuijp, Leonard. 2013. "The Dalai Lamas and the Origins of Reincarnate Lamas." In *The Tibetan History Reader*, edited by Gray Tuttle and Kurtis R. Schaeffer, 335–47. New York: Columbia University Press.

Veg, Sebastian. 2009. "Tibet, Nationalism, and Modernity: Two Chinese Contributions." *China Perspectives* 2009/3: 98–107.

Wang Gungwu. 1983. "The Rhetoric of a Lesser Empire: Early Sung Relations with Its Neighbors." In *China among Equals*, edited by Morris Rossabi, 47–65. Berkeley: University of California Press.

Wang Hui. 2011. *The Politics of Imagining Asia*. Cambridge, MA: Harvard University Press.

Wang, Mingming. 2012. "All under Heaven (*Tianxia*): Cosmological Perspectives and Political Ontologies in Pre-Modern China." *HAU: Journal of Ethnographic Theory* 2, no. 1, 337–83.

Woeser, Tsering. 2011. "Who Are the Real 'Orientalists'?" Translated by High Peaks Pure Earth. Posted on June 9, 2011. http://highpeakspureearth.com/2011 /who-are-the-real-orientalists-by-woeser/.

———. 2016. *Tibet on Fire: Self-Immolations against Chinese Rule*. London: Verso.

Woeser, Tsering, and Wang Lixiong. 2014. *Voices from Tibet*. Honolulu: University of Hawai'i Press.

Wylie, T. 1980. "Lama Tribute in the Ming Dynasty." In *Tibetan Studies in Honour of Hugh Richardson*, edited by Michael Aris and Aung San Suu Kyi, 335–40. New Delhi: Vikas Publishing House.

Yeh, Emily T. 2007. "Tropes of Indolence and the Cultural Politics of Development in Lhasa, Tibet." *Annals of the Association of American Geographers* 97, no. 3: 593–612.

The Planetary

Christine L. Marran

The return to "authenticity" . . . is a closed route.
—Masao Miyoshi, "A Borderless World? From Colonialism to
Transnationalism and the Decline of the Nation-State"

Conceptual Darlings

A grainy black and white photograph of Masao Miyoshi's three children playing on the beach in the North Bay region of San Francisco introduces "Planetary Thinking and Environmentalism" in his collection of interviews with Mitsuhiro Yoshimoto entitled *To the Sites of Resistance* (2007).
The effortless image of three children frolicking on a sandy beach smoothed
by frothy waves presents a personal attachment that a planetary perspective is challenged to maintain. Even if Miyoshi considers ecological totality
as the necessary frame for literary and cultural studies for the twenty-first

I am grateful to James Fujii, Shimpei Takeda, Christophe Thouny, and Reginald Jackson
for their comments on a draft of this essay. I also thank University of Minnesota Press
for letting me publish some passages from my *Ecology without Culture: Aesthetics for a
Toxic World*.

boundary 2 46:3 (2019)   DOI 10.1215/01903659-7614207   © 2019 by Duke University Press

century, the chapter opens not with a predictable image of the globe but with a photograph imbued with a personal sense of urgency, and Miyoshi did call this new ecocritical strand of thought his most important academic work. Certainly, his article "Turn to the Planet: Literature and Diversity, Ecology and Totality" makes no bones about the direction he thought cultural studies should take. He writes,

> For the first time in human history, one single commonality involves all those living on the planet: environmental deterioration as a result of the human consumption of natural resources. Whether rich or poor, in the East or the West, progressive or conservative, religious or atheist, none of us can escape from the all-involving process of air pollution, ozone layer depletion, ocean contamination, toxic accumulation, and global warming. . . . Literature and literary studies now have one basis and goal: to nurture our common bonds to the planet—to replace the imaginaries of exclusionist familialism, communitarianism, nationhood, ethnic culture, regionalism, "globalization," or even humanism, with the ideal of planetarianism. (Miyoshi 2001: 295)

Through the concept of planetarianism, Miyoshi introduces a critique of exclusionist concepts of belonging and identity that would hide the common vulnerability of the human species to climate change and other planetary changes induced by human behaviors. This essay addresses the critical potential of such a globalizing concept for area and comparative studies and suggests how it might be implemented in visual analysis.

Miyoshi introduced his concept of "planetarianism" nearly contemporaneously with a now frequently cited idea introduced by atmospheric chemist Paul Crutzen and biologist Eugene Stoermer to commence a new geologic epoch. Called the "Anthropocene," this epoch would mark the human capacity to fundamentally change earth and atmospheric systems like never before, although Stoermer had apparently used the term much earlier, along with a few others. The concept of the Anthropocene became the conceptual darling of this century in the humanities and sciences, in part because divergent groups can engage the concept. Those who believe in rationalism to solve the problem of radical change to earth systems and those who consider our future with grim, existentialist humility both exploit the theoretical range of the concept.[1] The recently expanded notion of the Anthropocene calls attention to the unprecedented levels of anthropogenic impacts to earth systems, including species extinctions and the slowing of

1. For a brief history of the use of the term *Anthropocene*, see Kolbert 2010.

biodiversification, ocean acidification, freshwater overusage, expanded and intensified land use, atmospheric aerosol loading, and chemical pollution (Thomas 2014: 1588).[2] As Rob Nixon (2014) points out, anthropogenic culpability was discussed openly as early as 1988. At that time, the director of NASA's Goddard Institute, James Hansen, stated in testimony at a Congressional hearing that science was 99 percent unequivocal that the world was warming and that we needed to act collectively to reduce emissions or risk a host of unintended consequences. What is different about this interest in anthropogenic change now, as opposed to twenty years ago, is the range of scholars and scientists ready to speak to the anthropogenic effects on the environment. In the humanities and sciences alike, this concept has served as a wake-up call to their disciplines. Miyoshi's turn to the planetary, a turn he made late in life, demands that all disciplines consider anthropogenic effects on the globe. In fact, that is exactly what is happening.

Whether there is sufficient geological evidence to warrant such a change of epoch nomenclature was evaluated by the International Union of Geological Sciences in 2016, but discussions continue to evolve regarding when we consider humanity's geophysical change to the planet to have commenced to reach the critical stage in which we find ourselves today. Options range from the start of agricultural labor in the early Holocene, to the invention and common use of the steam engine in the eighteenth century, to the 1920s, when radiation was first introduced into the earth's stratigraphy, or post-1945, when the use of chemicals and nitrogen fixation technologies soared.

Epoch name change or no, the urgent need to address a host of global environmental issues is clear, but what is particular about Miyoshi's planetary thinking? Miyoshi's concept of the planetary invokes Anthropocene discourse when he posits a global commons. This global commons is based on the idea of a universally shared climate crisis. All of humanity is subjected to this crisis leading Miyoshi to remark that "a new kind of environmental studies will need to decide whether human extinction is worth thinking about" (Miyoshi 2010: xxxi). The novel aspect of his writing on ecological totality lies in his demand to reconsider what we do in literary studies and the humanities based on this shared global condition. Impatient with the "internecine struggles" within the discipline of literary studies, Miyoshi suggests that we respond to the end of the Cold War, the start of the neoliberal global economy, and continued environmental deterioration by con-

2. Rockström and his colleagues (2009) developed these nine critical planetary boundaries or thresholds that should not be crossed. Cited in Thomas 2014: 1599.

sidering economic disparity with our shared environment as the impetus. In contrast to the descriptive term *Anthropocene*, his use of the awkward ideological term *planetarianism* projects a sense of agency, but having introduced it late in life, Miyoshi did not have a chance to pursue the full range of its conceptual possibilities.

He was not alone at the turn of this century in his desire to rethink the bounds of his own discipline through the specter of radical geophysical change to the planet. For example, in 2003, celebrated economist Hirofumi Uzawa released his book *Economic Theory and Global Warming*. In it, Uzawa theorizes an economic system based in the ecological event of global warming—one that would account for environmental disequilibrium, which impairs economic development in developing countries and "lower[s] the welfare of all people in all future generations decisively" (Uzawa 2003: ix). More recently in the popular book market, Naomi Klein has published *This Changes Everything: Capitalism and Climate Change* (2014) as her third volume in a sustained critique of contemporary global capitalism albeit without substantively critiquing capitalism as a system. The argument in *This Changes Everything* suggests that a different kind of capitalism—one that considers anthropogenic impact on a planetary scale—is the only way for human and nonhuman species to survive the future (although many nonhuman species have already been lost). In his field of history, Dipesh Chakrabarty (2009) has articulated how the discipline might respond to challenges posed by climatological change. Chakrabarty argues that narrow constructions of the discipline of history, ones that minimize geological perspectives, cannot account for humanity's global force (Thomas 2014: 1590).[3] The book series Critical Climate Change, edited by Tom Cohen and Claire Colebrook, offers multiple studies of art, architecture, and philosophy through the lens of anthropogenic change. In short, in the twenty-first century, we have seen a plethora of attempts to rethink disciplines in terms of a planetary scale.[4] In his last work for the field of comparative literature and cultural studies, Miyoshi also posited the planetary as his point of departure.

---

3. In *To the Sites of Resistance*, Miyoshi said about history that "we should end with thinking that history begins with human civilization," and we should theorize what physicists mean when they say that we sense space and time in the 11th dimension" (2007: 316).
4. More recently, Critical Climate Change, a new series published by Open Humanities Press, and edited by Tom Cohen and Claire Colebrook, publishes "experimental monographs that redefine the boundaries of disciplinary fields" in response to the symptoms of anthropogenic change. See http://www.openhumanitiespress.org/books/series/critical-climate-change/.

Discourses of the planetary suggest that the particularity means nothing without the totality, as Miyoshi himself argued. But historian Julia Adeney Thomas has illustrated that, in fact, scale can make all the difference in how we conceive of planetary changes like global warming. Microbiologists give us a radically different perspective on the problem of survival—who or what is endangered when the climate is in crisis (Thomas 2014: 1588). Thomas argues that the historian's role is to determine who the "we" of climate crisis is and by which measure we are in crisis. Miyoshi was clearly interested in a similar question in his work on ecological totality, brief as it was. For example, in his essay "Literary Elaborations," he opens with Stephen Jay Gould writing about scale: "We can surely destroy ourselves and take many species with us, but we can barely dent bacterial diversity and will surely not remove many million species of insects and mites. On geologic scales, our planet will take good care of itself and let time clear the impact of any human malfeasance" (Miyoshi 2010: 1; Gould 1993). The human agent—producer and consumer of global capital—is the "we" of this global crisis who is engaged in malfeasance. Yet, this relatively expansive, species-based definition of the "we" may ultimately be what undoes the power of the concept of the planetary for its inability to address the particulars of a social community. And, further, such an expansive perspective may mean that we can see nothing at all as far as ecocritical impact. As critical theorist Claire Colebrook has suggested, Anthropocene discourse is unwieldy: "We are at once mutations, at the same time as we come up against a complex multiplicity of diverging forces and timelines that exceed any manageable point of view" (Colebrook 2014: 11). This idea of an environment without any single manageable point of view, and an environment certainly not visible solely from a planetary perspective, invites a critique of Miyoshi's theory of the planetary. Put differently, however, Miyoshi's work seeks a new vocabulary for addressing climate change within his field. We could say that his theory engages humanistic inquiry at what environmental humanities scholar Timothy Clark calls the "hypothetical scale" (Clark 2012: 158), while his photography embraces a generational scale. Implementing the hypothetical scale in analysis changes what is deemed "important," according to Clark, who suggests that in such an analysis, nonhuman entities would play a role. Miyoshi instead focused on planetary scale to rethink humanistic disciplines. Taking Miyoshi's practice of photography as a provocation, I discuss the incongruities introduced by the concept of "planetarianism" for cultural studies and photography.

The Planetary as Critique

Miyoshi's call for new a scale of thinking in cultural criticism begins with a critique of identity politics—an argument rehearsed in several of his essays, including "Japan Is Not Interesting" (2000b). In his interview with Yoshimoto on the planetary, which he treated as a potentially productive movement through his use of the term *planetarianism*, Miyoshi stated,

> It all started with my rejection of identity politics. This means reject-
> ing alliances and dedication to one's own group beyond differences
> in history and geography. And once one refuses alliances to one's
> own group, where should one go from there? Clearly one must reject
> the group of one's nation-state. One cannot be satisfied with nation-
> state. As an intellectual concept it is not only bankrupt, but in reality
> in so many ways it has already been abandoned. Creating a global
> political economy and the protection of citizens are the only missions
> of the nation-state, but those are hardly realized. (Miyoshi and Yoshi-
> moto 2007: 314)

As Miyoshi explains it, his planetary perspective might best be considered description over theory at this point in time. His planetarianism describes the present situation under capitalism, in which the pursuit of capital has led the state to work for profit beyond national boundaries. In the process, it has abandoned its citizens. His quick example of this regards music art-ists who work outside the frame of the nation-state, making it wrongheaded to label music, in his eyes, as "Japanese" or "Korean." The nation-state, in this form, is not the site for producing identities and cultural knowledge. Furthermore, the state's fundamental lack of interest in citizens, along with the reality of artistic practice beyond the frame of the nation-state, requires that "we must dismantle, to the degree possible, the nation-state as a cul-tural concept. The way to do this is through environmental conservation-ism" (Miyoshi and Yoshimoto 2007: 317). Miyoshi had long questioned the category of the nation as the dominant unit for identity formation. As he stated in an interview, "What is important is the willingness to go outside one's national, cultural and disciplinary borders" (2010: 284).

Additionally, Miyoshi critiqued ethnicity-based identity formations as dependent on a false sense of homogeneity: "All ethnic and social groups have internal minorities who need the support of the outside world. We cannot distort world affairs for the self-interest of totalizing and totalized tribes and families and ownerships. In fact, we need to recall that ethnic or cultural groups are not private properties or corporations. We cannot let any ethnic groups privatize or monopolize its identity" (Miyoshi 2010: 204). Miyoshi historicizes his critique of identity politics by arguing that cultural studies was liberating in the first half of the twentieth century, when it was used to define experience against monocultural totalities. Now, however, comparative literature, gender, and ethnic studies have become spaces of atomization where incommensurable cultural or ethnically defined entities have no point of contact. This pursuit of gender and ethnic identity, he argues, is warmly embraced by transnational corporatism, which uses gender and ethnic identity toward the production of markets, while such atomization works against necessary alliances of neighbors who share an environmental predicament:

> The disintegration of not just comparative literature but literary studies as a whole may be already under way. If our fractured groups are engrossed in their self-interests, outsiders have good reason to feel repulsed by them. The general public wants to understand its place in the "globalized" world, and there is a deep concern with the waste-based economy. And yet those who have traditionally intervened in such issues are preoccupied with their internecine struggles conducted in a language of their own. The public is excluded and unwanted as long as it refuses to learn the jargon of partisans and to become partisan. (Miyoshi 2001: 294–95)

This concern that fragmentation is produced through ethnic and gender studies and will produce a weakening of oppositional political and economic action is reiterated in "A Conversation with Masao Miyoshi" (2000a).

This critical perspective that blames cultural studies for failing to be a productive agent of criticism and intervention is unacceptably reductive to critical theorist David Palumbo-Liu, who finds Miyoshi's critique of multiculturalism and identity politics "uncharacteristically ill-informed and totally unsubstantiated" (Palumbo-Liu 2012: 345). Certainly, Miyoshi could have discussed more thoroughly the ways in which global capital relies heavily on cultural constructions while ignoring environmental costs. Or, if partisan language produces rifts in the shared commons of the globe, just how this relates to environmental justice is a sticky problem, given that cultural and ethnic bonds have often formed the basis for all kinds of radical environmental action by conservatives and progressives. That said, Miyoshi is not an outlier in his critique of humanistic discourse as a culprit in global warming. Cultural theorist Tom Cohen, for example, has made the bold claim that the humanities have been so interested in the human subject, including human culture and identity politics, that humanist scholarship is complicit in global warming: "The mesmerizing fixation with cultural histories, the ethics of 'others,' the enhancement of subjectivities, 'human rights' and institutions of power not only partook of this occlusion but 'we theorists' have deferred addressing biospheric collapse, mass extinction events, or the implications of resource wars and 'population' culling. It is our sense of justified propriety—our defense of cultures, affects, bodies and others—that allows us to remain secure in our homeland, unaware of all the ruses that maintain that spurious home" (Cohen 2012: 15).

Comparative literature scholar Gayatri Spivak in no way takes the kind of totalizing approach that Miyoshi does in arguing for a global commons and defacement of disciplines. That said, she does similarly suggest that theory at the level of planetarity (her word) avoids the pitfalls of dogmatic and exclusionary storytelling that speaking through the voice of private authority of experience invites: "The old postcolonial model—very much 'India' plus the Sartrian 'Fanon'—will not serve now as the master model for transnational to global cultural studies on the way to planetarity. We are dealing with heterogeneity on a different scale and related to imperialisms on another model" (Spivak 2005: 85). Those "imperialisms on another model" are international compacts like the EU, GATT, NAFTA, and so on, but the scale that her planetarity introduces is an unsettling move for predictable subjects and finds its metaphor in the inhuman and unpredictable entity of weather: "One must not make history in a deliberate way. One must respect the earth's tone. One might be obliged to claim history from the violent perpetrator of it, in order to turn violation into the enablement of the individual, but that is another story. After the effacement of the trace, no project for restoring the origin. That is 'just weather,' here today as yesterday" (88–89). The planetary scale of address for Spivak is an opportunity to "turn identitarian monuments into documents for reconstellation." This is all toward a refusal of identity politics, which Spivak baldly suggests is "neither smart nor good" (92). History that has placed "itself in the forces of nature and thus away from the specificity of nations" is preferable because it displaces cultural props and the authority of identity-based collectivities (94).

Miyoshi and Spivak may write at the scale of the planetary in order to interrupt the literary and area studies' export of national or ethnic ethos, but there they part ways. Spivak's appeal to the weather seems designed to introduce a forcible movement against predictable entities in comparative literature. Miyoshi is invested in producing a new, transdisciplinary totality for thought and environmentalism. Shrinking coastlines, unequal access to water, ruined farmland, and other examples of shared climatological experience require us, as humans, to jettison particular claims to difference: "No one can escape from the environmental crisis, and no segment of life can be free from it (even though the rich will try to survive longer than the poor, of course)" (Miyoshi 2010: 14). While Spivak mostly stresses the need for relations to the world that identity politics and the current formation of comparative literature stifle, Miyoshi's planetary thinking is about articulating relations to a totality that is a fundamental condition of everyone. But with his parenthetical remark, "the rich will survive longer than the poor, of course," Miyoshi seems to realize that he risks throwing out the proverbial baby with the bathwater. Anthropogenic impact will deeply affect everyone, but especially those already living in poverty; and no one can deny that poverty is a gendered and racialized issue. Where one lives will also matter as sea levels rise, rice paddies are contaminated with cadmium from nearby factories, or local seas are emptied of fish from commercialized fishing. So, discourses of climate change may have enabled us to make a claim toward a certain kind of universalism, but we are still not all in this together, and this is not a new environmental problem. Those who have labored for capitalist modernity have lived in the shadow of capital. Many have already had their worlds destroyed right under our very noses.

How planetary discourse differs from earlier environmental discourse lies in the fact that we have come closer than ever to agreeing as a species that there is a problem. Even if we determine that cultural props atomize us so that we do not recognize our shared environmental predicament, we still have not adequately addressed the logics of difference that climate change both enables and disables. The attempt to imagine the human subject differently under global warming has an irony about it. Philosopher Frédéric Neyrat points this out when he calls Anthropocene discourse the ideological completion of a process that began with industrialism, capitalism, and the colonization of nonhumans. For Neyrat, the concept is trapped by a tautology of human exceptionalism and is therefore flawed as a site of critique because it performs what he calls a "constructivist euphoria." This "euphoria" identifies the human species as having produced global warming, ocean acidification, desertification, and species extinctions, while at the same time working primarily to find technological fixes toward maintaining human dominion (Johnson and Johnson 2014).[5] The critical gesture

5. Anthropocene discourse does invite a chain of thinking that is more apocalyptic when it suggests the very real possibility that *Homo sapiens* (some with Neanderthal DNA), as

made here is to critique the humanistic arrogance that would ignore the agency of the earth systems themselves.

Similarly, when Cohen addresses how current theoretical discourse is hard-pressed to describe our current climate condition, it suggests the need for the humanities to account theoretically for current conditions. Miyoshi's concept of planetarianism answered Jeffrey R. Di Leo's question, "Can theory save the planet?" with an "only if"—only if area and comparative studies' institutionalized practices are challenged.

Scale

Like Miyoshi, Timothy Clark critically considers his intellectual discipline through the environmental problem of global warming, but he argues that working at the scale of the globe can be confounding and problematic. Planetary discourses with their grand scale and breathless urgency can work paradoxically to undermine our capacity to react to our shared environmental condition. In his suggestive essay "Scale," Clark writes,

> With climate change, however, we have a map, its scale includes the whole earth but when it comes to relating the threat to daily questions of politics, ethics or specific interpretations of history, culture, literature, etc., the map is often almost mockingly useless. Policies and concepts relating to climate change invariably seem undermined or even derided by considerations of scale: a campaign for environmental reform in one country may be already effectively negated by the lack of such measures on the other side of the world. (Clark 2012: 148–49)

For Clark, we often make "deranged" jumps in scale in our environmentalist discourse, which lead to fantasies of agency—an issue addressed by Neyrat when he refers to the constructivist euphoria that addresses climate change as a problem to be solved in order to maintain business as usual. For Clark, the global or planetary involves a dizzying array of sites that expand or contract depending on the disciplinary frame through which they are discussed: "If that tired term 'the environment' has often seemed too

a species and as individuals, may not be able to control earth systems because terrestrial, oceanic, and climatological systems have become animated beyond human control. In this sense, perhaps Miyoshi's "planetarianism" offers even an Enlightenment approach to ecological totality because there is still a situation to be addressed and acted upon.

vague—for it means, ultimately, 'everything'—[then] the difficulty of conceptualizing a politics of climate change may be precisely that of having to think 'everything at once.' The overall force is of an implosion of scales, implicating seemingly trivial or small actions with enormous stakes while intellectual boundaries and lines of demarcation fold in upon each other" (152). At stake is the way in which the material aspects of the planet are rendered flat and undifferentiated based on the discursive approach to it. Clark is particularly attentive to the problem of what he calls "liberal criticism" (152).

The labor of reading is the productive site for Clark's ecocritical perspective on the general problem of the logics of difference in criticism and cultural studies for climate change. In his eyes, we have not been reading at the planetary scale. We have instead depended upon modes of thinking and practice that may be internally coherent or even progressive but treat the earth as if it is indefatigable:

> A nonhuman politics also raises questions about the dominant, liberal/progressive cultural politics of much mainstream professional literary criticism. The frequent method now is to read all issues as forms of cultural politics within an understanding of the text analogous to [the] way the liberal tradition sees civic society generally, viz. as an arena for the contestation of individual or collective interests, rights or identity claims. . . . Yet each, at the same time, is staking its own rights to air, water, space and material resources and to focus solely on the rights of the individual person or group elides the issue of the violence continually and problematically being waged against the earth itself, whose own agency is both taken for granted and disregarded. It is as if critics were still writing on a flat and passive earth of indefinite extension, not a round, active one whose furthest distance comes from behind to tap you uncomfortably on the shoulder. Modes of thinking and practice that may once have seemed justified, internally coherent, self-evident or progressive now need to be reassessed in terms of hidden exclusions, disguised costs, or as offering a merely imaginary or temporary closure. (155)

Clark offers scale as a way to overcome the limitations of liberal criticism. His "third scale," which he calls the "hypothetical," enables a different sense of time and place, and releases narrative from having to perform meaning at an always already humanistic scale.

According to Clark, literary analysis can occur at three scales. The first is the reading of humanist themes as they emerge through the narrator's world. This kind of approach leads to clichéd interpretations about a story's presentation of what "makes us human." The second scale is most common in cultural criticism and what Miyoshi and Spivak critique. It involves reading a text for ethnicity, culture, national identity, or through a "methodological nationalism" that jettisons what does not fit in cultural models. In this scale, gender, class, national identity, and so on, form the bulk of literary analysis. The third scale of reading is what Clark suggests we do to refresh literary analysis so that it is not subjected to a (limited) liberal critical approach. The hypothetical scale offers an opportunity to read for nonhuman agency and outside familiar critical coordinates of race, class, and gender so that "a kind of non-anthropic irony deranges the . . . story as any easily assimilable object of any given kind of moral or political reading" (161–62). This hypothetical scale helps us escape familiar frames of analysis that rely on national difference and the habits of area studies formulated from the cold war and may provide a sense of how we could further develop a practice of planetary criticism.

Photography and Scale

I have discussed the reading of literature and poetry at the hypothetical scale in a different context.[6] Here, I would like to return to Miyoshi's photograph of his children on the beach and consider the question of scale and interpretation for photography. He was, after all, a prolific photographer and even published a book with his photographs, writing in a brief introduction, "Within the borders of a photograph, all is self-enclosed. It has neither a beginning nor an ending. Let me repeat, it tells no story, it is not here. That is why a photograph can be evidence, but never history" (Miyoshi 2009: 8). From his perspective, what would this photograph that prefaced *To the Sites of Resistance* be evidence of? Three youth splashing in the waves certainly conjure up a sense of personal histories in the making— the carefree early stages of lives. Perhaps a reading at the first or second scale will do.

As a final thought experiment, I'd like to take up Miyoshi's concept of planetarianism and his appreciation of the photographic medium, and the practice of reading for scale, to consider a compelling collection of photographs by Shimpei Takeda (www.shimpeitakeda.com/trace/). Takeda's extraordinary photographic project "Trace" was created in the wake of the

6. See chap. 4 of Marran 2017.

nuclear meltdown in Fukushima on March 11, 2011. He was born in Fukushima but lived in New York at the time of the meltdown. After the meltdown, Takeda returned to Japan to embark on "Trace." In this inventive project, Takeda brings together a sense of geologic, human, and planetary history. His range of images, large and small, embody multiple scales of history in this long-term project. The combination of radiographs, polaroids, and soil images were produced through a very physically draining process on the part of the photographer-artist who hauled sixty bags of radiated soil from a vast range of locations in and near Fukushima prefecture to be the subject for radiographs.[7] Takeda's process was to create images by exposing photosensitive material of silver halide to radiation emitted from contaminated particles. Upon experimenting with a radioactive isotope disc from Tennessee and orange US-produced Fiestaware, which includes substantial amounts of uranium oxide in the material, Takeda then produced radiographs of radiated soil by exposing the photosensitive paper to the soil for ranges of time. The soil sample radiographs, including the most dramatic one pictured below (Figure 1), appear as far remote stars against a black velvet sky, some with more and some with less ghostly dots and milky smudges. The photograph below features radioactivity traced in soil taken from Lake Hayama's Mano Dam in Iitate, Fukushima, where the air registered 1.848µSv/h and the ground measured 6.438µSv/h (Figures 2 and 3). These radiation readings registered higher than any other of his soil samples from the first twelve locations.

Takeda's project does not end with radiographs of soil samples. He also took polaroids and soil close-ups of the contaminated areas from which he took bags of soil. Smaller polaroids show the art and architectural features in these locations. The engineered and architectural sites selected by Takeda are wide ranging. In polaroid #4, the Shioyasaki Lighthouse in Iwaki, Fukushima, is featured in a picturesque long shot along the Pacific Ocean. Polaroid #5 features a corner roof of the Nihonmatsu Castle in the bottom right-hand side of the frame. In #9, a centuries-old statue from the Zen temple of Nakano Fudoson in Fukushima City absorbs the full frame. In #3, a mounted gun represents a former naval air base of Kasumigaura. In #2, Takeda has chosen to feature only the natural grasses of a site that had been occupied by Kashiwa military base. Each medium or long shot of these specific locations, labeled with place names, represents human his-

---

7. The polaroid images and soil close-ups function only as smaller supplemental images in the project.

tory. The religious sites and war sites depict the institutions of cultural life and industrial modernity of generations. Using Clark's interpretive model, we can easily read them at the second scale. The sites that Takeda has carefully chosen represent significant sites of centralized power in human history: a castle, a military base, a lighthouse. The cannon depicted in the Kasumigaura photograph, when compared with the shot of grasses covering the Kashiwa airbase in Site #2, shows two paths taken. One shows the memorializing of militarism, the other suggests its waning.

Both, however, when subtitled with radiation levels of soil from that area and partnered with images of photographic traces of radioactivity and soil close-ups, produce a cold (war) irony. The spatially interesting radiographs offer a different sense of time, making it impossible to favor a second-scale reading that addresses only human generational time. These "Traces" of soil represent an ecosystemic futurity of a place—the long-term consequences of radiation on earthly elements that, in Takeda's words, "tell stories of much greater cycles of time" (Morse 2015: 89).

Takeda's multiple interpretations of single sites depict them as doubly wounded in terms of short- and long-term histories, but always as wounded. If we read them at the second scale, the visual records by Takeda of engineered sites and religious iconography show places as haunted by radiation for generations to come. They seem to represent a lost, once vivid past. At the hypothetical scale, the project "Trace"—with its featured radiographs, which contain no engineered or religious elements and no figures of any sort—suggests an entirely different scale of time. Human history has evaporated. The dots and smudges of white on the dark background produce an image of a seemingly endless past and future, with or without humans. Unlike Takeda, Miyoshi did not articulate his theoretical ideas of ecological totality through figureless images. His writing, like his photography, is deeply embedded in human history. The photograph of his three children frolicking on the sand depicts an environment for humanity. His planetary thinking was based in a rejection of exclusionary cultural identities and a call for new alliances within the humanities. Takeda's comparative photographic images project different senses of time with long shots of historical sites, on the one hand, and close-ups of soil samples that appear as limitless extraterrestrial space, on the other.

When Miyoshi introduced the term *planetarianism*, it was to describe an urgent need to dismiss parochial approaches within comparative literature and area studies—to develop a practice of considering our shared

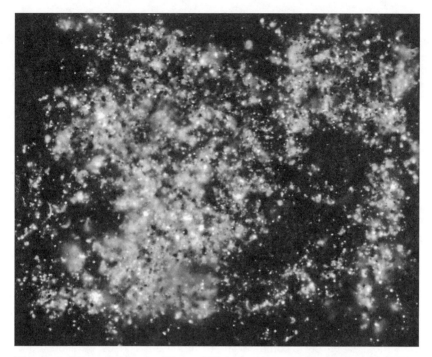

Figure 1. Shimpei Takeda. "Trace #16, Lake Hayama (Mano Dam)," 2012.

Figure 2. Shimpei Takeda. Location polaroid, Lake Hayama, 2012.

Figure 3. Shimpei Takeda. Soil close-up, Lake Hayama, 2012.

predicaments, including climate change and other systemic problems that occur at the scale of the planet. The route to authenticity is closed now, not because the world is transnationalized, as Miyoshi suggested when he wrote the sentence quoted in the epigraph, but because we find ourselves geophysically in a different time and space. Certainly, denizens of Japan are as subject to planetary changes as anyone else. And yet, parochial interpretations of Japan studies persist, including ones like the following: "Environmental debates in general and ecocritical discussions in particular have been reshaped by the concept of the Anthropocene over the past ten years in Australia, North America, and Western Europe whereas it has resonated less forcefully in other parts of the world, Japan included" (Heise 2018: viii).[8] The tiresome old saw that theory happens only in the West continues to riddle scholarship, including ecocriticism. Similarly, Japan continues to be read as a site of cultural peculiarities, and scholarship on Japanese texts can only be relevant for Japan. They are "a privileged launchpad for investigating how the narrative traditions and templates of a particular culture accommodate or resist crises such as deforestation, soil erosion, air pollution, species extinction, and toxic waste. As ecocritics around the world seek to contribute to the investigation of what narratives and images work most effectively to communicate environmental crises, detailed knowledge of such cultural specifics is clearly necessary and urgent" (ix). Here it is suggested that textual production is formed through national narrative traditions and relevant to its local context. Critical writing will then also primarily address that local context in a kind of feedback loop.

Miyoshi has pointed out that if we are in a fundamentally different, environmentally precarious situation, then area and comparative studies will eschew parochialism. Planetarianism, or planetarity, is useful for thinking because it relieves us from the confines of parochial relativism. There is no need to pretend that there is some constitutive exclusivity for an industrialized wealthy nation in the age of rising seas. Seattle sinks, Miami sinks, New York sinks, Tokyo sinks. Coming across some Anglophone critics, one might think that Japan scholars do not care about climate change and that the role of Japan studies is forever to locate the indicative characteristics

8. Comparative literature scholar and ecocritic Ursula Heise makes this comment in the foreword to a collection on environmental issues. Her beef with the volume is that climate change is not addressed. In this critique, one English-language volume on ecocriticism of Japan-related texts is made to stand in for all ecocriticism regarding Japan or Japanese-language texts.

that would allow us to continue to identify narrative traditions and "conventional narrative forms," which would be examined for how they do or do not produce some culturally unique perspective on the material world. All the while, what becomes at stake is cultural identification, the ethnos. This would be stale determinism for the archipelago in this age of rising seas.

Miyoshi's call to reframe disciplines around a planetary scale and Takeda's comparative photography collection "Trace" are invitations to think beyond predictable geopolitical identities in these geophysically unpredictable days. The planetary is useful for thinking because it leads us to ask whether there is any virtue in assessing environment through banal comparative terms framed in terms of ethnos or the nation-state. Miyoshi argues that we jettison structures passed down to us through systems of knowledge that would segment space and replicate selective collectivities given the unforgiving climatological changes wrought by anthropogenic impact. The material world itself, in quiet and dramatic ways, serves as a reminder that if we write for always predictable collectivities, then we limit who, or what, gets recognized as casualties of global change.

References

Chakrabarty, Dipesh. 2009. "The Climate of History: Four Theses." *Critical Inquiry* 35, no. 2: 197–222.

Clark, Timothy. 2012. "Scale." In *Telemorphosis: Theory in the Era of Climate Change, Vol. 1*, edited by Tom Cohen, 148–66. Ann Arbor: Open Humanities Press with Michigan Publishing—University of Michigan Library.

Cohen, Tom. 2012. "Introduction: Murmurations—'Climate Change' and the Defacement of Theory." In *Telemorphosis: Theory in the Era of Climate Change, Vol. 1*, edited by Tom Cohen, 13–42. Ann Arbor: Open Humanities Press with Michigan Publishing—University of Michigan Library.

Colebrook, Claire. 2014. *Death of the PostHuman: Essays on Extinction, Vol. 1*. Ann Arbor: Open Humanities Press with Michigan Publishing—University of Michigan Library.

Gould, Stephen Jay. 1993. "The Golden Rule: A Proper Scale for Our Environmental Crisis." In *Eight Little Piggies*. New York: W. W. Norton and Co.

Heise, Ursula. 2018. Foreword to *Ecocriticism in Japan*. Edited by Hisaaki Wake, Keijiro Suga, and Yuki Masami. Lanham, MD: Lexington Books.

Johnson, Elizabeth, and David Johnson. 2014. "On the Political Unconscious of the Anthropocene." Interview with Frédéric Neyrat. *Society and Space*. March 20, 2014. https://societyandspace.org/2014/03/20/on-8/.

Kolbert, Elizabeth. 2010. "The Anthropocene Debate: Marking Humanity's Impact."

Environment 360 (May 17, 2010). http://e360.yale.edu/feature/the_anthropo cene_debate__marking_humanitys_impact_/2274/.

Marran, Christine L. 2017. *Ecology without Culture: Aesthetics for a Toxic World*. Minneapolis: University of Minnesota Press.

Miyoshi, Masao. 2000a. "A Conversation with Masao Miyoshi." Interview conducted by Kuan-Hsing Chen and transcribed and edited by Steve Bradbury. In *Trespasses: Selected Writings*, edited by Eric Cazdyn, 263–84. Durham, NC: Duke University Press.

———. 2000b. "Japan Is Not Interesting." In *Trespasses: Selected Writings*, edited by Eric Cazdyn, 189–204. Durham, NC: Duke University Press.

———. 2001. "Turn to the Planet: Literature, Diversity, and Totality." *Comparative Literature* 53, no. 4: 283–97.

———. 2009. *This Is Not Here*. Los Angeles: Highmoonoon.

———. 2010. *Trespasses: Selected Writings*. Edited by Eric Cazdyn. Durham, NC: Duke University Press.

Miyoshi, Masao, and Mitsuhiro Yoshimoto. 2007. *Teikô no ba e—arayuru kyôkai o koeru tame* [*To the Sites of Resistance*]. Tokyo: Rakuhoku Shuppan.

Morse, Anne Nishimura, et al. 2015. *In the Wake: Japanese Photographers Respond to 3/11*. Boston: MFA Publications, Museum of Fine Arts.

Nixon, Rob. 2014. "Naomi Klein's 'This Changes Everything.'" *New York Times*, November 6, 2014.

Palumbo-Liu, David. 2012. "Crossing the Lines: Masao Miyoshi's Trespasses." *Criticism* 54, no. 2: 343–51.

Rockström, Johan, et al. 2009. "Planetary Boundaries: Exploring the Safe Operating Space for Humanity." *Ecology and Society* 14, no. 2: 32. https://www.ecologyandsociety.org/vol14/iss2/art32/.

Spivak, Gayatri Chakravorty. 2005. *Death of a Discipline*. New York: Columbia University Press.

Thomas, Julia Adeney. 2014. "History and Biology in the Anthropocene: Problems of Scale, Problems of Value." *American Historical Review* 119, no. 5: 1587–1607.

Uzawa, Hirofumi. 2003. *Economic Theory and Global Warming*. New York: Cambridge University Press.

Snowpiercer as Anthropoetics: Killer Capitalism, the Anthropocene, Korean-Global Film

Rob Wilson

A Crazed Capitalist Train

This worlding elaboration of Korean films will aim to draw out figu-rations and critiques of the capitalist body and (no less so) the urban/rural dialectics and the South Korea/US/global spatial, spectral, and worlding figurations. These tactics will be discussed as represented in the complexly global local as well as planetary Korean filmmaker and screenwriter, Bong Joon-ho (born 1969).[1] In an intertextual sense as well, I will build on my pre-vious work on global and local filmic dialectics that reflects on the works of two powerful Korean film directors, Im Kwan-taek (in *Inter-Asia Cultural Studies*) and Pak Chan-wook, versus "minor cinema" (in *boundary 2*), as well as on the "spectral aesthetics" of Korean global-local films (in *Com-parative American Studies*) (see Wilson 2009, 2003, 2001). Korean films, as articulated in generically distinct works such as Bong's *The Host* (2006),

---

1. This essay builds on an initial presentation on July 17, 2015, in the "Critical Turn of Global Korean Film" seminar at Yonsei University, Seoul, Korea, for which I thank the edi-tors of *Situations* journal as well as Korean American novelist and friend Gary Pak. It also draws on Wilson 2009.

boundary 2 46:3 (2019)   DOI 10.1215/01903659-7614219   © 2019 by Duke University Press

Mother (2009), and *Snowpiercer* (2013), register on the affective nerves and in the spaces of city, country, and planet some disorienting moment of national/transnational coproduction and global-local interface informing and deforming the shape of cinema, nation, subject, and (all the more so now) the endangered planet.

The Pacific Rim in South Korea has been lived in as an uncanny global-local space of techno-creative newness and creative-destructive postwar dynamism where all is in the mix, flow, and brash interface of codes, styles, languages, and genres. Film works like *The Host*, *Mother*, and *Snowpiercer* can help cosmopolitical citizens to mime, live inside, simulate, and decode this performative global-local interface as a social transformation of postmodern late capitalism that I have called, and would here explain again under dire conditions of the Anthropocene, "Killer Capitalism on the Pacific Rim" (Wilson 2007). With its class warfare–ridden train driving headlong through a frozen earth of climate-change apocalypse and immanent planetary disaster, the globally distributed Korean film *Snowpiercer* in particular haunts the contemporary moment of consumer pluralism (on sites like Facebook or Amazon) and techno-optimism (in Silicon Valley if not Wall Street) as some doomsday allegory of *killer capitalism*.[2] Visually striking and thematically reductive in didactic ways, this darkness-laden movie is set not just on the Pacific Rim or along the DMZ-divided Korean peninsula (as were Bong's earlier place-based movies) but along some lunar-like edge of doom with remnants of contemporary humanity cast between precarious survival and biosphere extinction. The appropriate framework for this film reflects the ecoscape and telos of the capitalist-driven Anthropocene, I will argue; hence, this is a work figuring forth the dynamics, perils, and affects of what cultural critic Margaret Ronda (2014) has called an "anthropogenic poetics" (called here *anthropoetics*), as this analysis will elaborate.

Well received by film critics and left-leaning cultural theorists in the United States and UK, *Snowpiercer* is a South Korean science-fiction

2. Immaterial seeming even more so than film or photography, Silicon Valley and its array of technologies and media are having a lasting impact on the geological earth: "For this reason [rare-mineral extraction], the long-lasting legacy of Silicon Valley will not amount to corporations or branding or creativity or individualism, but its soil: the heavy concentration of toxins that will last much longer than the businesses and remind of the geological afterglow of the digital hype, the residue of the tech companies' use of chemicals in the manufacturing of our devices. Benzene, trichloroethylene and Freon are not necessarily 'things' we associate with digital media cultural ephemerality, but they are some of the historical examples of health hazards caused from production of disk drives" (Parrika 2013).

action film that touches on issues of global warming and threats of ecological endangerment. Its plot is roughly based on a French graphic novel *Le Transperceneige*, by Jacques Lob and Jean-Marc Rochette, but cinematically engages with a broader range of transnational and ecological issues in a trenchant framework Masao Miyoshi had begun to call a "planet-based totality" (2010: 261).[3] Directed by Korean film director Bong Joon-ho, the genre-transformative maker of *The Host* and *Mother*, as well as two earlier mystery-thriller genre films, *Barking Dogs Never Bite* (2000) and *Memories of Murder* (2003), *Snowpiercer*'s screenplay was written by Bong himself along with Kelly Masterson.[4] Raw, evocative, and in-your-face mannerist in style, substance, affect, and language, the film is Bong's English-language debut as what Kyun Hyun Kim rightly has called a "blockbuster *auteur*," whose films are haunted nonetheless by "the social tension of the 1980s, a period of both political activism and economic prosperity" in South Korea as well as concerns with deformations of the natural landscape, watersheds, and rural life caused by the creative-destructive dynamism of a globalizing city like Seoul (see Kim 2013: 188–99). Approximately 80 percent of the film was shot in English; filming was done on train sets at Prague's Barrandov Studios to simulate the fury-driven autonomous motion of a world-encircling train speeding toward some arctic apocalypse, as if the train's circular motion and horizontalness was enacting the closure of a plantation-like world-system with no alternative to its death-driven social antagonisms.[5]

3. Titan Comics published the latest volume in the best-selling *Snowpiercer* series "in which the last human remnants explore the frozen earth" (Bocquet and Rochette 2015). For the original work, see Lob et al. 1982.

4. As critic Peter Sobczynski (2014) writes in a perceptive review of *Snowpiercer*, "[W]hile Bong may owe [Terry] Gilliam a debt of inspiration, this is no copycat effort by any means. In his earlier films, Bong has demonstrated a knack for taking standard generic premises and twisting them around in new and unusual ways that entertain genre expectations while subverting them at every turn. Even though the idea of watching people trying to push their way through an unstoppable train may seem to have certain visual and dramatic limitations, he and co-writer Kelly Masterson always manage to keep things [visually and thematically] interesting."

5. I thank Jin Jirn for his critical response to this paper (when first presented at Yonsei University) and his focus on the filmic "horizontalness" of the train's social organization as some deformed vision of the imagined-nation as one of solidarity, fraternity, and equality, in stark contrast to the looming vertical spatiality and techno-spectacles of foregoing urban-future films like *Metropolis* (1927), *Blade Runner* (1982), or *Brazil* (1985). J. P. Sniadecki's film *The Iron Ministry* (2014) depicts an overpacked train to portray social tensions in the PRC and has been called a documentary version of Bong's dystopian fantasy; Yeon Sang-ho's record-breaking film *Train to Busan* (2016) was hailed as a *Snowpiercer*

The film was broadly praised for its vision of global class warfare and ecologically Jeremaic tonality, and often named in film critics' top ten film lists of 2014. Initially planned for a limited screen showing, critical and popular response to what we can call this *Korean-global* film prompted the Weinstein Company to expand distribution to theaters globally and reluctantly run it through digital streaming services after Bong refused to make editing cuts of twenty minutes to shorten the film's length and soften plot impact.[6] Crazed with extremity of affect, thriller action, and a cosmopolitical style as befits the Korean-global blockbuster mode of hybrid production, the movie also prods its audience, inside and beyond South Korea, or the global "Korean wave," to confront looming conditions of global warming, ecological disequilibrium, and the larger horizon within the Anthropocene frame, as I will go on to elaborate.[7]

With a star-studded international cast ranging from Tilda Swinton and Ed Harris to Song Kang-ho and Jamie Bell, the movie takes place in the not-so-far-off year 2031 aboard a globe-spanning *Snowpiercer* train laden with tensions. This ill-fated Leviathan on rails coursing through the late-capitalist Anthropocene is driven by bad history and ruled by everyday savagery. Each train coach is loaded with the grubby lower-class or faux-elegant upper-class remnants of humanity after a misguided attempt to stop global warming through climate engineering has created a new ice age and a catastrophic future embodying (literally) what is now called the Great Acceleration of the nuclear era. Such technological hubris can only remind contemporaries of botched attempts to alter global climate through failed carbon regulation or the techno-driven science that has already altered the climate through petroleum extraction, carbon and resource overmining on land and sea, agrochemical manipulation, and species extinction across a denaturalized planetary environment that is in accelerating trouble.

---

with citizen zombies. Bong Joon-Ho's film *Okja* (2017) dramatizes environmental perils of genetically altered animals.

6. According to Hollywood reports, Weinstein disliked Bong's 126-minute cut and allegedly demanded the removal of twenty minutes before he would release it (Child 2013).

7. See Julian Stringer (2003) on the Hollywood-blockbuster industrial mode of production-cum-circulation becoming quasi-global norm after works like *Jaws* (1975), *Titanic* (1997), *Terminator* (1984), *Gladiator* (2000), and *The Lord of the Rings* trilogy (2001–3), among others, a mode becoming all the more hegemonic now with the opening of a huge China market with a taste for such *daipian* (big movie) spectacles. For localized counterviews in Stringer's collection, see Berry 2003 and Thompson 2003. In such generic terms, Park Chon-Wook's *Joint Security Area* (2000) is considered the first of several homemade Korean blockbusters.

If the outside weather we sense is arctic deadly all around the train, the inside atmosphere (as if crossing *Naked Lunch* with *Lord of the Flies* and *The Fountainhead*) on the lone last train is ominous with sadism, wacko humor, pulp-fiction caricature, drug addiction, stupor, mayhem, madness, and death. We are delivered into an endgame machinic world, where lines such as, "I know what people taste like and I know babies taste best" sound like mere everyday descriptions of a killer-capitalist need. To pierce the snow-sign ecoscape is to pierce the code for global capitalism and revolutionary necessity, to overcome left melancholy and reject liberal reformism, if not to derail the train. *Snowpiercer* is clearly projected as "an allegory for capitalism and revolution," refracting the by now normative dialectics of global polarization, as Aaron Bady (2014) has argued in "A *Snowpiercer* Thinkpiece, Not to Be Taken Too Seriously, but for Very Serious Reasons" for *The New Inquiry*.[8] *Snowpiercer*'s version of the Anthropocene is very much a fable of what has come to be called the present-day Capitalocene, a time frame conterminous with what Roy Scranton describes as "carbon-fueled capitalism [as] a zombie system, voracious but sterile" (2015: 23).

Class allegory on the train itself is palpably spatialized, weaponized into an antagonism, if not fashionized into a figuration of class warfare between grime and glitz. Curtis Everett (Chris Evans) plays the leading member of this lower-class tail section and its passengers, as he helps man up a crazed revolution-from-below to rise against a gloating elite in the front of the train. Darkened chambers prevail and block any kind of frontal vision, as the train speeds on through gloom and doom to further gloom, bloodshed, and doom. There is no middle-class section on this train; like the contemporary neoliberal state on overdrive, the social body is polarized into wealth and poverty. Capital dwells in light and security, and feeds on luxury and epicurean thrill; labor lives in darkness and need, close to penury, misery, intoxication, and death. The train speeds on indifferently, as if an embodied symptom of the accelerated capitalist system as such. In effect, Bong Joon-ho has become one of those artistic visionaries who, facing the global system in its rise, impact, and decay, is able to *see it feelingly* (to invoke Shakespeare's *King Lear*) in this and other films considered as affect, figure, setting, and form.

States of perpetual precariousness are materialized, enacted, and sped up on Bong's manic-depressive train ride through a snow-white arctic limbo that seems oddly aesthetic as it speeds by out the train windows,

8. Rothstein 2015 is more broadly focused on the capitalist global system and its "unseen" presence as the reified or sublimated infrastructure of everyday life. See also Han 2017.

like some Fredric Edwin Church painting on steroids. The perpetual-motion engine of this accelerated and robotic train, in effect, enacts the 24/7 telos of turbo-driven capitalism. *Snowpiercer* stages the massive inequity, moral indifference, and environmental plunder that is plunging "spaceship earth" toward climate disaster, multispecies displacement, and doom under the geo-historical framework we can now call the Anthropocene.

Defining the Anthropocene

"We are all covered in smoke and dirt from years and years of not washing and particles in the air, and we are all the same color if you look at it," as Octavia Spencer has remarked to explain her *Snowpiercer* character, Tanya (Mulligan 2014). World citizens are all covered, if unevenly, from Beijing to Harlem and Tuvalu Island, in what can be called Anthropocene grime and dust, dirty water, toxic air, and acidic ocean. What is this Anthropocene that has arisen, as geo-period framework of planetary unity, during the past two decades? Paul Crutzen, chemist and 1995 Nobel Prize laureate, posited and popularized the term *Anthropocene*: it originally arose in the natural sciences, but it has evolved into a discourse that now permeates the humanities and social sciences.[9] What has come to be called "anthropogenic climate disruption" is creating dire feedback loops between global warming, melting icebergs, and ice sheets in Antarctica and Greenland, and rising sea levels across the globe (see Jamail 2015; and Haraway 2016: 45–52).[10] Here I will further draw on two of its keenest advocates and critics, Naomi Klein and Donna Haraway, to set up the terms and syntax of this multiscalar shift toward understanding the Anthropocene, and turn to literary critic Margaret Ronda to help articulate a poetics and cultural politics relevant to the affects, plot, scene, and tactics in *Snowpiercer.*

As social biologist-cum-feminist cyborg scholar Donna Haraway has warned of our current planetary situation she calls "staying with the trouble,"

9. According to the framework of the Anthropocene, human beings (who only dwell on or exploit less than half of the earth's surface) have irrevocably transformed the geo-landscape as anthropogenic force since the Industrial era (and all the more so) given the use of nuclear force: oceans are warming and acidifying, tropical rain forests are disappearing faster than ever, thus altering weather patterns, ecosystems, and the geologic conditions of the planet (see Scranton 2015: 29–38; Haraway 2016: 44–57).

10. In a Truthout overview of the Anthropocene, Jamail 2015 draws on multidisciplinary research from *Anthropocene Review* to posit the year 2050 as the catastrophic telos of the ongoing climate crisis.

People joined the bumptious [planetary survival] fray early and dynamically, even before they/we were critters who were later named *Homo sapiens*. But I think the issues about naming relevant to the Anthropocene, Plantationocene, or Capitalocene have to do with scale, rate/speed, synchronicity, and complexity. The constant questions when considering systemic phenomena have to be, When do changes in degree become changes in kind? and What are the effects of bioculturally, biotechnically, biopolitically, historically situated people (not Man) relative to, and combined with, the effects of other species assemblages and other biotic/abiotic forces? No species, not even our own arrogant one pretending to be good individuals in so-called modern Western scripts, acts alone; assemblages of organic species and of abiotic actors make history, the evolutionary kind and the other kinds too.

But, is there an inflection point of consequence that changes the name of the "game" of life on earth for everybody and everything? It's more than climate change; it's also extraordinary burdens of toxic chemistry, mining, depletion of lakes and rivers under and above ground, ecosystem simplification, vast genocides of people and other critters, et cetera, et cetera, in systemically linked patterns that threaten major system collapse after major system collapse after major system collapse. (Haraway 2016: 99–100)

It is this hugely consequential geo-planetary *collapse* of climactic equilibrium and species loss Haraway points to that can rightly now be named—with full historical irony and teleological wariness of "anthropogenic" causes—the *Anthropocene*. This Anthropocene, as a near bad future we all face as precarious citizens fueled by a carbon-driven capitalist system hurtling toward the year 2031, becomes Bong's planetary setting and the ecological problem he tries to imagine beyond in a trans-species gesture of hope that closes the film. But, for most of the film, *Snowpiercer*'s darkened cabins hold passengers unfit to grasp, control, or affect the looming global ecological disaster. The scene of *Snowpiercer* is not just local and specific to one place or "historically situated," as in emergent frameworks of "Chinese ecocinema"; instead, the setting registers or speaks for the radical totality of space-time enclosure as framed under the looming horizon of the Anthropocene.[11]

11. In *Chinese Ecocinema in the Age of Environmental Challenge*, coeditors Sheldon H. Lu and Jiayan Mi make this summarizing claim: "Given the enormity of China's ecological

No recuperated "green world" looms on this future-foreclosed horizon of the Anthropocene in *Snowpiercer*: just bare life, social animus, and desiccated dream. In discussing the deformed humanity and blasted machinery as well as the desiccated ecology of *Mad Max: Fury Road* (2015), McKenzie Wark (2015) has asserted, "All cinema is [now] Anthropocene cinema, but not all cinema knows it."[12] Wark goes on to claim that the Australian director of these *Mad Max* films set in desert outbacks and a punk-dominated future, George Miller, has realized this apocalyptic horizon of planetary ruination all along. We could affirm as well that Bong Joon Ho has been making an "Anthropocene cinema," as specifically formulated by the Han River in Seoul.

The slogan on *Snowpiercer* film posters signals the class-warfare plot as a social Darwinist drive to dominate or be dominated: *Fight Your Way to the Front*, as the ad slogan for the movie claims, as this demand becomes radically incarnated all along the rail lines, *or you will die*. Transportation magnate Wilford (his name recalling Willard from *Apocalypse Now* [1979]) and his 1 percent cohort of corporate elites inhabit extravagant front train cars, while the 99 percent poor inhabit the cramped tail end of this techno-body train in squalid bare life. These lower-class minions are all watched over by Wilford's bullying guards, who materialize the viciousness of "killer capitalism," a social reality that can turn murderous in an instant, to invoke a phrase from Robert Stone's empire-haunted novel *A Flag for Sunrise* (1981). The anticommunist spirit of Ayn Rand from the 1950s hovers over the amoral ruthlessness here like some nihilistic code: eat or be eaten, dominate or be turned into subaltern meat fit for the kill inside the train or be thrown to the planetary freezer outside. The Anthropocene closure

---

challenges, China's ecocinematic imagination is necessarily historical situated" (2009: 2–3), showing that this Chinese genre thus tends toward documentary, locality, and specific environmental contexts and issues.

12. Wark (2015) finely describes the vertical class-haunted spatiality as well as the ideological closure he sees enacted through the spectacular visual effects in *Fury Road*: "This is a film then about the vertical, of a climb out of the base by labor, towards the superstructures, the desire to dwell in the utopian forms promised by a different kind of ideology, but the need to bring that vision back to the city, to use it to redesign the relation between the four liquids, the four flows. Even if the four flows (and their genders, masculine fuel and blood; feminine water and milk) do not quite come back together in equilibrium. It is not quite clear balance can ever be restored or ever existed, even in the green world. It is a film about history, then. One that refuses the option of acceleration. We can't keep fueling this machine forward forever expecting some green world to be at the end."

effect of bare life gets enacted as a gothic-sublime train racing along on retro-Fordist Industrial-era rails. Gallows humor gets madly mingled with consumer narcosis as the oppressed class might just seize the means of production, with tones of goofball terror verging on Hegelian triumph, as the movie prods the mongrel multitude to the activist eruption of *Occupy Train*.

As Nathan Lee (2014) summarizes the multispecies approach to enframing the Anthropocene as a planetary horizon of *trouble* for kith and kin, Haraway resists androcentric assumptions of human control, human endangerment, or mere human pathos or anxiety as inadequate to what is occurring across the species. In a response to "Donna Haraway: Anthropocene, Capitalocene, Chthulucene—Staying with the Trouble," Lee writes of Haraway's attempts to gesture beyond the enclosures of the Anthropocene:

> Drawing on science studies, science fiction, and eco-activist art practices, Haraway troubles the *anthro* in Anthropocene by arguing that the sciences of modern synthesis offer powerful tools for conceptualizing life in terms of copy and competition, but cannot account for the idea of "obligate[d] symbiosis." Her own symbiotic approach is to situate the Anthropocene in relation to the deep history of capitalism (the "Capitalocene") and the potential to activate poetic, destructive, powerfully vital practices of the "Chthulucene." Named for the ancient, unspeakably enigmatic, squid-like deity invoked by the horror writer H. P. Lovecraft, the Chthulucene marks, for Haraway, the possibility for the not-yet-finished, the ongoing, the dreadful but generative forces of the inhuman within the human. (Lee 2014)

This turn beyond the Anthropocene reflects what Haraway embraces in *Staying with the Trouble* (2016: 97–98) as the "sympoiesis" of queer-kinship belonging that would move beyond the human species and its androcentric pathos and need. Bong's movie does "stay with the trouble" of imagining class warfare and planetary endangerment as generated by the history of industrial capitalism. But the film's closing scene even gestures toward a trans-species affinity of sympoiesis with the return of the polar bear who bonds with the two multicultural survivors after the train wreck. Still, *Snowpiercer*'s framework of image, concept, affect, and action is largely androcentric. Its plot is driven by the human will to domination and control. This plot is raw in its class analysis, uses modern trains and rails as social synecdoche for the whole capitalist system, and finally calls on technology-inspired solutions to the climate crisis. That is, its filmic dialect is not so much minority language as the discourse of Marxist dialectics, which gives it social pungency in a time of the Occupy movements from Madrid to Oakland.

Along class-warfare lines inside this train's incarnated "Capitalo-cene," Curtis Everett has been guided by a shadowy, reluctantly Marxian mentor named Gilliam (played by John Hurt), whose portmanteau name can only recall dystopia sci-fi film director Terry Gilliam, maker of *Brazil* (1985). Curtis's mandate is to lead subaltern passengers in revolt during the delivery of its daily dose of soylent-green protein blocks.[13] Seizing the last few cars, Curtis and his class crew free Namgoong Minsu (Kang-ho Song) from his junkie sleep in cryogenic transcendence. In his pre-junkie days of techno-labor, Minsu had created the train's security system, but he is now doped into oblivion along with his clairvoyant if erratic daughter, Yona Minsu (An-sung Ko).

Curtis offers father and child more Kronole, a drug that induces states of what literary critic Sianne Ngai calls the late-capitalist affect of *stuplimity*: meaning a stupor-like narcosis of stupid sublimity not unlike the self-medicating denizens of a postmodern crack house or Wall Street wolf men addicted to crazed profits.[14] Both addicted by now, father and child will exchange work for dope, doing some smart labor for some stupid stupor. Namgoong is the only character that speaks Korean, which along with his drug addiction, techno-genius, and mute charisma give him an oddly transcendent presence, as if he stands in for the Korean director himself, who would rather mutate anthropogenic affects rather than slow down or explain his power-crazed ice world. As if an inside joke about using Korean in such a globally marketed film, Bong has admitted with joyous irony in an *Esquire* interview, "I was looking for a name that would be most difficult for foreigners to pronounce. Namgoong . . . it is difficult. There are some name-related jokes in the film" (Mulligan 2014). This touch of Korean language can be considered just one sign of Bong's recalcitrant reminder of otherness and the language of minority filmmaking.

The globalization-from-below forces are met in the middle of this claustrophobic train by security guards ordered by sub-Minister Mason; they suffer bloody overkill casualties worthy of a Sam Peckinpah Western or a Kim Kiduk Korean horror movie.[15] Curtis is forced to sacrifice his second-in-

13. Hurt was full of admiration for Korean director Bong in this and prior films, proclaiming, "Technically, he is as clever as Hitchcock" (quoted in Titze 2014).
14. See Ngai 2007: 248–97 on the affective dynamics of postmodern "stuplimity."
15. For a richly theorized and far-ranging study of such genres as Korean postwar and

command, Edgar, to end the fight, but Mason agrees to lead Curtis, Namgoong, Yona Minsu, and their class allies forward through the train toward
a humanity-domineering subject whom they plan to decapitate like some
Lacanian subject presumed to know the sublime substance of capitalist
ideology. After realizing that armed guards sent by Minister Wilford's right-
hand woman, Mason (a diabolical schoolmarm, Tilda Swinton), are not as
threatening as they appear, Curtis and Namgoong—along with their rebel
party that includes Edgar, Tanya, and Yona (her name in Korean echoes the
Old Testament prophet Jonah struggling inside this machinic whale)—set
off for a final confrontation in dark closed spaces and hothouses full of flora
and fauna. They will battle amoral patriarch Wilford (played by an oddly
mundane Ed Harris), the Hugh Hefner–like creator of the engine, to determine the fate of Planet Earth. Swinton, playing her character like some
postmodern pastiche of uncanny geopolitical recall, has said her persona
is a mix of Lady Margaret Thatcher, Colonel Gaddafi, Adolf Hitler, and Silvio
Berlusconi all done in a Yorkshire accent (Ehrbar 2014). Along these lines
of pastiche history, in a 2013 interview with *Ten Asia*, Ko A-sung (Lee 2013)
has said her own "weird English"—to invoke Evelyn Chin's term (2009) for
such "Chinglish" and related idioms like "Konglish"—was created from a
mongrel pidgin mix of US, Philippine, Inuit, and Indian accents, as if befit-
ting some border-collapsed language at the edge of the world. Such weird
English is deployed to unsettling effect, for example, in Korean American
poet Cathy Park Hong's bastardized tourist-worker pidgin in *Dance Dance
Revolution* (2008) and *Engine Empire* (2014). "I'mma double migrant," Park
Hong's Guide in *Dance Dance Revolution* says in tourist patois, "Ceded
from Koryo [Korea], ceded from Merikka [America]" (2008: 26).

But this rogue train's class system, as a synecdoche for world capitalism, works through some nexus of autocannibalism, bare life sustained in a
horrific closed ecology, like some moving internment camp. As Aaron Bady
claims of the film, "Even the revolution is an integral part of the train. . . .
Only the engine is eternal" (2014). In other words, even the possibility of
world revolution will endgame on this world-historical train, where *lack* and
satisfaction are built like illusions into the system as just cynical ploy, systemic motive. The train materializes an advanced state of late capitalism
that has swallowed humanity into its very head, bowels, and machinic body.

---

global obsessions, see Peirse and Martin 2013, especially sec. 3, "Contemporary 'International' Horror," for modes of Korean global hybridity and coproduction. More broadly
framed along the transpacific "remake" nexus, see also Chan 2009, particularly for ethnically recoded transformations of global genres.

Bady captures the decadent, world-weary nihilism of Bong's ruling-class power on what I have been calling this killer-capitalist train moving in circles around the Anthropocene scene:

> Let's not forget, after all, that while we see scores of lounging, decadent drug-addled first-class passengers dissipating themselves in pleasure, as our heroes navigate through the bowels of capitalism, we also see at least as many black-masked, hatchet-wielding thugs, first class passengers who are ready, willing, and able to kill on command, and who apparently live *for* that command. Even the party-raver passengers turn into a murderous mob when given the opportunity to do so. Even Tilda "Ayn Thatcher" Swinton pivots easily from punching down to punching up; given the opportunity, she's as happy to live by killing Wilford as she is to live by killing passengers. They are one and the same thing; killing is what makes her [come] alive. (Bady 2014)

For Bady, what we could now call the *global precariat* class will have their bad new day as well on this train, but they are hardly portrayed as some liberating Jacobin angels.[16] Bong's precariat is driven to desire, to become like the ruling class, but their impact is to lack, to suffer, to become cannibalized, and to implode. There's a certain postpolitical giddiness that *Snowpiercer* captures, in other words, as if the global system has already gone too far; there is no exit and no alternative, just wall-to-wall capitalist Anthropocene, and nuts-and-bolts adjustments until humanity is gone and the planet erupts into glorious posthuman ruination. Bong's concentration on spatial enclosure (the train going in circles) and foreclosed or de-realized temporality fits Fredric Jameson's diagnosis of an advanced global postmodernity of financialization—and a "curatorial" leftism of altered spatial practice—he associates with manic "aesthetic singularity" at many levels (Jameson 2015).[17]

16. On the Precariat as "the new dangerous class" unmoored from collective coalition, enduring ties to place, pension plans, labor benefits, and insurance plans that became normative under postwar Fordism, see Standing 2014.

17. As Fredric Jameson contends, "Today we no longer speak of monopolies but of transnational corporations, and our robber barons have mutated into the great financiers and bankers, themselves de-individualized by the massive institutions they manage. This is why, as our system becomes ever more abstract, it is appropriate to substitute a more abstract diagnosis, namely the displacement of time by space as a systemic dominant, and the effacement of traditional temporality by those multiple forms of spatiality we call

Bong's eco-catastrophic allegory is finally a bit too obvious, too pat, too literalized and closed in its bleak totality and locked-in ecosystem, and thus offers an androcentric framework closed off from hope or change or any reformist semblance of ecological hope, nation language, or social policy. As Bady theorizes *Snowpiercer*'s cinematic "time after the revolution," "How can [Bong's] train be a metaphor for late capitalism when it literally is, in the movie, the form that capitalism takes after climate change? It is the latest possible kind of capitalism, a capitalism that no longer makes anything other than pain and suffering. The train is the capitalism that has eaten up the entire world, and is now just living off its own stored reserves of fat" (2014).

Along the crazed revolutionary way leading toward the engine room of the train, Namgoong and Yona gather stashes of Kronole from the drug-inebriated passengers. They reach the final car before the engine, which is secured by a large door. Namgoong gathers the Kronole, which he knows is an explosive by-product from the train's operation, and plans to use it to blow off the side hatch of the train. Doped up or cosmically conscious, Namgoong believes that he has observed that the ice outside the train is thawing, and humanity can now survive. Curtis insists that he still must face Wilford to explain how and why the master subject created this kill-or-be-killed society on the train. An erotically slimy Wilford tells Curtis that he and his seeming opponent Gilliam have orchestrated the revolution he has led to control the population and manage scarce resources. Wilford then orders his men to kill 74 percent of the remaining tail-section population and suggests that he plans to have Curtis take over as new over-seer of the train. Yona pulls up a floorboard to reveal that Wilford has used children from the tail section as replacement parts for their failing engine. Curtis knocks out Wilford; nothing changes. With the passengers about to swarm him, Namgoong lights the fuse on the Kronole and races inside the engine room. He and Curtis use their bodies to protect Yona and Timmy from the crazed explosion. The noise triggers an avalanche outside, violent and sublime—the Anthropocene disaster long expected and awaited—thus derailing the lone train. Yona and Timmy emerge from the train wreck and, as one frail sign of earthly regeneration, see a polar bear moving along the vast snow: some trans-species sign (like the fabled Zen snow leopard) that remnants of animal life can exist outside the doomed train.

Still, some latent telos of modernity's death drive resides at the core

---

globalization. This is the framework in which we can now review the fortunes of singularity as a cultural and psychological experience" (2015: 128).

of Bong's Korean-global film, enacting a vision all but shorn of place, shorn of situation, shorn of any capable politics or resources of hope.[18] To quote the radically gleeful Bady, enjoying the annihilation of the capitalist system, as many dream of doing to move beyond leftist melancholy and socialist defeat, hoping against hope for the end of the system: "Nothing good can or will come from that train, and its total destruction is a relief. For the viewers, we get death without death: we don't actually have to destroy the entirety of humanity to enjoy the fantasy of all the things we hate about our-selves, as a species, being obliterated. By making that train the crystallized encapsulation of everything that is awful about late capitalism, *Snowpiercer* lets us watch it [the global system] burn" (Bady 2014).

Toward an Anthropoetics of Global Unmaking

This portrayal of the global system in such ecologically haunting terms is no small formal or conceptual feat: to try to imagine the planetary Anthropocene as a poetics and a politics within the Capitalocene, how-ever radically bleak, negational, or morbidly inhuman. We might consider this movie as a feat of what Margaret Ronda calls, drawing on the theories of major Anthropocene anthropologist Bruno Latour and invoking a range of nonnarrative experimental poetries from the contemporary overdevel-oped world, an "anthropogenic poetics" (2014). Drawing on minor writers like Juliana Spahr, Evelyn Reilly, Michael Leong, Jasper Barnes, Joshua Clover, Brenda Hillman, among others, Ronda summarizes, "What is dis-tinctive, perhaps, about the planetary anthropogenic *poesis* of the Anthro-pocene is both its irreversibility and its seemingly endless capacity to unmake" (109).[19] By *unmake*, Ronda invokes emerging tactics of erasure, disjuncture, species overlay, unexpected juxtaposition, semantic decre-ation, a near total refusal of neoliberal piety, and narrative tactics of conso-lation, restoration, sentimentality, and "end-of-nature" containment.[20]

18. We could still ask: What is specifically Korean or Korean-local about Bong's "big movie" vision and its cinematic take on the Anthropocene? The Korean-language ges-tures and names alluded to above seem small and ineffectual signals of cultural differ-ence and ethnic otherness to the blockbuster mode of spectacular effects.
19. On the need for art and literature to articulate conditions of environmental damage and social inequity that stakes more hope in "narrative," see Sze 2015.
20. As Margaret Ronda argues, "There is, in fact, an emergent literature of this 'end of nature' paradigm, engaged in these new modes of thinking—negative, indebted, ele-giac—necessitated by global ecological crisis: the field of ecopoetics" (2013). See also Ronda 2018.

While Bong is no end-of-nature poet as such, his movies enact what we could term *desublimating negation*. They would refuse and unmake the usual normative consolations of optimism, marriage, and success; imagined personal or communal triumphs; that everyday Hollywood-happy liberal code of the bored salary-man life taken as a gold-dreaming regime under what Lauren Berlant calls the masochism of liberal capital's "cruel optimism" (2011).[21] But such narratives of planetary calamity, economic austerity, and bleak immensity have become "our new sublime," as Paul Bové has put this literary and aesthetic of planetary endangerment; citizens face all but daily the economic risk of total collapse or environmental disaster.[22] Is this what we could call, and await more works of, the *killer-capitalist sublime*? Or what Naomi Klein has called the rise and spread of *disaster capitalism* (2008) as neoliberal life norm? Turning to the little Pacific island of Nauru as just one endangered site of resource extraction as situated early and late inside the deadly energies of the Anthropocene, Klein argues, in her ecological jeremiad of far-reaching documentation and environmental sway, *This Changes Everything*:

> The lesson Nauru has to teach us is not only about the dangers of fossil fuel emissions. It is about the mentality that allows so many of us, and our ancestors, to believe that we could relate to the earth with such violence in the first place—to dig and drill out the substances we desired while thinking little of the trash left behind. . . . This carelessness is at the core of an economic model some political scientists call extractivism. . . . Extractivism is a nonreciprocal dominance-based relationship with the earth, one purely of the taking. It is the opposite of stewardship, which involves taking but also taking care that regeneration and future life continue. (2014: 169)[23]

As William E. Connelly summarizes in his review "Naomi Klein: In the Eye of the Anthropocene" (2015), among many telling cases and examples like this one from Nauru, Klein zooms in on a once thriving and quasi-isolated Pacific island "that has been destroyed from inside out and out-

---

21. Like Ronda, Berlant often turns to postliberal filmmakers as well as nonnarrative poets like Claudia Rankine and Juliana Spahr to track and queer the affects, resistances, and syntax of everyday life under neoliberal capitalism.
22. Paul Bové, Facebook comment, re austerity mandates from Europe to Greece, July 2, 2015, used with permission.
23. On "disaster capitalism" and its killer dynamics of environmental catastrophe, creative destruction, and resource plunder, see also Klein 2008.

side in. It is [thus] simultaneously a sad reality and a powerful metaphor"—showing life under global capitalism as one spent inside the extremity and deadly endangerments inside the Anthropocene.[24]

South Korea goes on waking itself and accommodating its urban citizens to hyperactivated and all-but-futuristic modes of life under and as global capitalism. Hence, citizens in Seoul are at times walking inside states and affects of cosmopolitical stupefaction and (in effect) awakening not just to global militarism but to American-decentered forces of transnational globalization spreading across the Pacific Rim, if not across the entire global-climate planet, as *Snowpiercer* enacts. Citizens in Korea, as elsewhere, are awakening to the Anthropocene as a shared planetary horizon in California and Germany as in Nauru, South Korea, and across what Richard Smith outlines with grim detail and scope as "China's Communist-Capitalist Ecological Apocalypse" (2015). The death of the planet goes on spreading across Oceania and far beyond both sides of the Pacific that "zones the whole world about," as Melville put it in *Moby-Dick*. Calling out in such films like *Snowpiercer* or *The Host* as if some canary inside the Cold War coal mines of the DMZ, this Korean-inflected cinematic train drives on toward disaster, catastrophe, capitalist horror, through extremities of fire and ice, even if some unexpected remnant of redemption (like that polar bear) appears between the all-too-human rail lines of this film. We are all learning how to live, as well as how to die, inside the Anthropocene.[25]

Since I have drawn on literature and poetics to elaborate the tactics and figurations of Bong Joon-ho's *Snowpiercer*, allow me to end this filmic reading (or what I would call filmic *worlding*) with a piece of modern canonical literary history, a small yet prescient poem by the well-known American pastoralist from San Francisco and New Hampshire, Robert Frost.[26] Inspired by Dante's *Inferno*, with its ice-punished traitors and heat-punished lovers, as well as the modern science of planetary astronomy, the poem is called, starkly enough, "Fire and Ice." It was written and published in 1920, decades before the Anthropocene had a name or figured freezing or warming as a world-climate threat:

24. All the more influential in transdisciplinary impact. See Bruno Latour's Gifford Lectures at the University of Edinburgh on the Anthropocene as a Gaia Hypothesis, "Facing Gaia: A New Enquiry into Natural Religion" (2013).

25. See Scranton 2015 for an elegant polemic on planetary and personal mortality in the Anthropocene and Scranton's frail turn in the end toward the temporal pauses of philosophy and epic literature.

26. On tactics of "worlding," see Connery and Wilson 2007: esp. 209–23.

Some say the world will end in fire,
Some say in ice.
From what I've tasted of desire
I hold with those who favor fire.
But if it had to perish twice,
I think I know enough of hate
To say that for destruction ice
Is also great
And would suffice.
(2002: 237)

Maybe, in the specific contexts of the Anthropocene imagined as an ecological catastrophe disrupting all known modes of settlement and inhabitation, we could end with Chris Nealon's resistance to this "zombie apocalypse" of class warfare as raised to a planetary level in the year 2046, with its slight glimmer of hopefulness and comradeship on the horizon in *The Victorious Ones*:

And yes like every other poet with a child I have dreamed of mine
along some empty road in camouflage and tatters, scrambling for
potable water in 2046

But you know what? Fuck the zombie apocalypse

I'm going to imagine him with comrades
(2015: 9)

References

Bady, Aaron. 2014. "A *Snowpiercer* Thinkpiece, Not to Be Taken Too Seriously, but for Very Serious Reasons." *The New Inquiry* (blog). July 29, 2014. https://thenewinquiry.com/blog/a-snowpiercer-thinkpiece-not-to-be-taken-too-seriously-but-for-very-serious-reasons-or-the-worst-revenge-is-a-living-will/.

Berlant, Lauren. 2011. *Cruel Optimism*. Durham, NC: Duke University Press.

Berry, Chris. 2003. "'What's Big about the Big Film?': 'De-Westernizing' the Blockbuster in Korea and China." In *Movie Blockbusters*, edited by Julian Stringer, 217–29. New York: Routledge.

Bocquet, Olivier, and Jean-Marc Rochette. 2015. *Snowpiercer 3: Terminus*. London: Titan Comics.

Chan, Kenneth. 2009. *Remade in Hollywood: The Global Chinese Presence in Transnational Cinema*. Hong Kong: Hong Kong University Press.

Child, Ben. 2013. "Snowpiercer Director Reportedly Furious about Weinstein English-Version Cuts." *Guardian*, October 8, 2013. https://www.theguardian .com/film/2013/oct/08/snowpiercer-director-english-cuts-bong-joon-ho.

Chin, Evelyn. 2005. *Weird English*. Cambridge, MA: Harvard University Press.

Connelly, William. 2015. "Naomi Klein: In the Eye of the Anthropocene." *Contemporary Condition* (blog). March 15, 2015. http://contemporarycondition.blog spot.com/2015/03/naomi-klein-in-eye-of-anthropocene.html.

Connery, Christopher Leigh, and Rob Wilson, eds. 2007. *The Worlding Project: Doing Cultural Studies in the Era of Globalization*. Berkeley, CA: North Atlantic Books.

Ehrbar, Ned. 2014. "Interview: Tilda Swinton Based Her 'Snowpiercer' Villain in Part on Thatcher." *Metro*, June 24, 2014. https://www.metro.us/entertainment /tilda-swinton-based-her-snowpiercer-villain-in-part-on-thatcher/tmWnfx ---f2y8TcUiQwYg.

Frost, Robert. 2002. *Robert Frost's Poems*. Edited by Louis Untermeyer. New York: St. Martin's Press.

Han, Byung-chul. 2017. "Healing as Killing." In *Psychopolitics: Neoliberalism and New Technologies of Power*, translated by Erik Butler, 29–32. Brooklyn, NY: Verso Books.

Haraway, Donna. 2016. *Staying with the Trouble: Making Kin in the Chthulucene*. Durham, NC: Duke University Press.

Hong, Cathy Park. 2008. *Dance Dance Revolution: Poems*. New York: W. W. Norton.

———. 2014. *Engine Empire*. New York: W. W. Norton.

Jamail, Dahr. 2015. "The New Climate 'Normal': Abrupt Sea Level Rise and Predictions of Civilization Collapse." Truthout. August 3, 2015. http://www.truth -out.org/news/item/32131-the-new-climate-normal-abrupt-sea-level-rise -and-predictions-of-civilization-collapse.

Jameson, Fredric. 2015. "The Aesthetics of Singularity." *New Left Review*, no. 92 (March–April): 101–32.

Kim, Kyung Hyun. 2013. "The Blockbuster Auteur in the Age of *Hallyu*: Bong Joon-ho." In *Hallyu: Influence of Korean Popular Culture in Asia and Beyond*, edited by Do Kyun Kim and Min-Sun Kim, 181–206. Seoul, Korea: Seoul National University.

Klein, Naomi. 2008. *The Shock Doctrine: The Rise of Disaster Capitalism*. New York: Picador.

———. 2014. *This Changes Everything: Capitalism vs. the Climate*. New York: Simon and Schuster.

Latour, Bruno. 2013. "Facing Gaia: A New Enquiry into Natural Religion." Gifford Lecture Series, University of Edinburgh, February 18–28, 2013. https://www .ed.ac.uk/arts-humanities-soc-sci/news-events/lectures/gifford-lectures /archive/series-2012-2013/bruno-latour.

Lee, Cory. 2013. "Actress Ko A-sung." *Ten Asia*. September 4, 2013. http://en.tenasia
.com/archives/71940.

Lee, Nathan. 2014. "Form and Rhetoric in the Discourse of the Anthropocene." Art
& Education. https://www.artandeducation.net/classroom/66318/form-and
-rhetoric-in-the-discourse-of-the-anthropocene.

Lob, Jacques, Jean-Marc Rochette, and Benjamin Legrand. 1982. *Le Transperce-
niege*. Paris: Casterman.

Lu, Sheldon, and Jiayan Mi, eds. 2009. *Chinese Ecocinema in the Age of Environmental Challenge*. Hong Kong: Hong Kong University Press.

Miyoshi, Masao. 2010. "Turn to the Planet: Literature and Diversity, Ecology and
Totality." In *Trespasses: Selected Writings*, edited by Eric Cazdyn, 243–61.
Durham, NC: Duke University Press.

Mulligan, Jake. 2014. "The Man behind the Greatest Thriller of the Summer." *Esquire*.
June 27, 2014. http://www.esquire.com/entertainment/movies/interviews
/a29260/bong-joon-ho-snowpiercer-interview/.

Nealon, Chris. 2015. *The Victorious Ones*. Oakland, CA: Commune Editions.

Ngai, Sianne. 2007. *Ugly Feelings*. Cambridge, MA: Harvard University Press.

Parrika, Jussi. 2013. "The Geology of Media." *Atlantic*, October 11, 2013. http://www.the
atlantic.com/technology/archive/2013/10/the-geology-of-media/280523/.

Peirse, Alison, and Daniel Martin, eds. 2013. *Korean Horror Cinema*. Edinburgh:
Edinburgh University Press.

Ronda, Margaret. 2013. "Mourning and Melancholia in the Anthropocene." *Post45*,
June 10, 2013. http://post45.research.yale.edu/2013/06/mourning-and-mel
ancholia-in-the-anthropocene/.

———. 2014. "Anthropogenic Poetics." *Minnesota Review* 83: 102–11.

———. 2018. *Remainders: American Poetry at Nature's End*. Stanford, CA: Stanford University Press.

Rothstein, Adam. 2015. "How to See Infrastructure: A Guide for Seven Billion Pri-
mates." *Rhizome*. July 2, 2015. http://rhizome.org/editorial/2015/jul/02/how
-see-infrastructure-guide-seven-billion-primate/.

Scranton, Roy. 2015. *Learning How to Die in the Anthropocene: Reflections on the
End of a Civilization*. San Francisco: City Lights Books.

Smith, Richard. 2015. "China's Communist-Capitalist Ecological Apocalypse." Truthout. June 21, 2015. https://truthout.org/articles/china-s-communist-capitalist
-ecological-apocalypse/.

Sobczynski, Peter. 2014. Review of *Snowpiercer* on Roger Ebert's film review site,
June 27, 2014. http://www.rogerebert.com/reviews/snowpiercer-2014.

Standing, Guy. 2014. "The Precariat: The New Dangerous Class." *Working-Class
Perspectives* (blog). October 27, 2014. https://workingclassstudies.word
press.com/2014/10/27/the-precariat-the-new-dangerous-class/.

Stringer, Julian, ed. 2003. *Movie Blockbusters*. New York: Routledge.

Sze, Julie. 2015. "Environmental Justice Anthropocene Narratives: Sweet Art, Recognition, and Representation." *Resilience: A Journal of the Environmental
Humanities* 2, no. 2: n.p.

Thompson, Kirsten Moana. 2003. "*Once Were Warriors*: New Zealand's First Indigenous Blockbuster." In *Movie Blockbusters*, edited by Julian Stringer, 218–41.
New York: Routledge.

Titze, Anne-Katrin. 2014. "Snow Business: John Hurt on Snowpiercer and His Long
Career." Eye for Film. June 26, 2014. http://www.eyeforfilm.co.uk/feature
/2014-06-26-interview-with-john-hurt-about-snowpiercer-feature-story-by
-anne-katrin-titze.

Wark, McKenzie. 2015. "Fury Road." *Public Seminar* (blog). May 22, 2015. http://
www.publicseminar.org/2015/05/fury-road/#.VbUxqRd3ib4.

Wilson, Rob. 2001. "Korean Cinema on the Road to Globalization: Tracking Global/
Local Dynamics, or Why Im Kwan-Taek Is Not Ang Lee." *Inter-Asia Cultural
Studies* 2, no. 2: 307–18.

———. 2003. "Globalization, Spectral Aesthetics, and the Global Soul: Tracking
Some Uncanny Paths to Trans-Pacific Globalization." *Comparative American
Studies* 1, no. 1: 35–51.

———. 2007. "Killer Capitalism on the Pacific Rim: Theorizing Major and Minor
Modes of the Korean Global." *boundary 2* 34, no. 1: 115–33.

———. 2009. "Capitalist Body & Global/Local Space in Bong Joon-ho's *The Mother*
and *The Host*." Outline for undelivered talk at NYU Korean film conference.

But Then, What Is Culture?

George Solt

Trespasses (Miyoshi 2010) brings together some of Masao Miyoshi's principal writings from a career that traversed multiple disciplines and consistently scrutinized the politics embedded within various forms of cultural production. Published posthumously, the book consists of thirteen chapters, beginning with Miyoshi's final essay from 2009, and ending with a previously uncirculated interview from 2000. Eric Cazdyn's introductory essay provides a strong case for Miyoshi's enduring influence in Japanese studies and the humanities in general, and the foreword by Fredric Jameson captures the thrust of Miyoshi's impulse throughout his career to steer clear of fads in academic thought, critiquing both within institutions, such as the university, and in individuals the tendency to ossify and cower to pervading norms of self-censorship. Of the thirteen essays, five directly address problems pertaining to the study of Japan. While all the chapters reveal the evolution of Miyoshi's thought with respect to matters of concern to the field, chapters 3, 4, and 10, in particular, help us appreciate the critical interventions he made over different phases in his writing career.

Chapter 3, "*The Tale of Genji*: Translation as Interpretation," is a

boundary 2 46:3 (2019)   DOI 10.1215/01903659-7614231   © 2019 by Duke University Press

short review of Edward G. Seidensticker's 1978 translation of *The Tale of Genji* that addresses the problems inherent in translating classic foreign texts into modern English for contemporary audiences. Miyoshi's point is that in attempting to remold the ancient Japanese text into a coherent narrative in English that fits the expectations of its readers, the translator takes extensive liberties in rendering ambiguities in the text (particularly with respect to subject voices) into unambiguous actions and thoughts.

Chapter 4, "Who Decides, and Who Speaks? *Shutaisei* and the West in Postwar Japan," is an excerpt from Miyoshi's 1991 monograph *Off Center: Power and Culture Relations between Japan and the West*. Here he examines the debates surrounding the issue of subjectivity that became central to Japanese intellectuals in the postwar period. Despite the fact that the debates arose from an initial impulse of these intellectuals to confront their own complicity in promoting wartime nationalism, Miyoshi finds that much of the postwar discussion surrounding the notion of how to develop an independent philosophical core ultimately served to depoliticize many of those who became involved by encouraging self-contained contemplative thought and by producing an idealized and unrealistic sense of how subjectivity was formed and how it functioned in the West.

Perhaps the most relevant essay to the field of Japanese studies is chapter 10, "Japan Is Not Interesting." Miyoshi explains his use of the title as a means to pose difficult questions about the privatization of ethnicity, the use of cultural conformity as political control, and political apathy in both Japan and the United States. The essay concludes with a meditation on the question of representation that still concerns those engaged with the study of Japan, particularly in the United States. "Obviously, the representation of others is hazardous, because it always ends in misrepresentation. Yet one cannot forget that self-representation is not guaranteed to be right or authoritative either. Furthermore, even self-representation inevitably involves the representations of others. One should of course avoid deliberate misrepresentation of the other, which is rampant in both the media and academia" (204).

Learning Places: The Afterlives of Area Studies, which Miyoshi coedited with H. D. Harootunian (2002), is another text in which readers can find a thoughtful exploration of the problems confronting Japanese studies and Asian studies more generally in US universities. Miyoshi's critical interventions in the field of Japanese studies can also be appreciated in his other coedited anthologies, *Postmodernism and Japan* (1989) and *Japan in the World* (1993). Similarly, Miyoshi's now classic exposition on the modern Japanese novel, *Accomplices of Silence* (1974), is another site where readers can reacquaint themselves with his contributions to the field of Japanese studies.

Because of his centrality as a leader in the field of Japanese studies, it is all the more remarkable that Miyoshi's training and primary field of expertise was English literature, not Japanese, and that he began his academic career as a professor of Victorian literature at the University of California, Berkeley, where he produced his first monograph, *The Divided Self: A Perspective on the Literature of the Victorians* (1969). Miyoshi's timely contributions to the fields of architectural studies (chapter 7), globalization (chapter 6), and environmental studies (chapter 12) are also apparent in *Trespasses*. By bringing these divergent strands together, *Trespasses* represents an essential work that introduces many of Miyoshi's most significant writings over a career that covered a vast amount of intellectual terrain with the expressed purpose of deconstructing boundaries, disciplinary and other. The list of selected works provided at the end of the book is an excellent guide for further study of his writing and of his yet underappreciated role in stimulating a number of important conversations concerning area studies, the humanities, and the shifting role of the university in relation to changes in the political economy and the natural environment.

Reading *Trespasses* reminds us of Miyoshi's talent in asking deceptively simple questions and leading us down a path that leaves us with a deeper sense of crisis but also of new possibilities for imagining how to reconnect the dots.

References

Miyoshi, Masao. 1969. *The Divided Self: A Perspective on the Literature of the Victorians*. New York: New York University Press.

———. 1974. *Accomplices of Silence: The Modern Japanese Novel*. Berkeley: University of California Press.

———. 1991. *Off Center: Power and Culture Relations between the United States and Japan*. Cambridge, MA: Harvard University Press.

———. 2010. *Trespasses: Selected Writings*. Edited by Eric Cazdyn. Durham, NC: Duke University Press.

Miyoshi, Masao, and H. D. Harootunian, eds. 1989. *Postmodernism and Japan*. Durham, NC: Duke University Press.

———. 1993. *Japan in the World*. Durham, NC: Duke University Press.

———. 2002. *Learning Places: The Afterlives of Area Studies*. Durham, NC: Duke University Press.

Contributors

Tsering Wangmo Dhompa is an assistant professor in the English Department at Villanova University and a 2016–17 Andrew W. Mellon Foundation Graduate Fellow in the Chicano Latino Research Center at the University of California, Santa Cruz. She is the author of *Coming Home to Tibet* (2016) and has three books of poetry from Apogee Press: *My Rice Tastes Like the Lake* (2011), *In the Absent Everyday* (2005), and *Rules of the House* (2002).

Before his untimely death late in 2017, Arif Dirlik lived in Eugene, Oregon, in semi-retirement. In recent years, he held chairs and visiting professorships in Vancouver, Delhi, and Beijing, and maintained until the end, in scholarship and critical practice, his unwavering commitment to a better world. He mentored several generations of radical intellectuals in several continents, and his work on Chinese anarchism and revolution, postcolonial theory, globalization, and other topics has been translated into many languages. *Hougeming shidaide Zhongguo* (*Postrevolutionary China*, a translation of *Culture and History in Postrevolutionary China*) was published in Shanghai in 2015. A special issue of *Inter-Asia Cultural Studies* dedicated to the scholarly works and transdisciplinary impact of Arif Dirlik is forthcoming.

Harry Harootunian is Max Palevsky Professor of History, emeritus, at the University of Chicago, and adjunct senior research scholar, Weatherhead East Asian Institute, at Columbia University. Recent publications include *Uneven Moments: Reflections on Japan's Modern History* (2019) and *The Unspoken as Heritage: The Armenian Genocide and Its Unaccounted Lives* (Duke University Press, 2019).

Reginald Jackson teaches in the Department of Asian Languages and Cultures at the University of Michigan, where he specializes in premodern Japanese literature and performance. His research interests include Heian visual culture, Noh dance-drama, and contemporary choreography. His book, *Textures of Mourning: Calligraphy, Mortality, and the Tale of Genji Scrolls*, was published in 2018.

boundary 2 46:3 (2019) DOI 10.1215/01903659-7614243 © 2019 by Duke University Press

Mary Layoun is professor of comparative literature at the University of Wisconsin–Madison. She writes and teaches about intersections of politics, culture, and literature. Recent work includes "The Postcolonial: After a Category," "The Poetry of Constantine Cavafy and the Question of 'World Literature,'" "Here and There, Now and Then: Nations and Their Relations in Recent Palestinian-Israeli Cinema," and, in progress, "Worlds of Difference: Graphic Narratives and History."

Christine L. Marran is professor of Japanese literature and cultural studies at the University of Minnesota. She analyzes visual and literary texts from ecocritical perspectives, as illustrated in her *Ecology without Culture: Aesthetics for a Toxic World* (2017). She has published on ecocriticism, Japanese literature and cinema, film theory, and gender.

George Solt is associate professor at the Center for Global Education at Doshisha University in Kyoto, Japan. His work focuses on Japanese cultural history and US-Japan relations in the late twentieth century. He is the author of *The Untold History of Ramen: How Political Crisis in Japan Spawned a Global Food Craze* (2014), which has been translated into Japanese and Chinese.

Keijiro Suga is a Japanese poet and critic who teaches in the graduate program "Places, Arts, and Consciousness" at Meiji University, Tokyo. His anti-travelogue, *Transversal Journeys*, won the Yomiuri Prize for Literature in 2011. He has published five collections of poetry and read in Slovenia, Serbia, Kosovo, Lithuania, France, Germany, Spain, Ecuador, and other countries.

Stefan Tanaka is a member of the Department of Communication at the University of California, San Diego. His books, *Japan's Orient: Rendering Pasts into History* (1993) and *New Times in Modern Japan* (2004), focus on the interaction between pasts, time, and history in modern Japan. His latest book is *History without Chronology* (2019).

Chih-ming Wang is associate research fellow at Academia Sinica, Taipei, Taiwan. He is the author of *Transpacific Articulations: Student Migration and the Remaking of Asian America* (2013) and the coeditor, with Daniel PS Goh, of *Precarious Belongings: Affect and Nationalism in Asia* (2017). He is also the chief editor of the Chinese-language journal *Router: A Journal of Cultural Studies* in Taiwan. He is working on a book manuscript on Asian American return narratives and the post–Cold War.

Rob Wilson is professor of literature at the University of California, Santa Cruz. He is the author of *Reimagining the American Pacific: From South Pacific to Bamboo Ridge and Beyond* and *Be Always Converting, Be Always Converted: An American Poetics*, and is coeditor of *Inside/Out: Literature, Cultural Politics, and Identity in the New Pacific* and *The Worlding Project: Doing Cultural Studies in the Era of Globalization*. *Pacific Beneath the Pavements: Worlding Poesis, Cities, and Oceanic Becoming* and *Late Capitalist Weather on the Pacific Rim: Conjugations, Transfigurations, Speciations* are forthcoming.

Keep up to date on new scholarship

Issue alerts are a great way to stay current on all the cutting-edge scholarship from your favorite Duke University Press journals. This free service delivers tables of contents directly to your inbox, informing you of the latest groundbreaking work as soon as it is published.

To sign up for issue alerts:

1. Visit **dukeu.press/register** and register for an account. You do not need to provide a customer number.

2. After registering, visit **dukeu.press/alerts**.

3. Go to "Latest Issue Alerts" and click on "Add Alerts."

4. Select as many publications as you would like from the pop-up window and click "Add Alerts."